THE EAST COASTERS

Lois Nyman

THE EAST COASTERS

The Early Pioneering History of The East Coast of Tasmania

Second edition

With New Introduction by
Maureen Martin Ferris

Senior Vice-President of the Glamorgan Spring Bay Historical Society, and formerly Curator of the East Coast Heritage Museum, Swansea, Tasmania.

EER
Edward Everett Root, Publishers, Brighton, 2023.

EER

Edward Everett Root, Publishers, Co. Ltd.,
Atlas Chambers, 33 West Street, Brighton, Sussex, BN1 2RE, England.
*Full details of our stock-holding overseas agents in America,
Australia, China, Europe and Japan, and how to order our books, are
given on our website.*
www.eerpublishing.com

edwardeverettroot@yahoo.co.uk

We stand with Ukraine!
EER books are *NOT* available for sale to or in Russia or Belarus.

Lois Nyman
THE EAST COASTERS
The Early Pioneering History of The East Coast of Tasmania.

ISBN: 9781915115270 paperback
ISBN: 9781915115263 hardback

Design and production by Pageset Ltd., High Wycombe, Buckinghamshire.

ACKNOWLEDGEMENTS

I am indebted to Geoffrey Stilwell of the Allport Library and Museum of Fine Arts for his helpful critism of my manuscript. My thanks are also due to many friends for their help, among them Charles and Marion Shaw, Frances Cotton, Margaret Giordano and Frances Travers. Most particularly I should like to thank Ruth Amos (ex-Glen Gala for her enthusiasm and assistance with local history, and my lifelong friend, Geoff Groom, for his careful editing of my manuscript.

LN

The marked area is that portion of the East Coast that is covered by the book.

vi

PROPERTIES AND THEIR OWNERS

Allen Grove	John Allen
Apslawn	John Lyne
Apsley	William Lyne
Bamwell	Joseph Castle
Bellbrook	John de Courcy Harte
Belmont (Malahide)	William Talbot; George Meredith
The Bend	James King
Brooke Lodge	Patrick Duffy
Cambria	George Meredith
Coombend	Henry Lyne
Courlands	Joseph Butler
Coswell	John and Hugh Addison
Craigie Knowe	James Amos
Cranbrook	John Amos (Senior)
Egg Farm	John Allen
Enstone Park (William's Wood)	William Steel
Gala	James Amos
Glen Gala	Adam Amos (Senior)
Glen Heriot	John Amos
The Grange	James King
The Homestead (Picnic Point)	John Allen
Kelvedon	Francis Cotton
Lisdillon	James Radcliff
Mayfield	Thomas Buxton
Milton	John Allen
Muirlands	John de Courcy Harte; John Radford
Okehampton	Thomas Daunt Lord
The Plains	Joseph Allen
Piermont	Robert Webber
Ravendale	John Hawkins
Red Banks	George Meredith (Junior); Edward Carr Shaw
Rheban (Omoroe)	Richard Radcliff; James Radcliff
Riversdale	Richard Honner; George Merediff
Rostrevor	William Leard

Roy's Hill	Robert Hepburn
Sherbourne Lodge	Thomas Watson
Spring Vale	John Meredith; Charles Meredith
The Springs	Richard Allen
Swanwick	Robert Hepburn
Watermeeting	Alexander Reid
Woodstock	Peter Maclaine

ABOUT THE AUTHORS

Lois Nyman was an experienced historian and teacher whose poems, articles and short stories were widely published. She also wrote *The Lyne Family History* (1976), an east coast study.

Maureen Martin Ferris was until 2023 the Curator of the East Coast Heritage Museum, Swansea, Tasmania. She is a leading historian and genealogist and Senior Vice-President of the Glamorgan Spring Bay Historical Society in Swansea.

NEW INTRODUCTION

In 1642, the distinguished Dutch navigator Abel Janszoon Tasman christened the landmass "Van Diemen's Land" in honor of Anthony van Diemen, the governor of the Dutch East Indies at the time. This appellation endured until 1856, when the region's name was officially altered to Tasmania as a tribute to Tasman's pivotal role in its discovery.

The Eastern seaboard of Tasmania is replete with a diverse historical tapestry encompassing the realms of Aboriginal heritage, European exploration, and eventual settlement. In the early 1802, French explorers, led by Nicholas Baudin, embarked upon an expedition to the coastline of Van Diemen's Land. During this voyage, the explorers bestowed names upon various locales, such as 'Freycinet', while concurrently collecting a myriad of specimens, generating charts, and sketching landscapes. This undertaking assumed a paramount significance in the annals of Tasmanian Aboriginal history and particularly resonated with the Oyster Bay Nation due to its meticulous documentation and sketches of unprecedented detail.

The initial European settlement endeavours transpired in 1821 with the arrival of the Meredith, Amos, and Buxton families. With other families arriving shortly afterwards, these pioneers, having secured land grants, proceeded to erect unassuming dwellings, cultivate crops, and establish sheep and cattle farming operations. Access to water sources was of paramount importance, thus guiding their choice to settle near rivers or creeks. Simultaneously, the presence of convicts in the region became pronounced, with some eventually ascending to become landowners and innkeepers through a combination of rigorous toil and tenacity. Interactions between convicts and the landed gentry were facilitated by the establishment of Probation Stations in the 1840s across various locations including Buckland, Paradise, Maria Island, Rocky Hills, and the Douglas Apsley area. These stations, which harnessed convict labour, were designed to aid settlers in their endeavours.

The foundations of Swansea's military station were laid in 1827 at Waterloo Point. This establishment garnered its nomenclature from Captain George Hibbert of the 40th Regiment, a veteran of the Battle of Waterloo. The station, characterized by a flagstaff and whitewashed edifices including a gaol, police office, and magistrate's cottage, stood atop a rocky promontory projecting into the sea. It evoked the semblance of a miniature fortress from a distance, as eloquently described by the noted east coast author and artist, Louisa Anne Meredith, in her literary work 'My Home in Tasmania'.

Over the passage of time, the East Coast flourished, witnessing the emergence of various industries ranging from whaling, fishing, and wattle bark extraction, to boat building, and later, vineyards, orchards, and olive groves. Alongside these economic endeavours, the region's allure was augmented by its captivating beaches, opportunities for surfing, tranquil retreats, luxurious accommodations, and esteemed dining establishments, all of which collectively captivate the attention of visitors hailing from near and far.

Lois Nyman's book titled 'The East Coasters' initially debuted through Regal Press in 1990, but swiftly went out of circulation. However, it rapidly gained popularity and became a coveted resource for the historical narrative of the Glamorgan Spring Bay municipality.

The contents of Nyman's book encompass individuals, convicts, locales, and occurrences from the 19th century East Coast, supplemented by a collection of photographs, maps, an index, and references. This comprehensive work, 'The East Coasters,' stands as a culmination of numerous years of meticulous research. Notably, I had the pleasure of contributing my own family's history regarding the 'Radford and Castle families.' It's worth mentioning that Lois herself descended from the distinguished Lyne family hailing from Aspley/Apslawn.

A few years back, John Spiers paid a visit to Swansea, during which he expressed keen interest in Lois's book and its potential for re-publication. Following the subsequent closure of Regal Press, John took the opportunity to republish this historically significant enterprise.

Lois Nyman was not only a dear friend but also a devoted historian who artfully intertwined the tales of our forebears, enabling us to comprehend the lives and trials they faced. It brings me great satisfaction to know that this book will once again be made available through re-publication.

Maureen Martin Ferris   xii
August 2023

In his own estimation George Meredith was a person of outstanding importance and cleverness. Was he not descended from the royal kings of Wales? Had he not been raised, the son of a lawyer, in Castle Bromich Hall,[1] a manor house of some elegance? The world owed him success and he meant to have it.

When he was ten his father died, leaving his mother without enough money to have him trained in the legal profession as two of his brothers had been. Instead, he joined the Royal Marines and saw service in the West Indies, Egypt, America and the Mediterranean.[2] While recruiting in Berkshire in 1805 he met a pretty and gentle young heiress of seventeen named Sarah Hicks, and, being an eloquent and persuasive young man, induced her to run away with him, and married her that same year. As well as a private fortune, she inherited valuable buildings and land, so her husband resigned from the Navy - on half pay and with the rank of lieutenant - and for four years took upon himself the management of the property.

There had been no marriage settlement, and, living life in a fashion he considered suited to his birth and position, he frittered away a good deal of her money.[3] In 1809 he sold the estate for £20,000 and bought a property named Rhyndaston in the extreme south-west of Wales. It consisted of eight farms, one of which he managed, letting the others to tenant farmers.[4]

In 1813 Sarah Meredith, now thirty-one and with five children, engaged as a servant an eighteen-year-old village girl named Mary Evans, paying her £3 a year. She was capable and intelligent and had been reasonably well educated. She was also handsome and voluptuous, and did not escape the notice of George Meredith,[5] who, at thirty-five, was himself by no means unattractive.

From the beginning the two were strongly attracted to each other. In 1818 Mary gave birth to a son by him.[6]

Having been reared in a legal environment and an elite social world, followed by years at sea, George Meredith was ill-prepared for life on the land. Within five years of his buying Rhyndaston the estate had be-

Miniature of Sarah Meredith (nee Hicks) by Peat. (Courtesy Mrs L.V. Reisz, Orford)

come so run down that he either sold or amalgamated several of the original eight farms, reducing them to a mere three, none of which was well run. [7]Though an optimist by nature, he was forced to the realisation that he needed help, so he advertised for either a partner or a tenant to assist him.

* * * * * * *

Adam Amos was as canny with a penny as the next man, but there was so little money about in Scotland in 1814 that no matter how hard he worked he could only just keep clear of debt.

The lease which his late father had taken out on Heriot Mill Farm in 1776[8] had almost expired and he had to decide whether to renew it or move out of Scotland, as so many of his countrymen were doing. He started making enquiries as to what was offering.

Hearing of a 300-acre (120 ha) farm in Wales which was in need of either a tenant or a partner, he wrote to a friend, C. Pringle, in England asking his advice and requesting him to inspect the farm. The reply came that although the farm was two hundred miles (321 km) away he would be glad to visit it, but his advice was against entering into 'a partnership with the squire, as I do not think it would answer for a Genteelman and a furmer to lay out a joint stock in farming, for you must know Genteelmen is a little whimsicale.'[9]

Mary Evans the second wife of George Meredith (Private collection. on loan to Narryna Folk Museum. Hobart)

3

On receiving a favourable report later on Adam Amos wrote to the owner, Mr George Meredith*, and in the correspondence that followed the prospect appeared so promising that he decided to accept the offered sub-tenancy. A sale was held at the mill, in which everything from a three-year-old filly (£24) to 'old stuf' (4d) was included, and £375 was raised. He then went to the Heriot manse and asked the minister for his church clearance. It read: 'Adam Amos, gentleman, of Heriot, is a Presbyterian, a Communicant, and a man it will benefit all good Presbyterians to know.'[10] Finally the farm carts were packed with whatever was thought necessary for their future life; included was a supply of whisky and biscuits and an iron pot in case they needed to make porridge on the way.[11] So with his wife Mary and his six children, and his brother John and his wife Hannah and his two children, he set off on the long journey to Wales.

At the age of forty he was starting a new life.

Until his great journey Adam Amos had seldom left Heriot Glen. Once or twice he had visited nearby Edinburgh and once had gone as far as Dublin to see his brother James.[12] Therefore the three weeks' journey to Wales was full of interest to Adam, showing what a different world lay outside the small village in which he had been brought up. When at last they reached Wales and travelled through rich agricultural country to the market town of Haverfordwest his farming knowledge told him that good opportunities lay ahead. Driving the cart in the direction of Rhyndaston#, he prepared to meet his landlord, George Meredith.

In spite of the differences in their backgrounds and habits the two men got on excellently. They were both energetic and quick-witted, aggressive, ambitious and brave; they both had strong personalities and were quick-tempered and free of speech. Yet they never clashed. In the world of Adam Amos one agreed with the gentry immediately, regardless of one's private opinion -and that with no loss of self esteem; also, one never gave cause for dissatisfaction. George Meredith, who could manufacture dissatisfaction at will, was quick to see that in his new tenant he had an outstanding man and was therefore cordial to him, taking care not to antagonise him in any way.

John Amos, Adam's brother, lived with his family in one of the farm houses. Trained as a wheelwright,[13] he was an extremely handy man,

---

* Meredith is pronounced M'RIDDith in Wales.
# Rhyndaston in Tasmania was named by George Meredith's son Charles.

4

and soon settled down to make a living from building and repair work in the surrounding towns and villages; he also proved very useful to George Meredith, who used his skills to the full.

Once established at the farm, Adam was plunged into a welter of work in an effort to bring it up to the standard he required. In this he was helped by local labour, as well as his children when they were not at school. The rich soil responded well to his expert husbandry and when he held a sale of wheat and oats in 1816 he cleared £225 - an undreamed amount for him.[14]

His landlord, playing at farming and working at pleasure, continued to lose money. Forced to cut his losses, in 1818 he entered into negotiations with a Mr Andrew Burt to buy Rhyndaston. While the sale was proceeding the property was divided into two farms only. One was leased to Mary Evans' widowed mother, Nurse Martha Evans, the village featherbed-maker and midwife, with Adam Amos as her subtenant, and the other was managed by a bailiff appointed by Mr Burt.[15]

It was during this time that Mary Evans became pregnant. In an effort to keep it secret the Meredith household left Rhyndaston, Mary going to to Bristol to wait out the months before the birth and the others to Birmingham. After the baby Henry was born Mary arranged that he should be cared for and then rejoined her employers, after which they moved to London. From Wales, Adam Amos kept them up to date with news, concentrating mainly on Wrathall, the bailiff [16].

On April 28th, 1819, he wrote of him: *'The Sheep looks all prety whole and sound he has done his Dewty to them at least....He abused Mrs. Evans & you he called all the bad names - Swindlers & Hoare Masters & thratend to put Nurse in Prison etc - and take Law and all that. I will put Morgan James on him for calling Nurse a Hoare before two Witnesses.'*[17] This he did, but not before Wrathall had sold or taken all the moveables from the farm. Adam, suspecting that this had been arranged between him and Andrew Burt, wrote: *'I cannot think Wrathall durst do so without his employers live, unless Wrathall Destines as is not unlikely to take himself & family with what mony he can lay his hands on over the Atelantic (if he do so I hope he will find enough there to take him by the Throat).'* Little did he dream that he, too, would soon go over the Atlantic.

Things came to such a pass at the farm that in August of 1819 George Meredith was forced to come back. In no time he had entered into a law

5

suit with Mr Burt over the estate - a law suit which brought him little profit in the end.

While in Birmingham Sarah Meredith had given birth to her sixth child, who died soon after.[18] She was now pregnant again, and settled down at Rhyndaston to await the birth of her next baby.

By now her husband had announced his intention of emigrating. What he did not say in so many words to the Amos brothers was that he intended taking them with him. Skilfully he played on their secret apprehensions by dropping hints as to their uncertain future at the farm. More and more often he mentioned the free land awaiting possession in the Colonies and the wide-open opportunities there, so that gradually they were imbued with the same enthusiasm as he, and decided that they, too, would emigrate.

Another person George Meredith badly wanted to take with him was Mary Evans, but in the end decided it would be better to set her up in a country inn, so that she could earn her living by managing it and mind little Henry at the same time.[19]

He proceeded with his plans to leave England. Having been forced to discard plans to settle at Norfolk Island by leasing it as a free grant, he had deliberated between the Cape of Good Hope or Van Diemen's Land as his future home. Finally he decided on the latter,[20] making up his mind to settle in an entirely uninhabited part of the island and people it with settlers of his own choosing.

Realising that she was quite unsuited for life in the wilds, Sarah Meredith, a very feminine and softly-raised lady, was not as enthusiastic about emigrating as were the rest of the family. However, as usual she gave in to her strongwilled husband. Her baby was born in February, 1820. During the confinement she was attended by Nurse Evans, who, when difficulties arose, was forced to call in Hannah Amos, John's wife. Such were the complications, however, that both mother and child died.[21]

Her griefstricken children were sent for, and, after attending the funeral, were sent back to their boarding schools, while their father took Mary Evans to London to help establish a home base for them while he made arrangements for their new life in Van Diemen's Land.

Money with which to establish himself was all-important, but when he took stock of his capital he found that he only had £1500. Desperate for more, he approached his friends, through whom he was able to raise the amount to £5000. Upon calling at the Colonial Office in May 1820 he was given the customary letter of introduction to the Lieutenant-Governor of Van Diemen's Land by Earl Bathurst, who also, at his request, promised 2000 acres (800 ha) of land for each of his sons when they reached sixteen years of age.[22]

He corresponded with Edward Lord, a leading citizen of Hobart Town (known there as an arrogant, landgrabbing trouble-maker) and arranged for him to have cattle awaiting his arrival, and, once settled, to buy all the butter his two hundred cows could produce.[23] He then joined forces with a Herefordshire man, Joseph Archer,* and with him imported twenty-four hardy Saxon merinos, unaware that Governor Macquarie of New South Wales had already supplied pure-bred merino sheep from John Macarthur's stud to the island.[24] Six of these were his, two belonged to Adam Amos and two to John Amos. Next, he and Joseph Archer jointly chartered the 400-ton ship *Emerald* and set about getting a complement of passengers. Among them was Thomas George Gregson# and John Meredith, a son of Charles Meredith, a distant and wealthy relative.

At Rhyndaston Adam Amos held a sale. When he estimated his takings at its completion he found he had £260 worth of ironmongery, £195 in paints and painter's tools, £54 in saddlery and £800 in cash. In preparation for a life where medical attention might not be available his eight children were vaccinated against smallpox.[25] Then, with their belongings packed and every available corner of receptacles filled with corn and hawthorn berries, he and John and their families left Wales in August 1820 and sailed to London.

Once there, they found there were still three months to wait before beginning the next stage in their adventure, so they filled in the time by attending to such details connected with the emigration as were suggested by George Meredith's silver tongue.

At this time their ex-landlord had other things beside embarkation on his mind, for on October 30th 1820, eight months after Sarah's death, he married Mary Evans.[26]

His relatives were shocked that he should have married a woman of the servant class, even though he had now legalised a relationship which they had deplored. His children were bitter and resentful that he should expect them to regard her as their mother. He, confident

---

*Joseph Archer's brother Thomas was already well established in Van Diemen's Land.
#George Meredith and T.G. Gregson remained friends all their lives.

that the new Mrs Meredith would be accepted in the new land, disregarded all adverse comments.

She, obedient, adoring and full-blooded, was to continue to be the love of his life until the day she died.

CHAPTER 2

In the winter of 1820 the Meredith children were brought from their boarding schools and placed in lodgings in Chancery Lane in readiness for their trip.[1] Then, on the bitterly cold night of the 8th of November they boarded a Gravesend fishing sloop and joined the *Emerald* at the mouth of the Thames. Soon the young child who had been born to Mary and George Meredith was brought down the river to join his parents, passing under the name of Henry Moorely.[2] On board also were Joseph Archer, the Gregsons, Richard Compton, Dr Desailly (the ship's doctor), and others. There, too, were the Amos families, travelling steerage in order to put their money to better use than personal comfort.

The monotony of the journey was temporarily relieved when, shortly after the death of Napoleon Bonaparte, they saw a pirate ship near St Helena and reported her presence to the frigate Mona the following day. At the Cape of Good Hope a stop was made and the energetic Adam Amos, together with some of the others, climbed Table Mountain.[3] Storms and times of emergency were almost welcomed, for then the male passengers were expected to help the deck hands.[4] But time passed slowly for Adam Amos and as a result his spirits rose as they neared Van Diemen's Land.

It was not so with his brother John. Far from owning the £1484 in goods and cash that Adam was bringing with him, he had very little, and was depressed at his lack of prospects. In this outlook he was encouraged by George Meredith, who played on his worst fears and then, when his spirits were at their lowest, unfolded a plan whereby he could become a land-owner instead of remaining an artisan. This scheme had been so perfected that it was already drawn up in legal form. After reading it through John realised that although it almost totally favoured the other man, it at least offered him a chance to make a better life for himself than was otherwise possible.

The agreement read:

'...That as the said John Amos possesses no capital or means wherewith and whereby to establish himself as land holder,

9

Farmer and Artificer on his own account, or to entitle himself to any Grant of land on his arrival at the said Island or Islands...it is hereby fully understood and agreed upon that all and every grant or grants of land which may be made, given or assigned to the said John Amos, or in his name, to his heirs and executors, whether as a settler or otherwise, within the said Island, shall be and by this Agreement is conveyed, sold, made over to and assigned to the said George Meredith as his property and possession.'

It continued by specifying that on receiving his grant John Amos was to surrender all deeds and was to act as trustee, agent and manager, in return for which George Meredith was to place under his care and management a farm of three hundred acres and to provide money and stock for occupying the same for eight years. As well - keeping in mind how clever John Amos was with his hands - George Meredith included in the Agreement that:

'J. Amos will, for eight years, when required, make farming implements, carts, carriages, machines and all carpentry within the usual working hours observed in England, profits to go to the estate, of which he gets one-third annually.'

The agreement continued by stating that at the end of eight years George Meredith agreed to make over and assign to John Amos one hundred acres of land - part of the land already occupied by him - as a free gift.[5]

With George Meredith's young cousin John as witness, they both signed the agreement. The only copy was kept by its author.

Although they sighted Van Diemen's Land on March the 8th, 1821, wild autumn winds blew the *Emerald* off course so far that at one stage they found themselves off the North-West Coast. They anchored off Hobart Town on the 15th[6] and then, because a prison ship, the Medway, had arrived the same day and was unloading its prisoners,[7] they had to wait until the next day before they could land.

The reporter from the *Hobart Town Intelligencer,* interviewing passengers, was so impressed by George Meredith's person that he informed the public that *'General Meredith, Esqre., lady and family'* were on board. The mistake was not corrected.

On learning that accommodation was an acute problem, there being only about 420 houses in which to lodge some 2700 people,[8]

George Meredith appealed to Edward Lord to help him find a suitable place for his family. This he did by arranging with another long-time resident, Lieutenant G.W. Gunning, that they should occupy Belle Vue, a gracious house overlooking the bay at New Town.[9] Although dismissed by its new occupant as 'a small and unfurnished cottage',[10] he took pleasure in the fact that it offered *comforts superior to any our passengers have met with.*

Governor William Sorell. Wash by W. McLeod (Mitchell Library, State Library of NSW)

His family settled, he now sought an interview with the Governor. Colonel William Sorell, after four years in office, was recognised by the colonials as a very able administrator, having increased noticeably the safety and prosperity of the island. His own affairs, however, were not in such good order, for the lady with whom he was living was not his wife. This was well-known, but so popular was he that the situation was largely overlooked, although ladies did not visit at Government House.[11]

George Meredith found no difficulty in obtaining an interview, for William Sorell was the most easy-going of men - so much so that he often lingered about the gates of Government House chatting to whoever happened to be passing along that end of Elizabeth Street.

At his most affable, George Meredith outlined his idea about founding a settlement in an uninhabited part of the island. In agreeing to this, Governor Sorell suggested the East Coast as being a suitable location, remarking that he had received good reports of it. They went on to discuss the question of the running of the future settlement, and the Governor put forward the thought that George Meredith might act as a police magistrate there when it was established.[12] He arranged for him to meet the Deputy Surveyor-General the next day, when he was shown maps of the district as well as a report made eighteen months before by Henry Rice, a part-time servant of Lieutenant Gunning's[13] who was well-used to island conditions, having been one of the convicts who had arrived with David Collins in 1804. With two other men, Campbell and Watson, he had been sent to explore the East Coast and had brought back reports of good land there, which sounded so satisfactory to George Meredith that he decided to explore the area himself.

There was another important matter to be determined, and that was the amount of land to be allocated to him and the members of his party. After making affidavit as to the actual amount of property brought into the colony he was assigned 2000 acres, John Meredith 1000, Adam Amos 500 and John Amos 400. Location orders for these having been issued, arrangements were made for an exploratory trip to the East Coast, and on April 5th, 1821 a party set off in a hired whaleboat. The group consisted of George Meredith, his fourteen-year-old son George, Adam Amos and his sixteen-year-old son James, and two of the men who had explored the area in 1819, Henry Rice and Watson.[14]

When they reached the half-mile of land at East Bay Neck (Dunalley) they hauled the whaleboat across on wooden rollers[15] and then proceeded up the coast. Later when they landed at Spring Bay and were pitching their tents, to their surprise a man emerged from the bush and joined them. He told them he was a shepherd assigned to Silas Gatehouse, who had a grant of land there; he also told them a great deal about the surrounding country and next day led Adam Amos to the Little Swanport River, while the others rowed round the bays and found 'Prosser's River', which had not been marked on the map they carried.[16] Silas Gatehouse's shepherd was soon joined by a 'stockherd'*, and together they kept the group supplied with kangaroos. Living off the land was not hard; in one evening George Meredith brought down two ducks, a pigeon and two cockatoos, his experience in England at bird shooting now proving useful. Accompanied by the government men, on April 12th they rowed to the Little Swanport River. There, though attracted by the beauty of the scenery, they were disappointed in the quality of the soil, so, leaving their guides, they sailed northwards with a good breeze behind them.

Some time later they found themselves in the peaceful waters of Oyster Bay. To their right was the sheltering outline of Freycinet Peninsula, its ruggedness dominated by the cracked mosaic of the three granite peaks of The Hazards, while straight ahead the gentle curve of a bay (Coles Bay) merged into a long sweep of sand (Nine Mile Beach).

At the southern end of this they grounded their whaleboat, and just beyond the mouth of a creek (the Meredith River) they pitched their tents.

For several days they explored the area of Swan Port, willing captives to its beauty. Sixty-one-year-old Henry Rice led the party, ably followed by the forty-seven-year-old Adam Amos; George Meredith, five years younger, was soon lame, but although suffering from a severe bowel complaint, refused to give in. They found flat land and good forests, valleys and rivers; they found an expanse of land burnt by the aborigines ('The Burnt Plains', later Melrose); they found a large lagoon covering about a hundred acres in area which they considered held the possibility of being drained and turned into good land (Moulting Lagoon). They were, however, disappointed to find that the

---

*One of these men was probably John Radford.

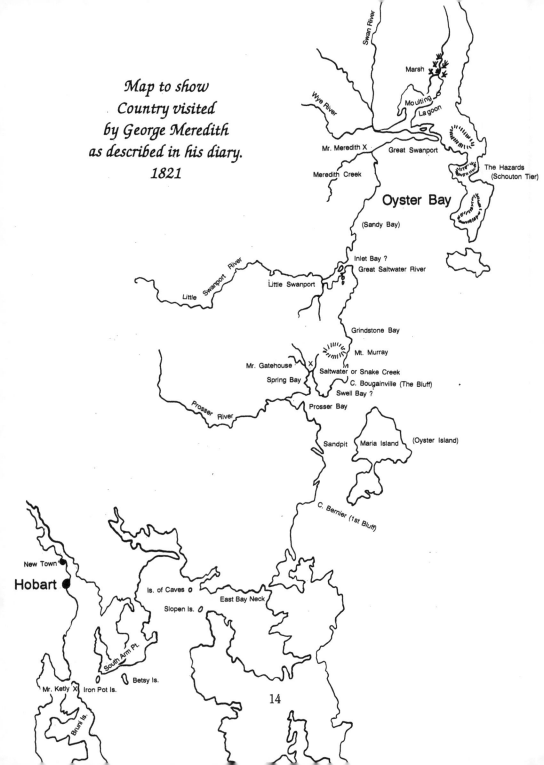

Map to show
Country visited
by George Meredith
as described in his diary.
1821

Swan River

Marsh

Moulting
Lagoon

Wye River

Mr. Meredith X

Great Swanport

The Hazards
(Schouten Tier)

Meredith Creek

Oyster Bay

(Sandy Bay)

Inlet Bay ?
Great Saltwater River

Little Swanport River

Little Swanport

Grindstone Bay

Mt. Murray

Mr. Gatehouse X
Saltwater or Snake Creek

Spring Bay

C. Bougainville (The Bluff)
Swell Bay ?

Prosser River

Prosser Bay

Sandpit

Maria Island

(Oyster Island)

C. Bernier (1st Bluff)

New Town

Hobart

Is. of Caves

East Bay Neck

Slopen Is.

South Arm Pt.

Betsy Is.

Mr. Ketly X   Iron Pot Is.

Bruni Is.

14

land was not nearly as good as had been reported earlier by Rice and Watson, though parts of it, well-served by rivers and creeks, promised well. An inland route over the Black Tiers (The Eastern Tiers) was traced, and they had already satisfied themselves that there was a good sea-route to the area. To their minds it had much to recommend it.

Behind all the advantages and disadvantages, clear in George Meredith's mind was the knowledge that here was a large expanse of virgin land ready for the taking - an ideal place in which to found the settlement of his dreams.

He wrote in his diary; *'I intend to fix our grants here.'* The others being of the same mind, each indicated the area that appealed to him.

George Meredith chose two thousand acres between Salt Water Creek (the Meredith River) and another small creek to the north (the Wye) - a sheltered and fertile area with glorious views of Freycinet Peninsula and Oyster Island (Maria Island). Adam Amos chose a five-hundred-acre pocket of good land directly across the creek from this (now the Red Banks Estate), while his brother favoured four hundred acres some three miles distant on the northern bank of the Wye.[17] A few miles to the north of this, at a section of land fed by springs and bounded by the Cygnet and Swan rivers, George Meredith selected for his cousin his thousand acres, naming it Spring Vale.

The next day the party of explorers started on their way home, eager to obtain official sanction for their grants. After four quick days of sailing with a following wind they reached Hobart Town. As they rowed past the settlement on their way to New Town the battery guns thundered out a salute - not to them, but to Governor Lachlan Macquarie, the Governor-in-Chief, who had just arrived from Sydney on board the *Midas* in order to see how things were faring in his southern colony.

George Meredith, not the man to miss an opportunity, quickly arranged for an interview with Governor Sorell, as a result of which he was desirous of obtaining favours from that gentleman's superior. All turned out as he hoped. Stating that he and his party intended to settle at Great Swan Port,[18] he said that neither his cousin nor the Amos brothers were satisfied with the amount of land allotted to them, each considering that he was entitled to a larger grant.[19] Mellowed by the additional information obtained by these men about the little-known East Coast, the Governor referred the matter, with his recommendation, to Governor Macquarie; he, to the delight of the claimants, promised to double the grants of John Meredith and Adam Amos and to allow John Amos a further three hundred acres, giving assurance that on his return to Sydney he would send official notification to this effect. Following this, Governor Sorell promised to send Deputy Surveyor-General Evans to Great Swan Port to measure out the various grants, allowing George Meredith first choice of land, his cousin second, Adam Amos third and his brother fourth.[20] Encouraged by his success, the settler-to-be requested that in view of his enterprise and vision he be given an order to select a reserve of a thousand acres adjoining his two-thousand-acre grant. To this Governor Macquarie agreed, pending approval from the British Goverment.[21]

Upon returning to New Town George Meredith wrote to his friends in England requesting that they petition Earl Bathurst on his behalf, emphasising his potential value as a settler and requesting that he be given the extra land.

The following month he made the acquaintance of William Talbot, an aristocratic and convivial Irish bachelor in his late thirties. He, after leaving Malahide Castle, County Dublin, where his family had lived since the 12th century, had landed in Van Diemen's Land in November the previous year and had then travelled to Sydney,[22] where on the strength of his assets of £6054 he had received a Location Order for the maximum grant allowed at that time - two thousand acres. While there he had personally chosen six convicts as his assigned servants and arranged for them to travel with him to Van Diemen's Land on the 90-ton brigantine, *Prince Leopold*.[23] On arrival he was introduced to a young Irishman who had also recently travelled down from Sydney. John de Courcy Harte, like William Talbot, belonged to a fine old family but had been sent down from his university in England on account of outrageous behaviour.[24] Equipped with a picturesque flow of speech and somewhat less than a thousand pounds, he was befriended by his fellow-countryman, who offered his assistance in helping to find him a place in which to settle.

On presenting his Location Order to the Lieutenant-Governor William Talbot was advised to discuss the potential of the East Coast with George Meredith, who, when contacted, gave such a glowing account of the area that he suggested that he and John de Courcy Harte join the proposed settlement. Recognising a man of quality,

George Meredith agreed. In a further interview with Governor Sorell, William Talbot was told that he could choose his two thousand acres at Swan Port and that if he built a hut and stockyard on it no one should have the right to dispossess him.[25] Stressing this, the Governor, perhaps suffering from a surfeit of George Meredith, said: *'Can Mr Meredith expect that everybody should be at Stand Still until it suits his convenience to chuse his land?',* upon which his secretary remarked, *'That's being King of Swan Port.'*[26] William Sorell then hoped that there would be no collision between the two settlers, adding that such a happening would be unlikely in an area where there were 60,000 acres of good land available.[27] He then gave the Irishman an Order of Occupation, dated 6th July,1821, which read as follows:

> *'Mr William Talbot has my authority to occupy Two thousand acres of land, the same being ordered in grant to him in the vicinity of Swan Port or Oyster Bay, subject to the Measurement of the said location by the Deputy Surveyor, when the tract of Country shall be surveyed. This authority to be considered as giving Priority of Claim to the particular land on which Mr Talbot may fix himself Except the reserves required for the Crown shall interfere.'*

Then Governor Sorell showed William Talbot an identical Order of Occupation made out to George Meredith, also dated 6th July 1821, and in so doing explained that he wanted to be fair to both men.[28]

The interview ended, in great haste William Talbot made his moves. He needed an overseer - an active and intelligent man capable of directing immediate settling-in operations at Swan Port. Upon making enquiries he was directed to a Derbyshire man, Thomas Buxton. He found him both energetic and talkative and only too willing to give details about himself;[29] he was thirty-one years old; he had a wife* and five young children and had been in Van Diemen's Land for two months; he had decided to continue the work he knew - farming - and had cash and assets enough to get a grant of 500 acres[30] but would prefer some experience of farming in the island before choosing his land. To William Talbot he seemed ideal, so he offered him £160 a year, with a house and provisions for his family as well, if he would establish a place at Great Swan Port for him.[31] To this Thomas Buxton agreed and at once set to work.

---

* It is said that Ellen Buxton, formerly Ellen Bott, had worked for Mr Buxton's family.

17

The thousand ewes William Talbot had bought locally and the twenty pure merino rams he had purchased in New South Wales[32] were put under the direct care of Alexander Reid,[33] a dark, tall young Scots farmer of a much superior type to the others; these, with the other stock, he directed should be driven by the other chosen assigned servants to Great Swan Port. He then hired a number of builders and set off with them by sea for Oyster Bay, accompanied by the same guides who had been with George Meredith on his trip.

On their arrival the men were shown where they were to build a hut for William Talbot. This was a spot about three-quarters of a mile (1.21 km)[34] north of the Meredith River and a mile (1.7 km) inland from the shore*,[35] and was in that two thousand acres (800 ha) that George Meredith had chosen as his grant.#[36]

For two months the workers had the whole of the district to themselves. They were kept fully employed. They cleared two acres of land and ploughed and sowed it. Then they erected for William Talbot a sizeable but quite badly made wattle and daub hut.[37]

This was the scene of activity which confronted Adam Amos in mid-September when he and his son James and his brother John arrived with mobs of cattle, some of which belonged to them and some to George Meredith.[38]

Thankful that the problem was not his, he set to work establishing his own grant. Being a farmer, he occupied himself with the stock while his brother, the builder, constructed a hut. This was a four-roomed, timber-framed building with thick walls of rammed turf and mud, a roof thatched with rushes and sags, and with two stone chimneys.[39] Then John built a smaller hut a short distance downstream for his temporary occupation,[40] for George Meredith had cautioned him not to build on that area to the north which he hoped to own until it had been measured and officially allotted to him; so he built within easy distance of the Meredith grant, knowing that soon there would be a multitude of tasks for him to undertake under the terms of their agreement.

A fortnight after the arrival of the Amos brothers George Meredith himself appeared, together with his young cousin and his eldest son. Outraged at what he found, he determined to fight for possession of the area.[41] In a burst of activity he laid claim to ownership by setting

---

*The site was opposite the present-day McNeils Road.

#William Talbot named this property Malahide.

Creek Hut. The old cottage at Red Banks from a sketch by Mrs Fanny Poynter (Meredith) 1846, presented to John Meredith. (Tas. University Archives, Parker Papers P1/35.)

John Amos to work building a hut for him on the north side of the creek and putting down foundations for a storehouse for clothing and food supplies, while he and his men set to work planting the fruit trees he had brought down with him. All this was in clear sight of William Talbot's hut but separated by about thirty acres (12 ha) of lagoon and wet, marshy land.[42] Then he had an area cleared beside his rival's two acres of cultivated land and set his men to plough it.[43] At once Thomas Buxton, hot in loyalty to his employer, ordered his men to plough beside them, and violent words followed.

Raging, George Meredith set off with his two relatives for Hobart Town, where he determined to continue the war. The night before they arrived there they put in at a small bay, and the next morning their thoughts were temporarily diverted by the arrival of six young aboriginal women. George Meredith, not failing to observe that two or

Crossing the mouth of Prosser's River — on the Sea — East Coast of Van Diemen's Land.   Sept. 1828.

7   6   5   4   3   2   1

Distance across in the Water
from ¼ to ½ Miles, along a
narrow ridge of Sand, the
deep Water on each Side —

Country - England, etc.

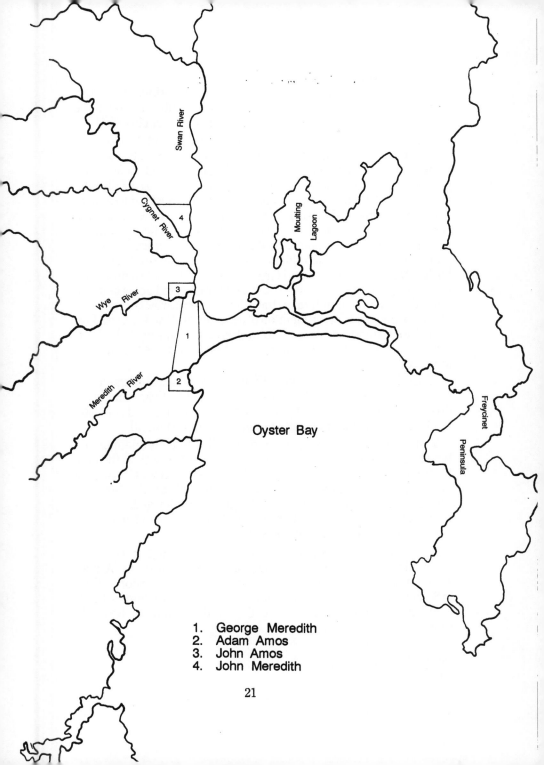

Swan River

Cygnet River

4

Wye River

3

1

Meredith River

2

Moulting Lagoon

Oyster Bay

Freycinet Peninsula

1. George Meredith
2. Adam Amos
3. John Amos
4. John Meredith

three were well-proportioned and relatively goodlooking, encouraged them to approach and soon had them diving for muttonfish (abalone) and crayfish, in exchange for which the men gave them bread.[44]

Once in Hobart Town, no time was lost in informing the Governor what William Talbot had done, and as a result the Deputy Surveyor-General was instructed to go to Great Swan Port and measure the grants of the settlers there, paying particular attention to the disputed area, dividing it into two distinct parts as seemed most fair to him. So in mid-November 1821 George Evans, cultured and clever, fleshy and careless,[45] set off to carry out the Governor's orders, taking with him his assistant surveyor, Thomas Scott. On arriving, he measured off the grants of the smaller landholders first. The seven hundred acres (280 ha) located to John de Courcy Harte* was situated over two miles from the Swan River and straddled the Wye, four hundred acres being on one side and three hundred on the other, while nearby, commencing at the northern side of the junction of the Swan and the Wye, was John Amos' four hundred acres.[46] John Meredith's Spring Vale** was surveyed, and then Adam Amos' five hundred acres+ below the Meredith River[47]

When he came to the disputed four thousand acres of open land between the Wye and Meredith creeks George Evans marked a dividing line north/south, which threw all the buildings and cultivated land into one grant - that apportioned to George Meredith.

William Talbot reacted strongly, demanding that his buildings and land be re-allotted to him.[48] Returning from his first visit to the area, he besieged Governor Sorell with letters and personal visits. So persistent and outspoken did he become that at last the Governor refused to deal directly with him any longer.[49] An intermediary, Father Philip Conolly, was chosen to represent him, and, being an amiable and convivial man, was acceptable to both.

For a while this worked well; then, to his future regret, Governor Sorell himself re-opened the correspondence by informing William Talbot that he had referred the land dispute to the Governor-in-Chief in Sydney, recommending that compensation be paid to him so that he could move somewhere else: he then ordered him to leave the property he was claiming.

---

*John Harte named his property Bellbrook.
#Now part of the Riversdale estate.
**The present Cranbrook-Syde estate was originally included.
+This area is now the Red Banks estate.

William Talbot refused. He, too, wrote to Sir Thomas Brisbane, putting his side of the case.

Now confident of the Governor's backing, in June 1822 George Meredith wrote a dictatorial letter to his adversary in which he ordered him to *'at once vacate the land he had taken by forcible possession,'* to which *'extraordinary notice'* he received the enquiry *'From whom have I taken the land by forcible possession'? From the aborigines of the island, or the kangaroos?'*[50]

Furious, George Meredith then put some of his stock to graze on the land cleared by Talbot's men and tore down some of his fences, following which he allowed his son George to set his dogs on the twenty pure merino rams while they were still in fold.[51] And now Thomas Buxton, newly appointed a constable, made his employer's battle his own by confiscating George Meredith's boat[52] for not having a port clearance. Such an outcry was raised at this that the Governor declared that Buxton had exceeded his duty and terminated his appointment, the position of Chief District Constable being given to Adam Amos instead, which raised a storm of protest.

In the winter of 1822 George Meredith received good news. His friends in England had petitioned Earl Bathurst so successfully on his behalf that he was to be given an additional 2000 acres (800 ha) adjoining his present land; this was to be a reserve and was to be granted provisionally for five years, after which it was to be given to him unconditionally should he have proved to be a worthy settler.[53] This meant that with William Talbot gone, as seemed sure, he could revert to his original choice of the best 2000 acres between the Meredith and Wye rivers and take his newly-granted 2000 acre reserve on the further side of the Wye. Since John Amos owned part of that, he would have to go.[54]

There remained one difficulty: the remaining portion of the land he wanted for his reserve was already taken.

It was occupied by Major Richard Honner. Arriving in Van Diemen's Land in November 1821, he had been advised by Governor Sorell to contact George Meredith with a view to joining his party at Great Swan Port. This he had done, presenting himself as a man of culture and means, and was welcomed as such. In January 1822 he and his family had moved on to 2000 acres of land lying to the north-east of John de Courcy Harte's Bellbrook and adjacent to John Amos' grant. There he had set to work building, fencing, and buying stock, and in so doing over-ran his finances.

Now, wishful to be rid of his new neighbour, George Meredith lent him money: he also let it be known among his stock-keepers that he would not punish them if any of his stock happened to break down Major Honner's fences and stray onto his property.[55]

Then something happened that robbed him of all complacency. In June 1823 a letter was received from Sir Thomas Brisbane in Sydney declaring that Mr Talbot had every right to the land he claimed and was to remain in possession of it. He enclosed a sketch re-aligning the two grants in such a way that William Talbot was given back all his buildings and cultivated land.[56]

George Meredith, his fighting instincts fully aroused, at once set to work in an endeavour to have the decision reversed. He wrote to the Governor; he wrote to the Governor's secretary; he wrote to the Governor-in-Chief. The letters contained no trace of his real feelings. They were respectful and diplomatic, apportioning no blame to any official, merely stating his claims and objections clearly and presenting facts that were quite true and others that were almost so.[57]

As soon as William Talbot heard the news that was so acceptable to him he requested that his grant be measured in accordance with the sketch received from Sydney. In reply the Governor told him that Mr Meredith had appealed against the decision and until he knew the result he could take no action.[58]

Restraint and diplomacy blown to the wind, the owner of Malahide wrote a furious letter, demanding his rights and accusing the Governor of favouring George Meredith.

And now the gentlemanly and affable governor, his patience at an end, replied in like vein, his quill screaming across the page.[59]

So began a war of words that went on and on, while the weeks turned into months, the months into years. Appeals were sent by both parties to Sydney, then to London, and with each letter the affair became more complicated. Many a time did William Sorell regret issuing an identical Order of Occupation, dated the same day, to both gentlemen.

CHAPTER 3

Ten months after landing the time had come for the families of the settlers to join their menfolk. A schooner, the *Mayflower,*[1] was chartered to bring them to the new settlement. After a trip of variety and excitement they arrived, and they and their furniture and belongings set off in bullock drays for their grants.

As soon as they were settled in, the *Mayflower* set off on her return voyage to Hobart Town. With the winds contrary they ran short of fresh water so dropped anchor out from Tasmans Peninsula and rowed ashore to replenish their supply. As they were rolling an empty cask towards a creek a number of armed bushrangers sprang out from the scrub and, seizing the men, ordered that they row them out to the *Mayflower*. There, taking possession of the vessel, they forced George Meredith and a carpenter into a small dinghy equipped with only one oar, and sailed off and left them.* Three days later, exhausted and with hands blistered, they reached the capital. Everything possible was done to find the runaways. A boat was dispatched after them but it was too late: the *Mayflower* was never seen again.[2]

A few weeks after the Deputy Surveyor-General had measured the grants at Great Swan Port in December 1821 Governor Macquarie sent the promised authority for the additional amounts of land he had approved for the settlers at George Meredith's request.[3] By the time the notification was received in Van Diemen's Land and had passed through official channels it was late autumn.[4] Once again a surveyor was sent to the area and the grants surveyed.

As William Talbot objected to John Meredith locating his additional land next to Malahide - for he feared at that time that he might be forced to move there himself - his extra thousand acres were taken at Jericho.[5]

Adam Amos, deciding that there was not the necessary available land next to his present grant, located his thousand acres about eight miles (13 km) to the north-east, his southern boundary adjoining that of Spring Vale. This he named Glen Gala Farm, the Swan River at his

---

*The area has from that time been known as Pirates Bay.

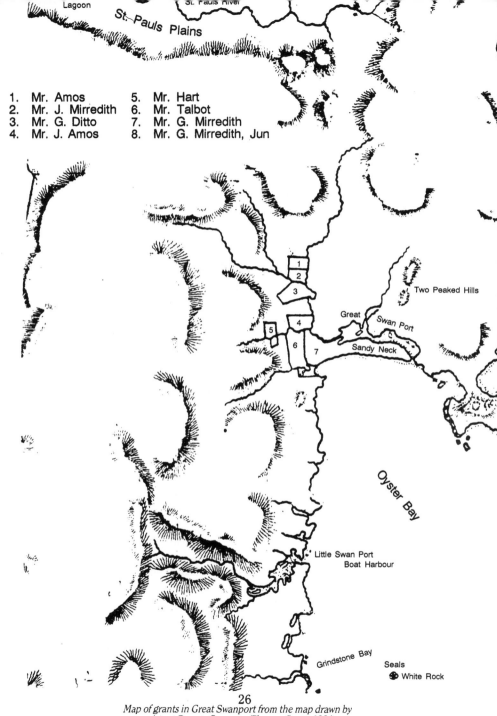

1. Mr. Amos
2. Mr. J. Mirredith
3. Mr. G. Ditto
4. Mr. J. Amos
5. Mr. Hart
6. Mr. Talbot
7. Mr. G. Mirredith
8. Mr. G. Mirredith, Jun

26

Map of grants in Great Swanport from the map drawn by assistant Deputy-Surveyor, Thomas Scott, 1824.

eastern border reminding him of the Gala Water beside which he had spent the first part of his life. There he built his chock-and-log hut, and on its completion moved his family to their new home.*

His brother John, now assured of his land, erected his residence on his 700-acre grant on the Wye, glad to be on his own land at last.[6] George Meredith, aware that the hut that Adam Amos had vacated was more comfortable than his own, moved across to it,[7] naming it Creek Hut.[8] The furniture he had brought out on the *Emerald* he stored in a windowless hut built by John Amos for the purpose.[9]

The Meredith boys, George and Charles, did not have an easy time. In one of his interminable letters to Sydney their father wrote: *'I am exceedingly conscious of the great change from their Native Land to a Colony such as this; and I owe to Mrs Meredith and to them my most anxious endeavours to make them feel the Change as little as possible.'*[10] His sons saw little evidence of this sentiment. No sooner had they arrived in Swan Port than the eleven-year-old Charles, delicate, pampered and frightened, was assigned the responsibility of finding extra food with which to supplement the government stores. Each morning he was roused from his tent outside Creek Hut and, often without breakfast, was sent out hunting kangaroo. The following year it became his duty to guard the valuable merino sheep while they pastured, during which time, terrified of aborigines, he flinched at every sound, expecting to be attacked.

The thought of snakes, too, occupied his mind, especially since John Amos had told him that once when 'at plough' without wearing any boots he had trodden on a large black snake, close to its head. Letting the bullocks take the plough where they would, he stood where he was until the snake had finished coiling round his leg. Then he had taken out his knife and cut off its head.[11]

One night he did not return home and his father, searching for him and the sheep, found them isolated in a winter flood; so cold and frightened was he that from then on he was allowed to sleep in the warmth and comfort of Creek Hut.

Much of the harsh treatment the children received was brought on by their refusal to accept their stepmother.[12] Conditioned as they were by their upbringing against tolerating such an unequal alliance, they could not reconcile themselves to her in her new role and were made

---

*Glen Gala is still owned by the Amos family.

to suffer in consequence. Gently reared, they were now forced to work as hard as did the Amos children.

To the north at Glen Gala Farm Adam Amos was in need of all the help he could get. With two square miles of virgin land to be brought under control, he was finding that getting a living from the unfamiliar country was both hard and perplexing. He and his family, hard-working though they had always been, were now forced to toil'more strenuously than ever. Their industry was apparent to any visitor; whereas most of the homes of the other settlers were surrounded by decaying wool and sheepskins, by bones, implements and piles of firewood,[13] their Scots thrift and neatness rebelled against such unsightliness and waste, so that their farm was always a model of neatness.

From May 1822 Adam's appointment as Chief District Constable increased his work, for there were many duties that went with his salary of £8.2.3 per year. He was expected to find and arrest runaway convicts and sheepstealers, hold a muster of all convict servants in the district each week, sign orders to allow any of them to move out of the area, and check that the settlers confined their stock within their often unfenced grants, as well as more minor duties.

In his diary* he listed all the convicts attending muster at Glen Gala Farm; six were from Major Honner, four from John Meredith, fifteen from John's cousin and six from William Talbot. At his property, Bell-brook, John de Courcy Harte - often absent at Little Swanport where he ran some stock on land owned by a man named Pritchard,-[14] rarely sent his men to the weekly check, for respect for regulations sat but lightly on his shoulders. Others complained of the distance involved and the time lost, as a result of which the musters were held monthly at John Amos' hut, *'that place being most sentrical'*.[15]

John had only one convict and Adam two, for neither was anxious to have *'free slaves'* under his command, the latter often remarking that if he had them about he never knew when he went to bed that he would not have his throat cut before morning.[16] For a while John was without help when the young convict assigned to him absconded. He was later found by stock-keepers at St Pauls Plains, to whom he admitted to being a runaway, and then *'fell a crying'*, after which he was taken in charge by a constable and sent to Port Dalrymple (Launceston) for trial.

---

*Adam Amos's diary is in the care of Mrs Ruth Amos, Swansea.

One of Adam Amos' government men had been borrowed by John Meredith in January to look after his stock at Jericho, and the other he often wished there. In his diary of 15th September 1822 he wrote: *'My servant Thomas Clare who hath been with me since May the 4th has shown great dissatisfaction and been very insolent for several weeks. Went off last Tuesday to go to Hobart Town to complain of want of Victuals we having had no bread for several days owing to the Vessel not arriving as we expected and no one in the Settlement has any except a little we ground from a little Spring wheat which we wished to preserve for sowing. He returned on Thursday night ... I reprimanded him for going & coming as he thought fit, he is one of the most hardened incorrigible Scoundrels ever I met with in my life. I wish from my Heart I were shot of him.'* A few days later he wrote: *'My servant Clare has been here since last Sunday. He only wrought on Monday and Wednesday and a little yesterday, having sold his jacket and burned his shoes so that he had no clothes to work with.'* A month later he was 'shot' of Thomas Clare when he was turned into the employ of the government.

On October 22nd 1822 Adam Amos recorded the departure of John Meredith for England, mentioning that the charge of his land and servants had been given over to George Meredith. He had shown delicacy in leaving Swan Port when he did, for Creek Hut, where he spent most of his time, was no place for a bachelor just then, for Mary Meredith was in the last week of her pregnancy. No complications were expected, it being her second confinement and she being healthy and reasonably young at twenty-seven. Nevertheless, her husband was rendered apprehensive through his love for her and arranged for the two nearest women, Ellen Buxton (who had just given birth to a son, George Swanport Buxton, on September 9th) and Hannah Amos (herself six months pregnant), to assist at the birth. All went well, and on October 31st 1822 the baby John, the second white child to be born at Great Swan Port, was delivered. The experience recalled to Hannah's mind the occasion two and a half years before when she had assisted in Wales at the illfated confinement of Sarah Meredith. She unwisely hinted to young Charles that Nurse Evans could have done more to save his mother,[17] which served to further embitter him in his attitude towards his father's second wife.

In December of that year Adam Amos recorded a change of location for a twenty four year old ticket-of-leave man, John Radford. A tall, fresh-faced labourer whose features were dominated by strongly-marked eyebrows, he had been sentenced at Exeter in 1817 to seven years' transportation[18] and on arrival in Van Diemen's Land the next year had been assigned to Silas Gatehouse's brother George, a man of good background who had himself been transported for seven years in 1803, but was now a respected and prosperous merchant in Hobart Town.[19] John Radford had been stock-keeping for him at Grindstone Bay, just north of Spring Bay, ever since,[20] but under his ticket-of-leave entitlement he was now free to work for William Talbot. This he did for a few months, being stationed near Little Swanport helping Alexander Reid mind his master's sheep, after which he voluntarily returned to his old position at Grindstone Bay.

On March 6th 1823 Adam Amos received a note from Thomas Buxton requesting his immediate presence at Malahide, as one of William Talbot's government men had been found dead. Sure enough, on arrival he found the convict, Thomas Hooley, *'quite dead'.*[21] *'It appeared on enquiry'.* he later wrote in his diary: *'that last night on the ingathering of the Harvest a Supper & Drink had been given and that the Deceased ate remarkably hearty, having had a gallon of rum amongst nine. They had all retired to rest. The deceased stumbled and fell as he went out. so did another who was going arm in arm with him; they would not be assisted by the others, who left them, expecting them to follow, but they had both layed on the place all night and was found by the overseer this morning, the one that was alive being unconscious of the other's fate. There being no other free settler there at the time we gave it as our opinion and Belief that Thomas Hooley had died by a Visitation of God, and gave orders that he should be buried on Saturday at Noon.'* On the Saturday he recorded: *'Went to attend Thomas Hooley's funeral. I asked before starting from Mr Buxton's whether anyone had any doubts or suspicion about the Death. Everyone appeared satisfied that he met his Death as we had before stated. He was buried on the line of march between Mr. Meredith & Talbot, about two hundred yards from where it is terminated on the South by a small river - in a coffin blackened -the grave about five feet deep. We put a fence of logs round it.'*

At this time George Meredith was in Sydney. Having optimistically plunged into various financial schemes which had all collapsed - including that of supplying butter to Edward Lord -he now owed that astute man of business an enormous amount of money. In such a financial state that he could not even pay the 25% interest, he had been served with a summons to appear in court, which, the colony being still under the jurisdiction of New South Wales, meant a trip to Sydney. There he was told that unless he could find bail to the amount of £1450 ($2900) he would be arrested.[22] At the trial it was conceded that the government itself had been the major cause of his financial distress by not having decided the exact area of land owned by him, which had prevented him from proceeding with any permanent undertakings. After detailing means by which he would repay his debts he was allowed to return to Hobart Town.

Once there, he sold to the Government Store, at a direct loss of £3 per head, all the cows belonging to him that had not been either stolen or lost, and also a thousand sheep at £1 each. When these were rounded up at Great Swan Port George and Charles, with two servants and no provisions, drove them in the depths of winter to the capital[23] - an ill-planned, ill-equipped expedition that impressed itself on their minds for life.

On January 19th 1823 Hannah Amos gave birth to twin daughters, Lavinia and Matilda. They arrived during a particularly difficult time at the farm, for the family was reduced to short rations, food being even more scarce there than at Glen Gala Farm, where they were living mainly on turnips, wallabies having eaten their first crop and the aborigines having stolen the potatoes they had planted.[24] There was no bread with which Hannah could build up her strength, for John was still feeling his way as to the proper seasons for sowing and was learning mainly by failures. Fortunately for mother and twins, when the time came to wean the babies Mary Meredith sent along some ships' biscuits, and these carried them through until the normal supply of wheat was available.

This food shortage had brought home to the Amos brothers the necessity for self-sufficiency and emphasised just how basic a need was flour to the settlement. Consequently, John drew up plans for a gristing mill, which was built at Glen Gala Farm and in the spring of 1823 was supplying meal to the settlers, as well as to the crews of schooners, constabulary parties and anyone passing through the district.

In February 1823 a forty-nine-year-old malcontent, Joseph Shaw, was being held in custody at the farm until he could be taken to Hobart

31

Town for trial, but so much trouble did he cause that one of the other convicts thrashed him and young John Amos, Adam's son, threatened to do the same. Upon this, he was returned to George Meredith, who sent him to help John Amos with the harvest - such as it was. On the completion of this work John returned him to his brother, but within a few days he had absconded. With him went Robert Gay, a red-headed young shoemaker who also worked for George Meredith - who, he complained, *used him ill*. Three weeks later they were picked up in Hobart Town, flogged, and returned to Great Swan Port. At the same time a nineteen-year-old convict named William Hollyoak, also employed by George Meredith, became ill and was sent to hospital in the capital, where he remained for a month.

In June, after sixteen months at Riversdale,* Major Honner left the district, loud in his denunciation of the treatment he had received there. When he had arrived, he said, he found that the whole country was distributed between the Meredith and Amos families, leaving no room for any further settlers with whom his family could associate; some things, he added, had transpired relative to one of Mr Meredith's family which prevented him remaining on friendly terms with them; also, he complained, Mr Meredith's cattle wandered at will through the country and had broken down many of his fences and were a deterrent to further farming efforts, and as a result he had been forced to leave the district and return to the capital, with his land still tied up at Great Swan Port.[25]

Richard Honner had not been long in Hobart Town before George Meredith contacted him. Telling him that he had been allotted a reserve grant of 2000 acres, he proposed that the Major should pass over to him the vacated grant, taking up another 2000 acres elsewhere instead. The Major was in a quandary: though reluctant to do George Meredith a good turn, the proposition was too good to miss. In the end he agreed, and terms were discussed, resulting in the value of the house and improvements (£120) being balanced against the Major's debt.

Young George Meredith, having turned sixteen the previous year, was now a landowner in his own right, though not to the extent he had expected. In spite of the fact that his father had been promised 2000 acres on his behalf before he left England, the largest area that could be extracted from the government was 500 acres.[26] This, as had been

---

* Riversdale was first known as Honner's Plains.

anticipated, was the land on which Creek Hut was built, and there young George continued to live with his parents, working his own land, Redbanks.

Other grants were approved at the same time - June 30th, 1823. Thomas Buxton, now confident that he had a working knowledge of farming conditions in Van Diemen's Land and thoroughly familiar with all the surrounding country, still acted as William Talbot's manager but had made application for 500 acres (200 ha) some twelve miles (19km) down the coast. Upon receiving authorisation to own the land, he named it Mayfield, after Mayfield House, his home in Derbyshire. Directly opposite the creek that formed his southern boundary (now Buxton Creek) a storekeeper from New Norfolk, James C. Cumming,[27] was granted a thousand acres, while back in Swan Port Joseph Allport, a lawyer in Hobart Town,[28] was officially allotted 1140 acres (456 ha) on the opposite side of the Swan River from John Amos' land[29] (now The Grange).

A settlement at Great Swan Port now being established, in October 1823 the Superintendent of Police, Mr Adolarius Humphrey, decided that a census should be taken, and General Muster forms were sent to Adam Amos. These he distributed among the settlers, and on reading them through after having collected them again he realised that George Meredith had entered all but his two younger children as being two years older than they actually were, but passed the form in without comment, knowing the reason behind it - that the sooner young Charles turned sixteen the sooner he would get his land grant. The return read as follows:

Wm. Talbot	(ship *Caroline*)	Mary Ann Amos	7 years
Thomas Buxton	(*Westmorland*)	Martha Amos	5 years
Ellen Buxton		Caroline Amos	3 years
Mary Buxton	10 years	Matilda)	
Sarah Buxton	7 years	Lavinia)	born 1/23
Agnes Buxton	5 years	John Harte	
Thomas Buxton	3 years	Henry Lee	
George (native)	1 year		
John Amos	(*Emerald*)		
Mrs Amos			
James Amos	16 years		
Ellen Amos	10 years		

George Meredith	(ship *Emerald*)	Adam Amos	16 years
Mrs Meredith		Margaret Amos	14 years
George Meredith	19 years	Helen Amos	11 years
Sarah Meredith	17 years	Mary Amos	9 years
Louisa Meredith	16 years	Janet Amos	5 years
Sabina Meredith	15 years	Robert Amos	3 years
Charles Meredith	14 years	Adam Amos	(*Emerald*)
Henry Meredith	6 years	Mrs Amos	
John (native)	1 (31.10.22)	James Amos	19 years
John Amos	18 years		

There were thirty-eight free persons and thirty-one convicts, including two females.[30]

With a total of nearly seventy people in the settlement George Meredith went to Hobart Town to press for the appointment of a magistrate, a constable and a lock-up for prisoners.[31] He came home disappointed in all respects, and furious in one - he considered it his right to be a magistrate, in view of the previous discussion held between him and Governor Sorell, and had failed to obtain the office.

CHAPTER 4

As news did not travel quickly in such an isolated district it was six days before Adam Amos heard of the first murder in his district. He entered the details in his diary: *'November 20th, 1823. I have heard that a large Mob of Natives has killed one of Mr. Gatehouse's men at Grindestone Bay and also Mr. Wm Hollyoak, who was on his way here from the Hospital, and wounded another who got away from them and fled to pitwater. His master and some of his men came after them to Mr. Talbot's, where they found them last night and fired on them, when they all scattered. A native of Sidney, Meskity as he is called, was with them and got off too, who is a dangerous fellow as he is ackwainted with fire arms and has the Natives at his command. One of his wives stopped and went with them to Mr. Gatehouse's home to show where the dead Bodys are hid.'*

The man who got away was the ticket-of-leave convict, John Radford. About sixty-five aborigines had been camped for a few days near the stock hut where he and a Tahiti native, Mammoa, lived; William Hollyoak was recouping there on his way back from hospital. When the blacks speared a sheep and began to roast it the stock-keepers objected, and a quarrel broke out. Mammoa and William Hollyoak were killed and then John Radford set off through the bush to save his life. A spear struck him, and, half pausing, he jerked it out, at the same time dragging off his boots.[1] As he set off again a second spear hit him and became so deeply embedded in a fleshy part of his person that it was impossible for him to pull it out and he was forced to endure the pain and presence of it until he reached Prossers Plains[2] (Buckland). When George Gatehouse heard what had happened he gathered men round him and set off in pursuit of the blacks.

After the attack the aborigines had proceeded eastwards and when they reached Redbanks had asked young George Meredith if they could camp there for the night. Next day they went on to Malahide, where they requested permission to camp for a few days. Unaware of the murders, William Talbot allowed them to stay. When the pursuing party of whites arrived they fired on them and a number escaped by swimming and wading across the lagoon, while others ran into the scrub. Among them was Muskitoo, who, wounded, made his way to Bellbrook where John Harte, in spite of knowing what had happened at Grindstone Bay, did nothing to detain him though he did nothing to help him either. A thorough search was made by George Gatehouse and his men but they were forced to return without any captives.

On the way home they called in at Mayfield, where they found that Thomas Buxton had completed building his sod hut and had moved in. Situated between Little Swanport and Great Swan Port, it was to prove a danger spot, being an ideal place for 'bolters' and aborigines to attack. Within a few weeks William Talbot's men had captured a bushranger there. Some twenty miles (22 km) to the north Adam Amos was notified of this and hurried down to take the man in charge. To his disgust on arrival he found that Thomas Buxton, after making the escapee, Gould, promise to give himself up to the magistrate at Pittwater, had let him go. Some time later he learned that the man had kept his promise.

Less than a fortnight later a party of aborigines visited Mayfield. Thomas Buxton was away at the time and learned on his return that they had set alight a brush fence which ran beside the hut, forcing a settler who had spent the night there to rush out and try to extinguish it, during which time he was speared in the back. The blacks then climbed trees and threw firesticks at the thatch, which caught fire. It was extremely fortunate that just then a military party in pursuit of escapees and blacks should arrive; at the sight of them the attackers disappeared.

They went to Glen Gala Farm. Adam Amos wrote of it in his diary: 'December 14th, 1823. The Natives who has been of late in the woods near my Hutt have this day set the Grass on fire near my farm. I thought it prudent to frighten them, having heard that they had thrattened at Mr Talbot's to burn my corn when sircumstances give them opportunity. I sent my eldest son who was joined by two of Mr. Meredith's men, who fired on them and wounded one. The Mob, who appeared numerous, fled over the hill. They purshoud them for some time & returned after dark with a quantity of spears, etc.' They came again the next night, and again a fortnight later, in attempts to burn the corn, but each time the fires were put out before they could destroy the crop.

In order to see what progress was being made in the new settlement Adolarius Humphrey required a Stock and Crop Return.

The completed form sent to him by Adam Amos read as follows:

STATEMENT OF CROPS AND STOCK IN SWAN PORT IN DECEMBER 1823

	Grant	Tillage	Wheat	Barley	Oats	Peas	Potatoes	Garden	Sheep	Cattle	Horses	Pigs	Assigned Servants
Wm Talbot	2000	40	22	9	6	-	3	1	3010	320	2	2	11
Thos. Buxton	500	-	-	-	-	-	-	-	-	-	-	-	-
J. Meredith	1000	-	-	-	-	-	-	-	-	-	-	-	-
G. Meredith, Jnr.	500	30	10	5½	4	4	5½	1	400	60	-	30	-
Adam Amos	1000	45	30	6	2	3	-	1	200	66	-	11	1
John Amos	700	8	3	1	-	1	2	1	100	60	-	18	1
John Harte	700	40	20	2	10	-	6	2	-	8	-	53	6

G. Meredith, Snr. 2000 acres ordered by Governor Macquarie and suspended by Sir Thomas Brisbane

Because in value a horse equalled about a hundred acres of land (40 ha), the only two in the district were owned by William Talbot, he being the wealthiest settler there. Whenever anyone had to visit Hobart Town he managed as best he could without a horse. Sometimes when a vessel called in at Oyster Bay the captain would take passengers back to the capital, but generally the travellers preferred to walk rather than suffer the discomforts of such a trip; usually, too, it was quicker, taking either three or four days, instead of up to a week, and sometimes longer, by sea. When walking it was the usual practice to spend the first night at Little Swanport, (where both William Talbot and John de Courcy Harte had stock huts), the second at Prossers Plains, and the third either at Richmond or Hobart Town, via Austin's Ferry.

Whenever George Meredith took recalcitrant servants to the capital for punishment, to ensure their safe arrival he preferred to travel with them by sea. In April 1824, accompanied by the still troublesome Joseph Shaw and another convict who had had the temerity to strike him, he prepared to set out in his whaleboat; however, at the last minute Shaw eluded him, and as he planned to attend an important meeting he was forced to leave without him. This meeting had been called to discuss the long delays in government business caused by having to refer it to New South Wales, with particular emphasis being placed on the necessity of having to travel to attend any case referred to the Supreme Court. He arrived in Hobart Town in time to attend the inaugural meeting to form a movement for the separation of the island from New South Wales, and, holding strong views on the subject, took a leading part in the proceedings.[3] In such a situation he was at his best, his fluency, knowledge of law and clear grasp of affairs enabling him to make a valuable contribution.

On his return home he found that after his departure Joseph Shaw had gone to Glen Gala Farm, where he complained that his master had not given him enough clothing, and that as he was forced to work without a shirt his health had suffered and he could not continue under such conditions. He was told that if he did not appear at the roll call next day in a shirt he would be reported; he turned up with just enough rags on him to make him respectable, and so passed muster.

In June 1824 Mary Meredith - frequently left for long periods to manage affairs alone, and hating it[4] - sent word to the Chief District Constable that the skipper of the Albion, an American negro named Richard Hazard,[5] had reported that his whalers had seen bushrangers in the district. Adam Amos at once appealed to the Superintendent of Police for a search party to assist in locating them, but the only help he received was one constable, who brought the news that fourteen convicts had escaped from Macquarie Harbour and were probably making for the more isolated parts of the island. The name of the leader was Matthew Brady. A warning was at once relayed to the settlers, as well as the skipper of the Albion.

It was not unusual for whaling ships to be in the bay, for in late winter particularly the waters about Freycinet Peninsula abounded with whales, the mothers coming to the calm waters to nurse their young and travelling through the Schouten Passage in an almost continuous line 'like pigs through a gate'.[6]

There was money in whaling, as George Meredith was quick to rea-lise. For five shillings (50c) a year he leased three acres of crown land situated about twelve miles (19 km) across the bay from Creek Hut and there set up a bay whaling station[7] which he named *The Fisheries*.* It was while he was in Hobart Town purchasing trypots, boilers, lines, cutting implements and boilers and hiring experienced whalers to supplement the pulling crew he would choose from his own men, that Mary was left to cope with the bushranger alarm.

Drawing of George Meredith with a whaling harpoon (Northern Regional Library)

*The Fisheries was at Coles Bay.

He had so timed this trip that he was able to attend a farewell dinner given for William Sorell in June 1824, for that official had been recalled. As a result of his unconventional domestic affairs having been reported to the Home Government official action had to be taken, and in spite of a strongly supported petition appealing against this the termination of his appointment was final.[8] George Meredith in particular was sorry to see him leave.

At the beginning of July the minds of the Great Swan Port settlers were diverted from thoughts of governors and whalers and escaped convicts by the news that one of George Meredith's stockmen, Robert Gay, had been murdered by the aborigines. He had been stationed at a stock hut near the head of Moulting Lagoon with another assigned servant, David Raynor. The latter went out with the cattle one morning, leaving his companion to go hunting in order to replenish their food supply. When Raynor returned that evening he was alarmed to see the dead bodies of their dog and cat lying near two unskinned kangaroos. On investigation he found that their hut had been plundered. There being no trace of Robert Gay he hurried to the stock hut at Spring Vale where his two brothers were stationed. In company with them and John Amos he returned, and for two days they searched before they were able to find Robert Gay's body. It was submerged in a pool about three hundred yards (274 m) from the stock hut, and only two fingers -the flesh of which had been eaten by crows - showed above water. Leaving the corpse undisturbed they reported the matter to Creek Hut, upon which Mary Meredith sent word of the tragedy to the Chief District Constable.[9]

Adam Amos found that the body had been horribly mutilated by the blacks. After burying it beside that of Thomas Hooley he organised a search party for the murderers. The number of searchers was swelled by the fortuitous arrival of some soldiers who had just captured seven members of Matthew Brady's gang. Under the control of Lieutenant William Gunn they set off for Creek Hut, where they were informed that whalers from The Fisheries had captured some aborigines who promised to lead them to Muskitoo, who had been among those responsible for the death of Robert Gay. Arriving on the peninsula, George and John Raynor went with two of the black girls, who showed them where they had hidden the dead man's rifle and the blankets and food they had stolen from the hut, but of Muskitoo and the men who had murdered him there was no trace.

Mary Meredith now reported that four whalers who were her husband's assigned servants had absconded. Adam Amos, in pursuit, followed their trail until he reached James Cumming's hut near the Buxton River, where he found them preparing to spend the night. Because he was alone he judged it unwise to attempt to arrest them, and the next morning set off for Hobart Town. Once there, he reported their escape and within a few days one was taken and sent to gaol for a month, but the others were not found.

On his way home he heard that the five remaining members of the Brady gang had been seen at the Prosser River, while further on James Cumming reported seeing three. From then on Lieutenant Gunn and his men ranged up and down the coast in pursuit, at times coming very close to capturing them. Guided by young James Amos, at one time they returned from St Pauls Plains with the news that the bushrangers had seized a convict and ordered him to lead them to Glen Gala Farm so that they could hold it up. An armed watch was kept all night but no absconders appeared. It was later reported by the captive guide that he had led the gang past the Amos's farm to a more populated area and had settled them down for the night near Malahide, hoping that the men working about would see them. This they actually did, but out of sympathy for fellow-convicts decided not to report their presence. Next morning the sound of crowing roosters nearby so alarmed the bushrangers that they forced their guide to lead them to Little Swanport, where, after ransacking Cumming's hut, they stole a boat and escaped, leaving their ex-captive to raise the alarm.[10]

Lieutenant Gunn and his men set out in pursuit. They failed to catch up with them, but near Grindstone Bay another search party under the charge of James Amos was successful in finding one member of the gang. Exhausted and hungry, he offered no resistance. When James covered him with his gun and shouted, *'Hands up and surrender or I fire',* he said, *'Fire and be damned to you',* and handed over his rifle.[11]

That night, safely back at Glen Gala Farm James looked out of the window and saw six armed men advancing towards the building. He shouted an alarm, and at once all the members of the family seized guns and took up positions at the windows. Adam Amos, rifle at the ready, called a warning to the men that they would be shot unless they surrendered. A hasty shout assured him that there was no need for alarm, as they were a police party sent for their protection by Mr Humphrey.

A week later Lieutenant Gunn arrived back at Oyster Bay. Though an enormously strong and active man, he was now ill from exhaustion and discouraged by his lack of success. In spite of this he continued to range the coast in pursuit of the runaways. Then, hearing that they were now terrorising the Huon Valley, he prepared to search for Muskitoo instead, when to his relief he heard that an aborigine who had been brought up in the home of Dr Luttrell had led two constables to him and he had been captured nearby.* On the point of collapse, he was persuaded to rest at a shanty provided for military use close to Creek Hut, where he was reported by Adam Amos to be *very poorly'*.

George Meredith, in contrast, was far from poorly; for him things were going well. He would soon be moving out of the cramped quarters of Creek Hut, for he had been given extra servants, among them a carpenter who was building him a small cottage (Redbanks) some distance behind his present home.[12] Mary had presented him with a daughter and had made a good recovery; and his whaling enterprise was succeeding under the administration of young George; indeed, so lucrative was it that he decided to venture into the sealing industry as well. He had a vessel, the *Cygnet,#* built on the left bank of the

The hut built by John Amos in 1821 in the foreground. The original Red Banks homestead & kitchen are in the Meredith Collection, State Library of Tasmania

---

* Muskitoo was tried for murder and hanged on February 25th, 1825.

The Cygnet was later wrecked on Maria Island.

Meredith River, just seaward of Creek Hut,* and in September 1824 entered into an agreement with three sealers that they should lead an expedition to the Straits Islands. Because he supplied the boats and equipment he specified that he was to have one-third of all the oil, sealskins, swanskins and feathers, but to his disappointment when the men arrived back in February 1825 they brought with them only 317 sealskins and no swanskins or feathers at all. But the next expedition proved more successful and as a result four casks containing 361 sealskins were exported to England, where each skin sold for twenty-five shillings.[13] So pleased was he with the *Cygnet* that he built another vessel, the *Black Swan*, which was slightly larger. However, after a few trips to the Straits Islands and South Australia she was wrecked in Bass Strait.[14]

William Talbot remained an ever-present source of annoyance to George Meredith. In an effort to relieve his feelings of frustration he impounded quite a number of his stock. In October 1824 Adam Amos, as Poundkeeper, advised the owner of Malahide that he held twenty-three of his cattle, upon which he received word that he could keep them. This spurred on George Meredith, and he kept rounding up more and more until there were over two hundred head of stock grazing Adam Amos's pasture. At this stage Thomas Buxton, who was still working at Malahide, came to collect them, but on failing to pay the fee returned without them. Then the owner himself arrived. Adam Amos recorded the event. *'Mr. Talbot arrived and after some mighty words asked Mr. Meredith's charges, or if there were any. I told him it was one shilling per head for all of an age to graze and he said he would pay nothing. I answered that he would not have the cattle without. He said he would not pay and would have the cattle too. Then gave me an order from Sheriff Abbott bearing date the second currant to deliver up Mr. Talbot's cattle as Mr. Talbot had entered into a replevin bond so I had no more to say. Only Mr. T. thought it proper to show a little of his rancour by saying that I had lost a number of his cattle and that I would not allow his servant on the day that the cattle were brought here to take the number of them, which two things I told him were damned lies. He thereafter made several ill-natured remarks on me and Mr Meredith which I took care to answer in the same style. I hope I shall have no more of him.'*

---

*The vessels built on the Meredith River had to be launched sideways, as the river was so narrow.

Sir George Arthur (an anonymouns miniature: Dixson Library, State Library of N.S.W.)

CHAPTER 5

Lieutenant-Governor Arthur was of medium build. He was dark and neat. His manner was courteous and distant. Any softness in his nature was centred on his God, his wife and his twelve children.[1] He drove himself and others hard, was efficient in all he did, and was fully in command of himself at all times.[2]

He took office in Van Diemen's Land in May, 1824.

Already he was well versed in details about the land dispute between the two leading settlers at Great Swan Port, Lord Bathurst having supplied him with page after page on the case. To his mind, Bathurst had said, the priority of choice should be assigned to Mr Meredith, but if Colonel Arthur found that the evidence did not support his opinion he would be glad of further information.[3]

Never one to procrastinate, soon after his arrival Colonel Arthur sent for Lieutenant Meredith.

The two men took an instant dislike to each other - a dislike that was to deepen with the passing of years.[4]

The interview that followed was the first of many. Sometimes the Governor met with one claimant, sometimes with the other, and occasionally with both together, but as he reported to Lord Bathurst...'*unfortunately, when brought together, their long cherished feelings of animosity always overcame their better judgement, and the effects equally deprived me of the possibility of correctly tracing up, as to time and circumstance, the points on which the question was to turn.'*[5] Tracing and deducting and surmising and discerning, he finally felt he was in possession of as many of the facts as he ever would be, and came to the conclusion that there was nothing in them that indicated one man having a stronger case than the other. But because he had to make a choice and because Earl Bathurst had supported George Meredith's cause, in August 1824 he decided in favour of him.[6] Consequently he directed William Talbot to place his house and lands under the ownership of the government, and gave George Meredith authority to occupy the original 2,000 acres (800 ha) he had chosen on his exploratory trip in 1821, the only requirement

45

being that he pay for any improvements that had been made on them since then.[7]

William Talbot accepted his decision without argument, vilification, or threat of legal action, a response so gratifying to the Governor that he granted him an additional thousand acres to add to the two thousand to which he was entitled. He took care to emphasise that in doing so he was taking into account the fact that nearly a thousand pounds had been spent on the property.[8] He also made it quite clear to both men that neither had any claim on the government and that the thousand acres given in no way represented compensation. Rather to his surprise and certainly to his gratification he received letters from both settlers thanking him for the patience and impartiality with which the investigation had been carried out.[9]

After some months of searching William Talbot chose for his grant an area in an unsettled district. It was close by the South Esk and Break-o'Day rivers - a place superior in every way to the property he had been forced to leave. Keeping intact the links with his place of birth, this selection, too, was named Malahide.[10]*

In his official capacity Adam Amos, early in 1825, was required to assess the improvements William Talbot had made at Old Malahide.

Malahide (Alport Library & Museum of Fine Arts.)

---

* Malahide, a most successful property, is still owned and occupied by a member of the Talbot family.

Ever curious, he undertook the task with enthusiasm. The old roughly made hut that had been thrown together in 1821 had collapsed and in its place was a five roomed residence with bound doors and glass windows. With the underground dairy, the outbuildings, the fences and the cultivated areas, he estimated the total improvements at a modest £700. He then carried the keys to Redbanks and handed them over to George Meredith for safe-keeping.[11]

Never did keys fit more snugly into any man's hand.

Now all that George Meredith needed was to pay the £700 and decided the exact boundaries of the land he was to own. Already he had received permission to locate his 2 000-acre reserve in that part of Riversdale that Major Honnor had occupied, so he mentally re-arranged the boundaries so that they would enclose the richest land possible. As this included the land occupied by John Amos he sent for him and told him that he must move from there,[12] promising to give him the extra one hundred acres (40 ha) mentioned in the agreement as compensation.[13]

He now possessed 4 000 acres of land, and had assumed ownership of John Meredith's 2 000 acres as well, but his passion for land was unsatisfied and he lusted for more. His busy mind conceived a possible way of acquiring some. He wrote to Lord Bathurst requesting that he should be given a thousand acres of land, as had been the case with William Talbot, pointing out the trouble and inconvenience that he had experienced because of the government's blunder.[14] He then reconciled himself to the long wait before he could expect a reply.

John Amos, now with eight hundred acres (320 ha) to locate instead of seven hundred, held half in abeyance when he persuaded his nephew James to let him have his own recently acquired grant on the eastern bank of the Swan,[15] opposite the mouth of the Wye. There, for the third time since his arrival in the district, he built a residence for himself and family.*

About this time the inhabitants of Great Swan Port learned that there was to be a considerable increase in the number of government men in their vicinity. Although about two-thirds of those in the colony were housed and maintained by settlers, difficulty was being experienced in accommodating the rest. Not only were barracks and prisons overflowing, but more offenders were arriving all the time.[16]

---

*There is no trace now of the early residences built and occupied by John Amos

To relieve the pressure Governor Arthur looked about for a suitable place of secondary punishment for the less dangerous criminals, and decided on Maria Island. Preparations for the penal settlement were carried out, and early in 1825 the *Prince Leopold* conveyed the first prisoners to the island - fifty convicts and their overseers, under the command of Lieutenant Peter Murdoch.

There was difficulty in establishing the settlement. The men proved to be both lazy and unskilled in agriculture,[17] and the endeavour was so frustrating to Lieutenant Murdoch that late in the winter he left. His place was taken by Major Lord.

Major Thomas Daunt Lord was no stranger to George Arthur, having served under him for a number of years when he had been in command of an establishment at Honduras on the Central American coast.[18] Nine months after his arrival in Van Diemen's Land he had obtained the position of Commandant, and, once on the island, undertook his duties with military precision. Under his discipline the men improved in their work, for he was not one to overlook slackness.

As more and more convicts were sent to the island tenders were called locally for food to be supplied to them and George Meredith was the successful tenderer for meat. At £2,000 a year the new enterprise proved lucrative. He had plenty of government men on hand to kill and dress his innumerable cattle and sheep, and his son Charles, now nearly fifteen, was of a size and age to take charge of the *Cygnet* on its trips to and from Darlington.[19] Near Old Malahide a tannery was built to deal with the hides of the sheep and cattle, as well as those of kangaroos, seventeen bales of which were exported to England in August, 1825.[20]

It proved a setback in progress to the district as a whole, and certainly to George Meredith personally, when it was discovered by officialdom that the *Cygnet* was being used by a man named John Arney to carry stolen government property from Maria Island, visiting vessels then conveying the goods away from the vicinity.[21] Furious, Governor Arthur forbade any ship at all to enter Oyster Bay - on the 'pretence', as George Meredith termed it, that smuggling was being carried out. Unable to remain passive under the slur, he set about building the largest vessel he had yet attempted - a schooner - and when it was completed set it to trading between the East Coast and Hobart Town. He named it *Independent*.

In July 1825 bushrangers appeared again at Great Swan Port. The settlers first became aware of their presence when George Raynor reported that a large number of sheep had been driven from the flock he was tending for his master, and at once a search party was organised by James Amos, who was now an assistant constable. *'They followed the sheep tracts about 30 miles to the Sea Beach near St. Patricks Head',* wrote Adam Amos in his diary, *'and there the sheep had been killed, the heads and feet burned and the Bellys remaining on the grass. James also states that they found a cow that had been shot and the Ball fell out of her belly as they turned her over.'* That was the only trace they found of the bushrangers at that time, but a few days later more of George Meredith's sheep were missing. This time he put young George in charge of the search party, but when they had followed the tracks to within ten miles of St Patricks Head he turned back, saying they would re-examine the area already covered. Although no one agreed with his decision not one of the party - even Adam Amos himself - cared to go against him for fear of incurring his father's displeasure. When they reached Moulting Lagoon the Chief District Constable, lame from rheumatism in his knees and with a temper that threatened to erupt, left them and went home, where he wrote, *'It is the worst managed business ever I saw or heard of, as we neither followed the sheeps tracts nor went to the place where the last were slaughtered.'* Young George, too, returned home, leaving the remaining members of the party free to trek up the coast again. When they came near the place where the previous sheep had been killed they caught sight of a man cutting up a seal cub. Creeping up on him, they seized him, and, tying his hands, forced him to lead them to the others. *'He informed them,'* wrote Adam later, *'that there were six besides himself - five of them at the time, sleeping under the Sail on the Beach. My son and party, consisting of three, went up to the men asleep and ordered them to surrender, which they did and delivered up their arms. My son took and bound one but before they had any more secured and while one of my son's party was aside planting the people's arms, the fellows made a rush and over-powered James and party, and took from them their arms and ammunition, and bound the three. When the other man returned they also bound him, and shortly thereafter took to their boat, leaving the party's arms and called to the man that was not bound that he might loose them. They had made the arms useless by wetting them. They took all the ammunition they had found on our party so they had nothing further to apprehend.'*

Upon his returning home, James, after receiving a blistering lecture from his father, was sent to Port Dalrymple to report the matter, following which a party under the charge of Lieutenant Gunn arrived.

Every day they went out in search of bushrangers, but on October 8th 1825, some hours after they had left their head-quarters the Brady gang descended on Redbanks. George Meredith himself was in Hobart Town - perhaps fortunately, for he was an extremely brave man and had he been there the attack would not have proceeded as smoothly as it did. Mary, seeing the party approach, sent a man on horseback after Lieutenant Gunn's military party, and no sooner had he set off than the bushrangers broke into the hut. Placing the servants under armed guard, Matthew Brady assured Mary and her stepdaughters that they would not be harmed; however, they were quick to obey when he ordered them to cook a meal and serve it.[22] Their hunger satisfied, the men started looting. Boxes were broken open, valuables piled in heaps, the store raided and supplies of food put aside. Then the wine and spirits were discovered and much was consumed on the spot. Launching two of the owner's whaleboats in the creek, they started filling them with load after load of stolen goods. Each time they returned to the hut for a fresh supply a half domesticated young aborigine who was often about the place helped himself to whatever items appealed to him. These he hid among the bushes, where they stayed undiscovered until a later time, when, upon his trying to sell them, the cache was disclosed.[23] The bushrangers, by now tipsy, failed to notice that their hoard was diminishing and continued to add to it. It was then that Charles Meredith, returning from a hunting trip, saw them. Hurrying to where David Raynor was minding stock some distance away, he sent him off to Glen Gala Farm for help. Then, stealthily making his way to the shelter of some scrub on the bank of the creek, he watched as the robbers, accompanied by one of the assigned servants*, rowed away out of sight. Among the stolen goods in the boat was some valuable silver which had belonged to his mother and which was later discovered buried in a distant locality, with Brady's sign, an x, scratched on each item.[24]

The runaways were well on their way before the frustrated William Gunn arrived at Redbanks. With no boat available for them the military party was forced to walk overland in the direction of Thomas Buxton's property. It was there that luck favoured them, for a schooner

---

*That night Henry Hunt was killed in a drunken brawl.

was anchored offshore. Boarding her, they set off under full sail and it was not long before they caught sight of the bushrangers. But the bushrangers also caught sight of them. Heading for land, they beached the boats, burdened themselves with their loot, and disappeared into the bush. There, no amount of searching located them.

The escapees' supplies lasted a fortnight and then, audaciously, they went to Pittwater, where Lieutenant Gunn and his men had made their headquarters. Nonchalantly taking over the house of Robert Bethune, for two days they lived the lives of gentlemen,[25] and then, hungry for excitement, raided the gaol. With fine liberality they set the prisoners free and then filled the empty cells with civilians and soldiers, after which they returned to their temporary home. During the raid the gaoler, keeping his distance, had seen what happened and ran to tell Lieutenant Gunn. He, with more valour than sense, set off to capture the gang singlehanded. When his six foot seven form (200 cm) loomed out of the darkness the sentries on guard had no difficulty in recognising their enemy. They shot him in the arm, effectively handicapping him, and made their escape.[26] The arm later had to be amputated, earning for him the nickname of 'Wingy' Gunn.

At Great Swan Port no more was heard of the bushrangers for a while, and the attention of the settlers turned to two new arrivals, Hugh and John Addison. They were builders from Scotland who had landed on the island in 1825. Within a short space of time John had been appointed Superintendent of Government Masons,[27] but wishing to be landowners as well as builders, they applied for and were given a location order for six hundred acres (240 ha) at Great Swan Port. On arriving there, they set about looking for a site. The land they chose was about four miles south of Redbanks, bounded on the south by the small Stony River and to the east by the waters of Oyster Bay. They named their country retreat Coswell and then, owning the land but not belonging to it, returned in December to the capital, where their building skills were in immediate demand. Once immersed in their trade, they learned that they were no longer required to work with George Evans, for Governor Arthur, almost bemused at the ineptitude and laxity of his Deputy Surveyor-General, had encouraged him to resign, suggesting he give rheumatism as a reason for his retirement.[28] At the same time the Governor was relieved to learn that Van Diemen's Land was now a separate colony from New South Wales, a fact which was also welcomed by most of its settlers, among whom was George Meredith who had worked hard for the island's independence.[29]

The bushrangers did not stay away from the East Coast for long. Soon eight of them took the Maria Island meat boat and sailed to Oyster Bay, where they transferred to a schooner, sank it, and made

John Addison

their way ashore to the Schoutens - that area of land between the eastern part of Moulting Lagoon and the sea. Leading a military party sent from Hobart Town, Adam Amos set out after them. All day the men searched, and the next day as well. Then towards evening as they approached George Meredith's stock hut the door burst open and eight figures broke from it and dashed into the bush. The weary pursuers raced after them but the gathering darkness left them no chance of finding them and they returned to the hut. There they found the captain of the sunken schooner, bound and lying on the floor. He told Adam Amos that the escapees were planning to rob Glen Gala Farm. Thoroughly alarmed, Adam hurried off to defend his family and property, and so upset was he that, when caught in a severe thunderstorm, he lost his way. *'I was much grieved,'* he wrote later, *'thinking the fellows would be at my house before me. I at last made out the way and on my arrival was informed that two of the robbers, Murphy and another, had made their appearance within two hundred yards of my house with fixed bayonets - that my son and men, along with my brother's son and men, made them take to their heels which was all they could do, having only one piece. I was now in full belief that I would be attacked and made all ready, keeping two sentries all night, but nothing happened.'* The military party arrived from the stock hut and stayed there next day in case the bushrangers returned, and then, to Adam's dismay, were ordered by George Meredith to station themselves at a hut at Redbanks in order to guard his family. That night the last entry was made in his diary: *'So I am left to my fate'.**

By this time, however, the bushrangers had realised that their presence in the district was too widely known for comfort and had moved inland, where it was officially estimated that close to a hundred other escaped prisoners were at large.[30] In Hobart Town report after report was received of attacks, depredations and killings. It was no longer safe for a free man to travel: neither was it safe for him to stay at home. The audacity of some gangs led them to go even into the capital itself, where the citizens became so alarmed that they offered to take over the duties of the local police and military, releasing them for duty in country areas. Their offer was accepted by Governor Arthur, who not only took part in the hunt himself, but also released prisoners to help, offering undreamed-of rewards to any who would give information leading to arrests, especially of members of the Brady

---

* No more diaries of Adam Amos have ever been found. but there are many letters which he wrote from Hobart.

James McCabe. Lithograph by or after Thomas Bock.
(Allport Library & Museum of Fine Arts.)

gang. With the offer of high rewards the released prisoners began infiltrating the gangs and information started to flow through. Soon arrests were made. James McCabe, illclad and barefooted,[31] was caught and hanged on January 1st, 1826, but Brady continued at large until finally a new member of his gang led police to his hiding place in the north of the island and he was wounded. Though he escaped that time he was captured shortly afterwards by John Batman and hanged in May,1826.[32]

So concentrated and effective was the search for the bushrangers that their tyranny became a thing of the past, and at last the people of the colony were able to go about their daily business with little fear of attack and many who had left their farms and fled to the town for safety now returned to the country.

CHAPTER 6

Early in 1826 Adam Amos sent a letter to William Pringle, a friend in Scotland, telling him all that had happened since coming to Van Diemen's Land. *'But even after all I have undergone,'* he wrote, *'I think my constitution has improved by it and is better now in my 52nd year than when I was 25.'* His three eldest sons, James, John and Adam, he said, were now strong men and the two eldest girls, Margaret and Helen, were taller than their mother, and all were a great comfort.

The farm, he added, had five hundred acres of poor sandy soil covered in trees called Stringy Bark, the timber of which was harder than oak and sank like a stone in water but split well and was good for fences and flooring; the other half had some very fine soil *'as fat as a dunghill',* with a deep river forming a natural fence on one side. The animals were very strange, many of them having false bellies in which the young were conceived and kept until they could shift for themselves. There were devils in plenty, resembling the badger in Scotland, and they had once caught a kind of ostrich, which he believed would soon be extinct.

Of the aborigines he wrote: *'The natives are the very last of the human species in arts or in anything that is like comfort. They know nothing. They go quite naked. In bad weather they take the bark of a tree and put it over them. They are covered in scabs. The men are, however, mostly strong and agile and throw a wooden spear of a heavy kind of wood sharpened at one end to the distance of fifty yards with force sufficient to kill a man, or rather to give him a mortal wound. Four convicts have fallen a sacrifice to them in our settlement and one settler was much wounded but recovered. They are much dangerous and troublesome; if they fall in with a white man or two, unarmed, it is only a miracle if they escape. It does not appear that they are numerous, perhaps five or six hundred in the Island.'*[1]

In March 1826 a group of between eighty and a hundred aborigines camped across the creek from Mayfield. Some who could speak English came over to the Buxton's hut, saying they were 'tame blacks'

- meaning that they were peaceable. However, later in the day when two of the Buxton girls saw that their leader had marked himself with red ochre - a sign that they meant war - they rushed over to where their father and his men were thatching a haystack and warned them. Dropping everything, they rushed towards the hut to get their guns, but they were too late; even as they ran they saw blacks streaming from the building, laden with guns and stolen goods. Flinging themselves into the hut, they found one aborigine still there clutching to himself a loaf of bread. Infuriated, Thomas Buxton seized him by the throat and shook him until he dropped it.[2] Just then another of his men staggered in, badly wounded, saying that his mate had been killed.[3] Completely outnumbered and helpless, with their only weapon a pistol that one of the girls had hidden, they were forced to stay where they were, but when night came one of them slipped out and hurried to Swan Port for help. Young George Meredith gathered a number of his father's men together and, well armed, the party made their way to Mayfield.

With the dawn the blacks returned. Firesticks in hand, they were seen running towards the haystack - that one lone haystack that represented months of hard work. Upon this, Thomas Buxton, shouting and brandishing a gun, broke from the hut and rushed at them. Behind him streamed the others, and the blacks, confused and alarmed, darted off. But the harm was done: the haystack was alight. Giving up all thought of pursuit, the men started putting the fire out, but that night, having found where the blacks were camped, they attacked, killing several and recovering most of the property they had taken from the hut. The return of their food and bedding was a great relief to the Buxtons, who realised how lucky they were not to have lost everything - belongings, haystack and hut, for it had been a hot summer and the ground was parched, and had the fire not been put out it would have spread.

The possibility of fire occurred also to George Meredith as he looked at the long grass surrounding the hut that housed his furniture. Apprehensive at the thought of anything happening to his possessions, in spite of government regulations prohibiting it, he decided to burn off.[4] Calling Mary to help him, he set fire to the grass some distance away, but to his alarm the flames leapt up and spread in a flare towards the hut. Realising that the danger lay in the low hanging roof thatch, they set to work pulling it off and throwing it as far away as possible, but the oncoming flames reached it, consumed it, and with added fury attacked the hut. The owners watched, helpless and frantic, as the roaring blaze reduced its contents to ashes.

The Merediths were inconsolable - the children because their mother's lovely furniture was gone and with it some of her remembered presence, Mary because the house they planned to build would not be graced by such beautiful things, and George Meredith because of the utter loss - the absolute and never-to- be-replaced loss, and this with no other possible person to blame but himself.

After some days, determined to make capital out of his loss, he wrote direct to Lord Bathurst, ignoring the rule that all correspondence must pass through Governor Arthur's hands. After informing the Earl that his 'warehouse' had been burnt and with it all his goods, he stated that this, together with the setback caused by the long-drawn-out land dispute, had almost brought him to his knees. As a result he was no longer able to afford to buy Mr Talbot's house and improvements at the prohibitive price the government was asking. In fact, he wrote, he was in such bad straits that he feared he must leave the land and seek employment as a public officer with the government. Apart from that solution there was only one thing that might save him. Were he to waive his claim for the thousand acres needed to equal the compensation given to Mr Talbot and instead be allowed official recognition of the two thousand acres his cousin had given him, he would be able to sell some of it and so recoup a portion of the £1200 he had lost through the fire.[6] He then wrote to his friends in England, asking that they contact the Earl on his behalf, requesting him to grant this favour. This they did, and their pleas added to the letter caused Bathurst to write to Governor Arthur directing him to transfer ownership of Mr John Meredith's land to his cousin and to allow him to have Mr Talbot's house and improvements without payment. Explaining his reason, he cited the great loss Mr Meredith had suffered because of the fire, and added that if he, Governor Arthur, was reluctant to settle affairs in this way he could choose the other alternative - that of availing himself *of Mr. Meredith's Services in any situation of moderate emolument for which he may be qualified.'*[7]

George Arthur, who had no desire at all to have George Meredith on his payroll, promptly carried out the orders. He then requested details of the fire from Adam Amos, which were supplied in full.[8] Relaying this information to England on September 1st, 1826, he also passed on a number of facts about Mr Meredith of which His Lordship was unaware, pointing out 'the extraordinary indulgence and accommodation' which had been shown him, and adding: 'If this gentleman had not by other measures afforded me a good insight into his character, I should be quite surprised at his venturing to ask for indemnification.'[9] In February 1827 Lord Bathurst, outraged at having been duped, instructed Governor Arthur to inform Mr Meredith that he would not be disposed to favour any further application he made on the subject.[10]

Still rapacious for greater stretches of land, George Meredith exchanged one of the five hundred acre blocks at Jericho for six hundred acres (240 ha) at Great Swan Port. This was owned by a man named Cogil[11] and was situated to the south of the Wye, the Swan forming its eastern boundary. This meant that he now owned an eight-mile stretch of land from the Meredith River to the junction of the Swan and Cygnet, the only exception being a small area of poor quality forest land, which he used in any case.

Those who lived on the East Coast were heartened to learn that in September 1826 a military station was to be established at Swan Port. The news was a relief to all, but especially so to Adam and James Amos, for with an increasing population and intensified attacks from aborigines they were unable to cope with the duties of their office.

The number of militia who first came to protect the area was not impressive, consisting as it did of a corporal and four soldiers, but within a year it had increased to twenty-three privates.[12] In charge of them was Captain George Hibbert, an officer who had served at Waterloo. The site he chose for the military station was a windy promontory a mile and a half south of Redbanks. Taking every possible precaution to ensure against the surprise attack of the future establishment, the Captain set his men to work cutting down every tree for a mile around. Peppermint, cherry, honeysuckle, wattle - all were cut off within a few inches of the ground. The resulting scene was desolate in the extreme, and one of the soldiers who had been at Waterloo eleven years earlier remarked that it reminded him of that battlefield, with the dead bodies stretched out in all directions. When the sergeant reported this to Captain Hibbert it struck an answering chord and he named the station Waterloo Point.[13]

Four new settlers were soon to benefit from the increased protection afforded by the soldiery. One of these was William Lyne.

He came from an old Gloucestershire family, well-to-do since the 16th century and holding large estates. But times and patterns of rural ownership had changed,[14] so that in 1790 it was estimated that three-quarters or more of English land was managed by tenant farmers rather than owners. As a result William had been brought up on an estate that did not belong to the Lynes - the thousand acre property of Coombe-End - and had grown up in the 14th century monastery that was the manor house. When his father, the lessee-manager, died in 1815 William took over his position. But in 1826 when the lease expired his mother renewed it again under the stewardship of a son-in-law, so passing William over. Of proud disposition and high temper, he refused to remain in a subordinate position at Coombe-End, and, with five children to support, turned his thoughts to a future quite different from his previous expectations.

Friends of his, Michael Steel and his sister Jane, had migrated to Van Diemen's Land in 1823 and had sent back good reports of the opportunities offering there. Half minded to follow them, he went for advice to Lord Bathurst, who lived four or five miles away at North Cerney.[15] Bathurst encouraged him, but pointed out that the island had a problem with bushrangers and hostile aborigines and recommended that he go to New South Wales instead, promising him a letter of introduction to Governor Darling, Sir Thomas Brisbane's successor as governor. His mind now fully made up, he started preparations for emigrating. As a last link with his home, he had his men make a coffin for him from an old oak tree on the property, and this he filled with lead, pewter and ironmongery for use in the new land. He packed five swords, six guns, five pairs of pistols and a large quantity of flints, as well as a barrel each of gunpowder and shot. He dismantled and packed his organ and the music he had composed, leaving out his flute and violin for use on the voyage.[16] He filled huge crates with his cider press,* a blacksmith's anvil and bellows and a copper furnace. Then, grieving, he shot his beautiful riding horse, not trusting anyone to care for it as he had done.[17]

It was full summer in 1826 when William Lyne and his wife Sarah and their children stepped on board the 450-ton sailing ship, the *Hugh Crawford*. Had they known of her unseaworthiness they would have stepped off again, for her timbers were so rotten that when a knife was stuck into her hull on her return voyage it sank up to its hilt.

---

*Now on display at the Bark Mill. Swansea.

"Hugh Crawford" from an original painting by G. L. Tuthill, 1824.
(Courtesy Mr. Max Atkinson, Hobart).

However, she carried them safely, the only unfortunate happening on board being the death of the wife and child of William Gatehouse, travelling to Van Diemen's Land to join his brothers, George and Silas. The ship made a fine entry as she approached Hobart Town, with the deck aswarm with thirty officers and men and the six musicians among the passengers sending English tunes sounding through the streets of the large village.[18]

Once on shore, William Lyne lost no time in contacting Michael and Jane Steel. Michael, a stout bachelor in his thirties, was blessed with a gloriously optimistic nature and laughed at the notion that the island was dangerous enough to drive his friends to New South Wales. While admitting that up until the previous year the bushrangers had been troublesome- so troublesome, indeed, that at his land at Swan Port he had lost hundreds of sheep to them and had been forced to move his flocks from there - he declared that at the present time there was not one bushranger at large. The aborigines, he admitted, were a different story. Although there appeared to be not many hundreds in the island, they were dangerous, though rarely to be seen. Weighing the advantages against the disadvantages, he had no hesitation in advising the Lynes to settle in Van Diemen's Land.[19]

Emboldened by this advice, William sought an interview with Governor Arthur. With some want of diplomacy he repeated what Lord Bathurst had said about the island and showed him a note from Lord Apsley, the Earl's son, in which he recommended New South Wales as 'safer soil' for him. The Governor, proud of his success with the suppression of bushrangers, took offence and subsequently wrote to Under-Secretary Hay requesting him to let Lord Apsley know that bushranging in his colony was now under control. He concluded: *'I hope he will form a better opinion of Van Diemen's Land henceforth than to deprive me of that Class of Settlers, which of all others is decidedly the most suited to improve the moral character of the people, and infuse a proper feeling and some industry into the Colony.'*[20]

Upon discovering that William Lyne was a surveyor, the Governor's mind immediately swung to George Meredith and his multitude of acquired acres. Realising that the new arrival was competent to differentiate between the land 'the King of Great Swan Port' claimed and that to which he was actually entitled, he suggested that he

Hobart Town, 1826, sketch by Thomas Scott. (Mitchell Library, State Library of New South Wales).

61

located the 1500 acres (600 ha) due to him in that area, at the same time making him aware of the situation.[21] Together they pored over a chart of the land round Swan Port, working out just which land was available and which had been officially allotted already.

Within a few days William Lyne, accompanied by his fifteen-year-old son Will and a guide, set off for Oyster Bay. Reaching it four days later, he tramped over the whole area, eager to explore everything. Seven miles to the east of Glen Gala Farm he found what he wanted. It was a warm valley of lightly-timbered land covered in fresh spring grass and fed by several small streams and a large river, which emptied itself into a tidal marsh at the edge of Moulting Lagoon. Though the soil was not fertile, remembering the Fens he thought it possible - as had George Meredith before him - to drain a portion of the Lagoon and so gain rich land. Enthused by his discovery, he set off for Hobart Town, calling in at Redbanks on the way and introducing himself to George Meredith. After some preliminary coversation he was asked where he intended to settle, so, spreading out his chart, he pointed to the spot. Upon this, George Meredith, recognising George Arthur's small angular writing and notations, at once realised what had happened. Cooling his affability to freezing point, he advised his visitor to forget about his tentative choice and take his grant at the Break-o'Day Plains instead.[22] With a painful sense of diminished consequence William Lyne took his leave, and on arrival back in Hobart Town made immediate application for his grant. Even when this was approved, so apprehensive was he of future trouble that he gave the Surveyor-General, Edward Dumaresq, five pounds to make quite sure of his boundaries.[23] Then, his fears lessened, he allowed his enthusiasm for Great Swan Port full rein.

So elequent was he about the area that two of his fellow-passengers on the *Hugh Crawford*, John and Richard Allen of Somerset, became interested and asked permission to go with him on his next trip to the East Coast, for as farming folk they were anxious to settle.

They were a closely-knit family, and John, accompanied by his widowed uncle Richard, had come out to join his brother Joseph, who had been ill for most of the four years he had spent in the colony.[24] Comforted by having some of his family about him, Joseph had suggested that the three of them settle close together. As there was no prospect of gaining land near his own 640-acre (256 ha) at the Big

62

Plains near Campbell Town,[25] he was more than willing to follow them to Great Swan Port if they found the area to their liking, and take his secondary grant there.

John Allen, slight, dark and small-featured, was alert and energetic. Well versed in farming, he had all the potential necessary for the making of a good settler. He had brought with him enough capital to secure a small grant, but there was one obstacle - he was only nineteen. Waiting until after his twentieth birthday in November 1826, he applied for permission to locate his four hundred acres (160 ha) at Great Swan Port.[26] Faced with his undoubted maturity and self-confidence, officialdom unbent, and he was given the permission he sought on the understanding that the grant would not be given public sanction while he was still a minor. Satisfied, he prepared to visit the East Coast with William Lyne.

For £25 a boat, the *Scotchman*, was chartered, it being the only vessel available at the time. She was a small craft of about nine tons and was generally used to carry river lumber. By the time she was loaded there remained only two feet of clearance between the gunwhale and the water,[27] so that the passengers were fortunate to be still afloat after they encountered wild winds and rain that lasted for three days. When at last they neared their destination and sailed into the sheltered waters of Oyster Bay, the flat bottom of the *Scotchman* made it possible to cross the sandbar at the mouth of the Swan, and they cautiously made their way up the river and turned into Moulting Lagoon. Finally they became stuck in the mud at a spot they named Christmas Point, and in heavy rain conveyed themselves and their belongings to land. It was there that they spent their first Christmas Day in the new land.[28]

They were now four or five miles from the grant allotted to William Lyne. Richard Allen, who was an excellent carpenter,[29] helped to construct a rough wagon, using a pair of wheels bought in Hobart Town, while others of the party formed a makeshift road by felling trees, moving boulders and clearing scrub. A pair of fine bullocks was bought for £30 from their nearest neighbour, Adam Amos, and so, load by load, the goods were finally transported to the grant.

On arrival the family was delighted with their surroundings, and even Sarah, uprooted against her will and hating the new country,[30] had to admit that it was a pleasant spot. They named it Apsley* after

* Apsley is now known as Apslawn.

63

Lord Bathurst's son,[31] and set to work to build a sod hut in which to live. When it was completed John and Richard Allen, who had at first meant to apply for grants next to the Lagoon and help to drain it, now changed their minds and turned back towards the main settlement. There they began exploring vacant land.[32]

John Allen chose his four hundred acres in a well watered area on the western bank of the Cygnet, opposite the northern half of Spring Vale. This he named Milton after his home in England. Immediately to the south-west of it he measured out a square mile of land with a view to recommending it for his brother Joseph, while his uncle Richard took up his three hundred and forty acres (140 ha) adjoining it and fronting on the northern bank of the Wye, to the east of Bellbrook.[33] This became known as The Springs Farm.[34]

At Glen Gala Farm, to Adam and Mary Amos it was a heartening thought that in a region still sparsely populated they now had at Apsley respectable neighbours whose children's ages approximated those of their own. Deciding that they would officially welcome them, one summer evening at the beginning of 1827 they and their eight children walked across to greet them and were welcomed into the sod hut by William and Sarah Lyne. It was a tight squeeze when all were inside, for

The Springs Homestead

64

Glen Gala, built in 1860 to replace the previous building which was destroyed by fire in 1858.

the members of both families were all large people.[35] It was not long before someone leaned too heavily against the still-soft turf wall, which collapsed soggily about them. All formality dissolved as everyone set to work to rebuild it. Under the expert help of the Amoses it became stronger than it had been before.

A few months later the Amos family was forced into building their permanent home when their chock-and-log hut was burnt down. A weatherboard double-storey house replaced it, and with its verandah, cellar and shingled roof was easily the finest and largest in the district. By the end of the 1828 it was finished, together with a store, a dairy, a log millhouse with a boarded granary above the mill, a log barn* and a log hut for the servants. Together these were officially valued at £830.

Infinitely smaller than the Amos's house but equally as strong was the log cabin# the Lynes built at Apsley. So alert were they to danger that it was almost a stockade. Measuring twenty feet square (six metres), it was constructed of large logs scooped out at the ends so as

---

* This barn is still in use.
# The ruins of the Lyne log cabin are still standing at Apslawn. A corner of it is on display at the Bark Mill at Swansea.

to fit together closely. The ceiling, like the walls, was logged horizontally to bear the weight of the attic and to prevent the cabin catching fire easily in the event of the blacks throwing spears on the roof with lighted punk attached. For protection there were six small apertures through which to fire guns, and the doorway was very low so as to baulk any intruders who might attempt to enter in a hurry. Little Betsy and Susan and their parents slept in the two attic rooms, the boys and the servant they had brought out from England slept under 'a roof-looking hut thatched to the ground with oak boughs,'[37] while the sod hut was retained as a kitchen.

They had built their cabin early in 1827. Towards the end of that year another settler was similarly occupied some twenty miles (32 kms) to the south. This was Robert Webber,[38] a fifty-year-old farmer from Dorset, who, with his wife Mary and six children, had been fellow-passengers with the Lynes and Allens in the *Hugh Crawford.* During the voyage he had been persuaded by the captain of the vessel, Lieutenant Langdon, to go into partnership with him at a location near Gretna but the arrangement broke up almost at once when difficulty was experienced in finding a suitable grant and the captain

Apsley Log Cabin

66

failed to keep his part of the agreement.[39] Having sufficient capital of his own for the purpose, Robert Webber obtained a location order for a thousand acres at Great Swan Port. He then requested permission for passage for himself and Mary to the area by one of the government ships that was about to sail there.[40] This was refused, so he and his sons - William (23) and John (18) - walked from the Clyde to Waterloo Point, driving their cattle before them, while Mary and the other members of his family finally embarked on another vessel.[41]

The land he selected was on the southern side of Stony River, opposite the Addison brothers' as yet unsettled grant.[42] Piermont, the name Robert Webber gave his property, shared with Coswell the breathtaking view of Oyster Bay and Freycinet Peninsula, the waters of the bay breaking on their eastern boundaries. For six months the family camped at the mouth of the rivulet, after which they moved into more adequate housing on rising ground further inland, on a spot sheltered from the sea breeze by a thick growth of Oyster Bay pines.

CHAPTER 7

Still another settler was moving house at this time. William Talbot's residence* had remained empty since the beginning of 1825. Letter after letter had passed between George Meredith and the government on the matter, and at last in 1827 Governor Arthur had given him permission to take possession of the building. Immediate arrangements were made to move into it, and their belongings were transferred by both manpower and bullock wagons across the mile that separated the two residences. The name of the new abode was changed from Malahide to Belmont, and although it was not the Castle Bromich Hall of George Meredith's youth it was certainly bigger and more comfortable than Redbanks. Young George moved in with them for a short time, during which Redbanks was enlarged and improved, and then returned to live there alone.[1]

Yet another settler was soon to arrive in the district, for in March 1825 Lord Bathurst had received a letter from a Mr James King, gentleman, of Middlesex. This read as follows:

'My Lord,

'As myself and son are preparing to go out to Van Diemen's Land, I am desirous of obtaining a grant of land there or on one of the Islands adjoining for the purpose of breeding Rabbits...As I shall take out £3000 to the Colony, I further beg for an allotment of other Land for the purposes of Agriculture, Dairying, and keeping fine wooled sheep, as I have a number of fine Merinos there, under the care of my Shepherd and Dairywoman, who went from England with them. My son, who goes with me, has been for the last two years with one of the most respectable Woolstapling houses in Leeds learning the sorting and qualitys of Saxony and other wools.

'For any other information that may be required I respectfully beg leave to refer to Lord Dacre, the Honble Wm Lamb and the Revd Philomen Pownell Bastard.'[2]

---

* There is no trace of the Old Malahide/Belmont house now, though the site is known to be opposite McNeil's Road.

This letter was passed on to Governor Arthur, who gave it as his opinion that Betsey Island would be ideal for the raising of rabbits, so when James King and his son James arrived in the colony early in 1826 the island was granted to him. The following May he stocked it with a breed of rabbit known as silver-greys (regardless of the fact that their fur was black), whose skins were destined for the China market[3] and he had a stone house built there.[4] A location order for 2000 acres at Oyster Bay was also issued to him. The grant he chose was on the opposite side of the Swan from George Meredith's reserve of Riversdale. Included in it were the 1140 acres (456 ha) issued to Joseph Allport in 1823 and which had not been improved in any way.[5]

James King, middle-aged and in ill-health, was carrying out all these arrangements in order to give his son a chance to make something of his life - an opportunity accepted reluctantly by young James. On March 30th 1826 the older man went to a leading solicitor in Hobart Town, Gamaliel Butler, and made a will in which he left Betsey Island and the 2000 acres at Great Swan Port to his son on the condition that he remained in Van Diemen's Land for ten years. Then, accompanied by the unwilling James and thirteen assigned servants, he arrived at Great Swan Port and commenced operations. He set his men to clear an area of fifty acres and to grub out every stump on it. In an effort to induce James to view the place more favourably he also superintended the building of a residence that was *'the most commodious hut in the colony'.*[6] He then applied for permission to rent a further two thousand acres adjoining his eastern boundary, and then, having done all he could for his son, returned to England. Thereafter the inhabitants of Great Swan Port saw but little of James King, Junior.

The arrival of the Kings threw the Amos brothers into a state of complete consternation. Years before, Governor Sorell had promised their sons that as each one turned twenty-one he should be given a grant of a hundred acres, even though they might not possess the money to warrant it. Deputy-Surveyor George Evans had marked the particular areas on a map which was never seen again. As these areas were threatened by the arrival of the Kings, in the autumn of 1827 the brothers contacted the Colonial Secretary, only to be told that as there was no record of their claim it could not be allowed.[7]

At the same time John Amos requested permission to locate his two four hundred acre grants in two separate areas, as his present location contained insufficient arable land. *'I have a large family to provide for,'* he wrote, 'and my Sheep are too much for the Land I now have.' To this the Colonial Secretary replied that there was no record in the office of Governor Macquarie ever having promised him any land extra to his original grant.* [8] This threw him into despair, but upon Governor Arthur stating that he believed Mr John Amos to be a respectable man who would not tell an untruth the Surveyor-General went down to Oyster Bay in August 1827 so as to get a clear picture of the situation. Upon his reporting back the Governor let it be known that he had such a good opinion of Mr John Amos, whom he stated to be a very industrious settler, that he felt authorised to not only sanction his eight hundred acres and confirm his sons in the land promised them by Governor Sorell, but to grant him an additional two hundred acres as well, making his acreage equal to that of his brother. He also gave authority for him to move from his present position and choose his grant elsewhere. [9]

Elated, John Amos made his selection further up the Swan almost directly opposite Glen Gala Farm, the river forming his western boundary back as far as James King's land. On this he built his fourth residence since coming to the country. It was the largest and strongest of all, being a chock-and-log hut of seven or eight rooms. He and Hannah named it Cranbrook House, as a link with the village in Kent where Hannah had been born.

To the north-east of them the Lyne family toiled at clearing their land of timber, which they stacked and burned, tending the fires far into the night. They realised that if they were to plant wheat that season they must hurry, so it was a relief to William Lyne when he started ploughing in the spring. Both young Susan and Henry were delicate, for in England, at a time when one-third of all deaths in the rural areas were caused by tuberculosis, [10] they, too, had been threatened by it. Ever mindful of this, their father made a small seat and attached it to the plough and often strapped the six-year-old Susan into it so that she could smell the good earth at close range as he turned the furrows. [11]

One day as he was ploughing, one of George Meredith's shepherds came running towards him in great distress, crying out that his companion had been murdered by the blacks. Leaving the plough, William ran with him to a valley about a mile inland,# and there he

---

* This approval was found in the Sydney office of the Surveys Department ten years later.
# The shepherd was murdered at Coombend.

found the dead man with a spear four and a half feet long (137 cm) stuck in his back. There was another protruding from a nearby tree, so deeply embedded that about six inches broke off as they pulled it out.* In the clearing also lay the body of a dead aborigine. This they placed against a log and covered with timber as a protection against wild animals before carrying the corpse of the shepherd away. Next day they called in at the spot again and found that the body of the black man had been removed. They could only guess that the aborigines had come and taken it so as to dispose of it according to their usual rites.

On a hill overlooking the lagoon was a growth of tall Oyster Bay pines, and each night a member of the Lyne family climbed one of these to see whether any aborigines' fires were visible. One night John, the eldest son, saw a sight so unusual that he ran back and called the others to see it. Writing of it years later, he recorded:[12] *'It has been doubted if the native blacks worshipped any superior Being or not. For my part I rather think they adored the moon, for in the year 1828 a tribe camped on the face of a hill about two miles away in front of our house at the time when the moon was full, and we could see them capering before a large fire - a thing quite unusual, for they generally made small fires in a circle and lay in the centre.'*

The Lynes themselves never neglected their Sunday worship. When the day of rest came William dressed in his best clothes -oldfashioned long before he left England: his ruffled shirt and elaborate neckcloth, his breeches that fitted into his black cloth stockings, his large square silver-buckled shoes, his waistcoat and longtailed coat. Bibles and prayerbooks were spread around and the family took their places in the little cabin and joined in morning prayer, giving thanks to the Lord for their continued preservation in a hostile land.

Well might they do so, for there was danger all round. At Belmont they were made aware of that fact when at the end of October 1827 young John Meredith was in the midst of enjoying his fifth birthday when one of the government men rushed in to say that aborigines were attacking the house. Snatching up their guns, George Meredith and young George and Charles ran outside in time to see a number of blacks throwing on to the roof spears with burning grass attached to them. The thatch was already alight and the attackers were so jubilant

---

*This spear is held at Narryna Folk Museum. Hobart.

71

and excited that they showed fight, killing one convict and wounding another before they could be driven off.[13]

It was fortunate that it happened to be one of the times when George Meredith was not in Hobart Town. His business affairs, coupled with his aptitude for public matters, still caused him to spend a good deal of time in the capital. Another reason for his frequent presence there was the need to launch his daughters into society, for they were young ladies now, Sarah twenty, Louisa nineteen and Sabina seventeen. It was a delicate situation, as it was necessary for him to play the part usually reserved for the mother, but with his daughters' willing co-operation he became quite adept in this paternal duty. Mary, though invaluable as the wife of a pioneer settler in a way Sarah Meredith could never have been, was nevertheless a person to be kept in the background when this game of matrimonial stakes was being played. Thus it became somewhat difficult for her husband to find excuses whenever in her frequent letters she expressed a wish to join the family in Hobart Town. Still young at thirty-two, she longed for a little light amusement as a change from the many dangers, decisions and tasks that made up her day at Belmont in the absence of her husband.

In July 1827 George Meredith sat down to gently discourage her leanings towards a holiday in town. *'My own Dear Wife',* he wrote, *'I must now indulge in a little conjugal chit-chat, the only relief I enjoy from the annoyance of this most stupid place & all its vexations - and yet you wish to come up here!'* He closed by saying: *'If we are successful in the approaching Whaling Season the product may be expected to go far towards liquidating our English Debts and then Dearest M., we will build our House, furnish it, and set up something like the establishment befitting a Gentleman's family - we will then visit Hobart Town.'*[14] But they never did.

He was most anxious that in every detail Mary should practise to improve herself. Her letter-writing worried him. Although she expressed herself clearly and wrote a far more legible hand than he, she sometimes left out words or made slight mistakes. He wrote to her: *'By writing and re-writing names and addresses over and over again you will soon be able to make your letters to me distinguishable for the penmanship. Indeed, my love, I am more anxious about these things than you seem to be aware of. There is nothing that escapes my observation emanating from you....but I refer to my idea of what should be written, said, or done, by a Lady.'* Gently chiding, gently encouraging, he continued: *'Even from the moment when I first pressed your virgin lips, and took you to my bosom and to my heart, had you but then ... said to yourself,'Although circumstances foiled the fond hope of realising every wish of my heart, still I feel it my Duty to act as if it were otherwise and to qualify myself ... worthy of the behests of fortune.' If, my Dear Maria, you had so acted from the first moment we plighted our mutual troth, what Lady could now claim precedency of you as a Lady.'*[15]

In the meantime he was content that she should manage his rural affairs for him in the seclusion of Great Swan Port, there practising her airs upon the servants, soldiers and settlers.

CHAPTER 8

With the passing of years the road from Hobart Town, such as it was, now reached to within twelve miles (19 km) of Little Swanport.[1] It was along this road that towards the end of 1827 there travelled a new settler. Joseph Castle was on his way to choose his grant.

He was the son of John and Phoebe Castle of Somerset, who, besides being well-established landowners in the village of Banwell,[2] owned a brewery. In 1815 at the age of twenty-five Joseph had married a seamstress, Edith Day, and by 1827 had four children - John (12), Robert (10), Phoebe (8) and Joseph (6). It was quite obvious to him, as it was to all agricultural people, that farming in Britain was at a low ebb, it being impossible to avoid the effects of post-war depression with its low prices for produce, high taxation, and the heavy burden of tythe and rent and poor-rate. Besides this, he was the youngest son and had no hope of inheriting much. He decided that the best future for him lay over the seas. Arrangements were made for departure, goodbyes were said, the family boarded the *Orelia*, and they set off for Van Diemen's Land.

They arrived in Hobart Town in August 1827 and soon afterwards Joseph presented to Governor Arthur his introductory letter from Under Secretary Hay *('Mr Castle is a very respectable farmer, with practical experience as a land surveyor')*. His location order directed him to the south section of Little Swanport and within a short time he set out to select his grant.[3] The five hundred acres (200 ha) coastal land he decided on had a magnificent view but the soil, sandy and infertile, was vastly different from that which he was used to. However, he was not afraid of the hard work he knew lay ahead and was well content in the knowledge that he would be working on a place that was his own. He named it Banwell and returned to Hobart Town to arrange the necessary details of ownership. Conscious of the complete rawness of the place, Edith and the two youngest children remained where they were, while Joseph and the two older boys walked to Banwell and set to work. Busy days followed as they settled in.

At the time that they were busying themselves with the initial work another new settler, Robert Hepburn, was making his way up the East

Captain Robert Hepburn
(Courtesy Mrs. Peg Davis, Elderslie)

Coast, passing well to the north of them. This latest arrival had an interesting history.

His father, William Hepburn, born in 1738 in Scotland, and reputed to be a descendant of the fourth Earl of Bothwell, had joined the Navy and became a captain in the Marines. When he was twenty he was married at Ayton* (the parish of his father, the Reverend Patrick Hepburn), to Penelope Newels. Shortly afterwards the young couple left for Jamaica, where the Newels owned plantations. It was probably at one of them, 'Wellekens', that a slave named Isabella lived. She was the daughter of Nana (King) Kromantse of the Diamenti tribe, a strong and fearless people from the Gold Coast of Africa who were much sought after by slave dealers. Princess Isabella had earlier either married or co-habited with Gregor McGregor, the great grandson of Rob Roy McGregor.#4 They had a daughter, known as Mary Ann Roy, and it was this half-caste girl who, some twenty years or so after his arrival in Jamaica, caught the attention of William Hepburn. She became either his second wife or his mistress, and in 1782 their son Robert, the future Van Diemen's Land settler, was born.

*Near Berwickshire.
#Gregor McGregor was a sea captain in the West Indies trade between 1750 and 1770.

While very young this child was sent to Scotland, where he was cared for in Edinburgh by his grandmother, the widow of the Reverend Patrick Hepburn, and at her death in 1792, by his aunt.[5] Later he joined the Royal Navy, where he rose to the rank of captain. He found that naval life offered much in the way of adventure. Once, when chasing smugglers, his excise cutter ran aground and he and the hundred men under his command were rescued by the crew of a French privateer, which he immediately claimed as a hostage of war, it being in the middle of the Napoleonic War. Another time, while in charge of a man-of-war he captured what he strongly suspected was a slave ship and had her captain, William Kermode*, paraded before him, but to his disappointment was forced to release him when his papers were found to be in order.[6]

As soon as Robert Hepburn saw middle age beckoning he decided to defy it with one more adventure, so leaving Elie, his property in Scotland,[7] he migrated. With his wife Jacobina and his three sons and five daughters he set sail in the *Greenoch,* arriving in Van Diemen's Land in January 1828.[8] A man of action, he went straight to work and within ten days had obtained a location order for 2560 acres on St

View from the beach near Swanwick showing Freycinet Peninsula

---

* In 1819 William Kermode emigrated to Van Diemen's Land, bringing with him goods and cash to the value of £15,000.

Pauls River, thirty miles (48 km) to the north of Waterloo Point. There he chose his grant, naming it Roy's Hill. It did not take him long to realise what an infertile area he had chosen and he soon made application for a secondary grant, stating his opinion that Roy's Hill was suitable for nothing but garden walks. As a former seafaring man he particularly requested that his new grant should be on the coast, and in April 1829 he obtained a secondary grant of five hundred acres (200 ha) within sight of Waterloo Point. It was a beautifully situated area on the eastern side of the entrance to the Swan River - an area which included a small rocky island suitable as a breakwater for his boat - and there he built a stone house which he named Swanwick*. He then set his convicts (now dressed in naval wear instead of government issue) to work constructing a road# between his two properties. Upon its completion he acquainted the Governor of it existence, pointing out that *'the road has now opened up the inland St Paul's Plain to Great Swan Port and the commerce of the world'.* The commerce of the world was inclined to be in danger whenever there was a flood, for parts of the road he had surveyed became submerged at such times, but he re-routed these places so that they were above the reach of the water.

His adventurous spirit was responsible for the naming of a river which until then had always been referred to as the Big River. Detailing the events that led to this, in December 1828 he wrote as follows to George Frankland, the Surveyor-General: *'In search of a grant I went on 27/11/28 to the source of the St Paul's River, which rises out of a marsh two miles long on top of the Tiers. I followed it until it was blocked by big rocks. I found the source of another river which joined the Swan River and proceeded across to Moulting Bay, past Mr Lyne's and up that river, when I found that the river which I was obliged to quit and the one I was on was the same. The river requires a name. Mr Lyne requested me to mention Lord Apsley, but he presumed His Excellency would decide that point.'*[9] Official sanction for the name was given and the Big River became the Apsley. It was not long after this that Lord Apsley sent William Lyne a fine gun.* *

Guns were becoming more and more a part of the lives of the settlers. The aborigines were becoming extremely dangerous - so much so that it was quite commonplace to hear of settlers who had

---

* The original Swanwick homestead, with additions, is still used as a residence.
# This was the original Old Coach Road.
* * This gun is now at Gala.

been murdered by them. For safety's sake it became the practice to always carry arms, even when ploughing, and as far as possible to leave someone near each homestead in case of attack. Hampered though they were by these restrictions, the men had to continue their work, and every available person was called on to help them.[10] So in February 1828 little Susan Lyne and her ten-year-old sister Betsy were given the task of watching some young calves near the marsh to see that they did not stray. So engrossed at play did they become that they failed to see seven or eight blacks creeping up on them. Their first indication of their presence was the shadow of a waddy as one of them raised it and struck Susan on the head, causing her to fall unconscious half in and half out of the shallow water of the lagoon. Betsy, terrified, ran screaming towards the nearby cabin. Her father and brother John came running out, guns loaded and ready, and fired at the disappearing forms of the aborigines, but they had already reached the bush and were disappearing. Fearing that Susan was dead, they carried her back to the cabin, where to their relief she eventually regained consciousness and after a few days was allowed out again.[11]

After leaving Apsley the aborigines went to George Meredith's stock hut a few miles to the north, and at the sight of them the assigned servants stationed there made their escape, leaving the hut free for the blacks to plunder. Emboldened, they made their way towards John Amos's place, but his little girls saw them and raised the alarm, at which the aborigines made off in the direction of Milton.

For several months after Joseph Allen had been granted New Plains* he had been content to stay there near his relatives, but by now he had left. Richard, his uncle, working hard at The Springs Farm nearby, was gradually turning bush into grazing land, while young John had worked to the limit of his endurance from the day he had taken possession of Milton. Sleeping with his musket beside him, for nine months the only time he had taken off his clothes, other than his smock#, was when he had changed on Sundays for his day of rest. With the help of his convict labourers he cleared land, planted crops and built a house for himself. In February 1828 he gained his reward when he gathered in his crops and made his first wheatstack. On that particular Sunday when the blacks were about he sent his men to report at muster and went to visit his uncle Richard, leaving only a

---

* Now known as The Plains, this land was granted in January 1827.
# John Allen's smock is at the Hobart Museum.

young boy at Milton. When he returned he found his house a smouldering ruin and his crops burnt.[12] The terrified lad came out of hiding to tell him that a party of blacks had first robbed his house of guns, books, papers, bedding and provisions and had then set fire to both the building and his wheatstack.

Sick at heart and furious, John Allen stormed down to Waterloo Point and reported his loss to the Assistant Police Magistrate, Captain Dalrymple,[13] who immediately sent out a party of soldiers in what turned out to be a fruitless pursuit of the aborigines. Then the magistrate requested an estimate of the damage, which Adam Amos put at £300, and a statement to this effect was given to John Allen. Never lacking in confidence and drive, he took it to Hobart Town and presented it to Governor Arthur, whose expressions of sympathy did little to pacify him. He requested further land in compensation for his loss. Referring to this by letter ten years later he wrote, '*Your Excellency was Compassionately Pleased to Promise an Additional Grant if I continued to Persevere on my Farm as I had done before, and Your Excellency having received Several Testimonials on my Unwearied Perseverance as before was very Humanely Pleased to order, in the latter post of that year, Two Hundred Acres Extension of my Grant as a Remuneration for the Aforesaid Loss, and not for Improvements that was then made on my Original Grant.*'[14] This additional land was taken where William Lyne had originally suggested he settle - on an area at the head of Moulting Lagoon, opposite and in clear view of Apsley. This he named Egg Farm. The Governor also promised him a secondary grant in compensation for his losses, and this he kept in abeyance, awaiting a more opportune time in which to locate it. He then set to work and built another house for himself, a double-storey stone building, not easily to be burned, but this was robbed in December when the aborigines came again. He was forced to fight them alone until help came eight hours later.

Towards the end of 1828 he and John Amos were sworn in as special constables,[15] while Alexander Reid, a free man for a year past and still living at Little Swanport (where he acquired what money he could as a paid man) was made a divisional constable for the southern part of that area.[16]

Regular visits to the Oyster Bay district each year were part of the age-old pattern of life to the aborigines, and this the white men well knew. As a consequence, as the time for their next migratory visit in

Milton, from a photograph taken in 1928, a hundred years after it was built.

John Allen repulsing the aboriginal attack at Milton in December. 1828. Artist unknown.
(Courtesy Mr. John Allen, Dysart)

1828 drew near some of the settlers had gathered at Moulting Lagoon to await their arrival. They came, and ten were shot dead and three taken prisoner. Following this, the black people's animosity reached fever pitch and they considered it their patriotic duty to injure or kill as many whites as they could.[17] One day at Apsley they came close to succeeding.

As William Lyne stooped his huge form to enter the low door of his log cabin he automatically glanced behind him and was startled to see a number of aborigines creeping down the hill about seventy yards (64m) away. Quietly calling a nearby shoemaker to join him, he went inside. There, handing him a gun, he explained the situation to both him and Sarah. Knowing the necessity of putting on a bold front, he hurriedly draped one of his long caped travelling coats on his wife, pulled one of his hats over her hair, thrust a gun into her hands and led the way outside. The aborigines, now almost upon them, were disconcerted to find three armed 'men' suddenly menacing them, and, intimidated, ran away. *'Had they got to the house'*, John Lyne wrote later, 'not one would have been left alive. The blacks at this time, from 1826 to 1831, were never known to give quarter. No doubt they had much reason to be exasperated, for it was said that before the arrival of Governor Arthur in 1824 the convict stock keepers were known to entice the black gins away from the tribes and if their husbands went to seek them they were often shot. But in Governor Arthur's time I believe it must have ceased, for he would hang free or bond if they killed a black except in self defence.'[18]

That same year, 1828, a new settler arrived in Little Swanport. Lieutenant John Hawkins had been given a grant in the southern part of the area,* inland from Joseph Castle's property of Banwell and adjoining the three hundred acres (120 ha) occupied by John Harte. Soon after he had settled in he heard that the position of Superintendent of convicts at Maria Island had become vacant, so he applied for it. His application being successful, he was appointed as from March of 1829.[19] Joseph Allen had also applied but was passed over when it was said that he had a drinking problem.

By now the aborigines were so dangerous that Governor Arthur was very seriously concerned. He had tried many things -attempting to confine them to certain unsettled areas, proclaiming a state of emergency, sending roving groups out to try to capture them, and establishing a line of military posts near settled areas, as was the case with the Waterloo Point Military Station. He, accompanied by a few officials, visited these posts, travelling about among the settlers at the same time and familiarising himself with his colony as a whole.[20] It was November 1828 when he made his way towards the East Coast. After a night spent at Ravensdale he arrived at Mayfield in time for a meal. Ellen Buxton, an excellent cook, dished up such a feast that her husband, upon being granted an additional seven hundred and eighty acres (312 ha) the following month, swore that it was because of that meal.[21]

When Governor Arthur reached Waterloo Point he was so impressed by its beauty that he said it must surely possess one of the finest views in the colony. He pronounced the station to be well laid out with substantial buildings, with adequate accommodation for soldiers and huts for prisoners.[22] Evidently there was not adequate accommodation for the vice-regal party, for a Dr Scott, who was travelling with them, was sent on ahead to Belmont to arrange for

---

* John Hawkins named his property Ravensdale.

82

them to stay the night. Upon his arriving there George Meredith, who knew him well, greeted him cordially and invited him in to dinner. When he said that he had a friend with him he was told to bring him too, but when the name of the 'friend' was disclosed George Meredith informed Dr Scott that Governor Arthur would never cross his threshold.[23] After the news was broken to His Excellency the party rode on to Glen Gala, where they spent the night. Next morning as soon as the noise of their horses' hoofs had died away Adam Amos made out an application for a further grant of two thousand acres, listing all the improvements he had made to the thousand-acre grant that he had occupied for seven years. Within a relatively short time the application was approved, Governor Arthur noting on the form: *'I have personally examined the improvements made by Mr Amos and I have satisfied myself that there is not a more useful or more thriving Settler of his class in the colony.'*[24] Adam chose the land immediately east of Glen Gala and stretching to the north, naming a square mile of it Melrose after the place of his birth.[25]

In 1825 Lord Bathurst had directed that Van Diemen's Land should be divided into counties, hundreds and parishes in order to facilitate the location of new arrivals and also to make it possible for the government to derive a reasonable quit rent based on the differing values of the land. Governor Arthur was ordered to appoint three land commissioners whose duty it would be to traverse the whole of the island for this purpose. They were also required to make observations about locating future roads, townships, schools, and so on. Edward Dumaresq, the Surveyor-General, was chosen to be one of the land commissioners, Peter Murdoch another and Roderic O'Connor the third; only the last two did the actual travelling, and it was Roderic O'Connor who made most of the entries in their journal.[26] He was a friend of the Governor's and was a contentious Irishman who had arrived in the colony with his two natural sons in 1824, having beforehand informed Lord Bathurst that he preferred any part of the globe to his miserable distracted country.[27] He had settled on a thousand-acre grant close to the Archers in the north of the island, but because of his interest in affairs of the colony was often in the capital attending meetings, as was George Meredith, whom he did not like.[28]

Towards the end of 1828 the two land commissioners set off to make their reports about the southern part of the East Coast, travelling by way of St Pauls Plains and Break-O'Day. The Macquarie River was in high flood and had set their cart and bullocks afloat, wetting their belongings, so that they were out of temper when they called in at Roy's Hill. There Roderic O'Connor found Robert Hepburn to be a gentleman every bit as haughty as himself, which pleased him not at all. He refused to be impressed by anything he saw. He wrote in his journal: *'He has built a curious Weatherboard House* and has been indefatigable in his exertions, but unfortunately for him the place he has selected is one of the most miserable in the colony, totally unfit for any purpose. The old saying, 'Let the cobblers stick to his last', is very applicable to many who arrive here as settlers...Mr Hepburn will soon find that all his capital will be insufficient to yield him any return, and he and his large family left in a state of destitution.'*[29] This was one of the few points on which the two men agreed, hence his application for his secondary grant of Swanwick.

Leaving Roy's Hill, the party succeeded with difficulty in manoeuvring their belongings across the Black Tiers (the Eastern Tiers) and down to Apsley. Here William Lyne took them round the property, showing them the preparations his men were making to lay the huge pipes that were scattered about, for he had already started his

Roy's Hill, from a sketch by Emma von Stieglitz in 1835.

---

* Roy's Hill (later Roy's Lea) homestead was burnt long ago.

84

Swanwick (University of Tasmania Archives)

project to drain the lagoon. The next day they left *'the very industrious, honest man'*[30] and went on to inspect Glen Gala. They were full of admiration for what they found there, summing up their opinion by writing: *'Were all settlers like Gatenby, Amos, Terry and Nicholas the Government should either support all the Convicts, or desist from transporting them altogether.'*

On crossing to the opposite side of the Swan they expressed surprise that John Amos should have been seven years in the colony and yet have such an undeveloped farm. They were given a guarded, though heated, reason why this was so, and rode into Meredith country ready to focus on anything that could be criticized. Passing through Spring Vale, they took care to note for His Excellency's attention that its owner had ignored Lord Bathurst's instructions that improvements must be made there. They found it in marked contrast to the grant of James King, which they extolled.

At Milton they were impressed by the amount of work young John Allen had done, and, riding through New Plains (now occupied by William Worthy) they arrived at Bellbrook. After observing that John Harte had about a hundred acres under tillage they came to The Springs Farm, where they found Richard Allen busy erecting fences and breathing out invective against George Meredith for allowing his cattle to wander at will.

Upon arriving at Riversdale they observed that the land first granted to John Amos was extremely fertile and had about eighty acres(32 ha) of corn sown on it. It was now let to the ex-convict George Raynor, who gave George Meredith half the produce from it.

After passing through the six hundred acres (240 ha) that Cogle had exchanged with George Meredith they noted that nothing had been done with it, and then travelled through a belt of second-rate Crown land and found themselves at Belmont. *'Mr Meredith is a great man', Roderic O'Connor wrote, 'At least he wishes to be thought so. We are apt therefore to look perhaps more minutely into all his operations. We expected to behold wonders, we were miserably disappointed. We first encountered his Stock yard, worse than that belonging to any old Norfolk Island Settler. His House had been thrown up by Mr Talbot who as a Bachelor and Bon Vivant cared little for exterior appearances provided the Cellar was well stored. At the back of the House a fine marsh, which if drained would make the choicest pasture, is retained for the Mansion as a Swannery and Duck Walk. At the front a large Lagoon capable of being easily drained still in a state of nature. Proceeding, we saw attempts at clearing timber here and there, at some distance a Tannery below a Blacksmiths' Shop, without either Coals or Iron. On crossing the Meredith River, we entered Mr Meredith jr's farm, he has lately come to reside on it, and seems anxious to improve it, he was busily employed stumping a very fine piece of land. Arrived at Waterloo Point, saw a vessel on the Stocks, Mr Meredith the Builder.*[31] We had often heard of a Man having too many Irons in the fire, and burning his fingers, Mr Meredith seems to be a happy illustration of the saying. Mr Meredith undertakes everything and accomplishes nothing. He is also a Whaler, and having possessed himself of so large a tract of land, conceives that he is entitled to the exclusive privilege of fishing on the waters of Oyster Bay.'*

Continuing their inspections, the land commissioners, though impressed by the beauty of Waterloo Point, deplored the poor quality of the land, all of which was rented by young George Meredith. The military station was commented on and a recommendation made that two thousand acres be reserved for a township.

---

* The Hobart Town Courier of November 1818 described this as a 50-ton vessel.

Moving southwards, they inspected the Addisons' six hundred acres at Coswell and found nothing to say other than that an overseer was in command* and that the land was too poor for anything. Their opinion of the land at Piermont was the same, but they noted that Robert Webber was hardworking and had leased White Rock (opposite Grindstone Bay) for sealing purposes but was rapidly plundering it.

Great difficulty was experienced when they reached Rocky Hills, for they found it almost impossible to guide their animals and the cart across the precipices that stretched for almost two miles before they reached Mayfield. On arrival there they found a newly completed large and comfortable home and were impressed by the amount of work Thomas Buxton had done. It was not so with the property immediately across the Buxton River (now the Kullaroo Estate), nor, as they found the next day, with the five-hundred-acre property at the southern head of Little Swanport (Seaford), which was also owned by James Cumming, for the two men in charge there were bad characters and were making no attempt to improve the two grants; also, the land commissioners discovered, they were selling their master's sheep and keeping the money for themselves.

Passing on to the nearby Two Mile Creek (Lisdillon Rivulet), they spent the night at the military station there. Upon exploring the coastal region the following day they were well aware of its beauty, describing the surroundings as *picturesque to a degree*.[32] They recommended that five hundred acres (200 ha) be reserved for a township between there and Boomer Creek (now Lisdillon and the Salt Works), as it was the best land to be found between Oyster Bay and Little Swanport; they also recommended that a further five hundred acres be reserved for the same purpose on the grant taken by James Simpson,# who they said should be allotted land elsewhere.

Crossing the Little Swanport River, they found themselves near the salt boglands adjoining the land used by John Harte. On being invited into his hut they found it stripped of everything by the aborigines, the only furniture, as their host needlessly pointed out, being that which was supplied by Mother Nature -namely, the ground.[33]

Across the creek (Ravensdale Rivulet) they found at John Hawkins's home a much greater degree of comfort. Nevertheless, they were

---

* At this time John Addison was submitting a design for the new Government House, which was not accepted; the building, after several false starts, was not completed until 1858.

James Simpson was the Police Magistrate for the Campbell Town district. His first grant was where Pontypool is now located.

Coswell. Photograph taken in the 1960's (State Library of Tasmania)

surprised at his choice of land, stating their opinion that a worse selection or a more dismal place they had yet to behold. The following day they were hardly more impressed by Joseph Castle's Banwell, saying that he had but little to expect from it and that he evidently realised this himself, for he proposed to establish a fishery there.

Finally, Peter Murdoch and Roderic O'Connor finished their two-month survey of the East Coast by suggesting that the best means of communication between Hobart Town and Oyster Bay by land would be by the Eastern Marshes. The settlers at Oyster Bay, they said, generally received their letters once a month; however, if a messenger were stationed at Oatlands to receive the mailbag he could go and return in time to connect with the messenger travelling between Hobart Town and Launceston, which would mean that the East Coast settlers would receive their mail as punctually as those in any part of the interior.[34]

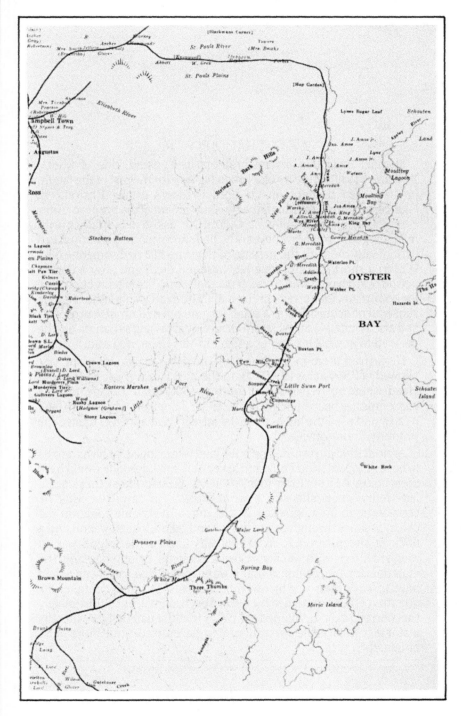

Map of Oyster Bay and surrounds as drawn by Land Commissioners

CHAPTER 9

Michael Steel had several brothers in England, one of whom, William, was fifteen years older than he. As with the rest of the family, he had been brought up on Lord Brassey's estate, Enstone, in Gloucestershire, where his father was sub-tenant of the property. After completing his education at Oxford he assisted his father with managing the property. For years he had shown marked attention to a certain lady but with the passing of time she married someone else. Within a short space of time her husband died, and after a decent period of mourning she looked expectantly in William's direction. She looked in vain, for he was a proud man. The death of his father and the subsequent acquisition of a small fortune opened up new prospects and also pointed to an escape from an embarrassing situation, and he decided to join his brother and sister in Van Diemen's Land.[1]

He arrived there in 1829 and obtained the maximum grant now allowed of 2560 acres (1060 ha) on the East Coast above St Patricks Head, where he lived in a small fourteen-foot-square cottage near the coast; this has been built by Dr Alexander Thomson, who owned land nearby and used the hut as a coastal retreat. William Steel named the property Thomsonville.[2]*

As no settled port existed near his land he arranged for all his goods to be sent to Waterloo Point and asked William Lyne if he would have them conveyed from there to his property. William chose the delicate lad Henry - now almost a man at fifteen - to carry out what he considered to be a light task in clearing a thirty-mile route up the coast, at times through dense bush,[3] and take a loaded wagon and a flock of sheep through. When all was packed the wagon was so weighed down with William Steel's personal belongings and the materials for a large house that it was decided that the sheep would have to work their way by carrying the nails; so a bag containing a quantity of them was tied to the neck of each animal, but unfortunately the morning dew so softened the paper that the nails fell out, thereby making it impossible for a house to be erected until more were obtained.[4]

---

*The property, later named Enstone Park, remained in the hands of the Steel family until 1970.

In the winter of 1829 a forty eight year old ticket-of-leave constable came to Great Swan Port in search of bushrangers.[5] He was the most complex, the most bewildering type of man the settlers in that area had ever encountered. Highly educated, he had mixed in society with men such as Goethe, Sir Joseph Banks and Lord Castlereagh, but was equally at ease with the lowest criminal. He was brilliant, attractive, unscrupulous, and had lived a life of headlong adventure. He had worked as a British spy, had once proclaimed himself king of Iceland, and had been mate in David Collins' ship, the *Lady Nelson*. In London in 1826 he had been convicted of petty thievery and transported to Van Diemen's Land, where he had obtained his ticket-of-leave the following year.[6] Now he was stationed at Oatlands, on his best behaviour, with his mind fixed on the possibility of a pardon. His name was Jorgen Jorgensen.

While he was searching the Oyster Bay area for bushrangers he made his headquarters at the home of the Chief District Constable. He found Adam Amos to be *'an honest and industrious man, hospitable, and such as one could wish every Van Diemen's Land settler of his rank to be. But his maxim is 'Let me alone and I will leave you alone.'*[7]

Runaway prisoners were leaving the East Coast alone just then so the Swede did the same, but three months later returned with a search and capture team, intent on finding aborigines. They found themselves short of supplies so called in and made requisition to Paddy Harte for a few pounds of meat, at the same time explaining their mission. They found the Irishman entirely unco-operative and not backward in giving reasons for his attitude, stating *'that the natives never came to any harm anywhere except when they knew that the d - d soldiers and constables were in the huts, and that he would not give a d - n for a receipt for the Commissariat.'* Yet they obtained what they needed in the end.

For all Paddy Harte's championing of the blacks they burned his stores at Great Swan Port a few months later,[8] after which his men reported that they had been in the habit of calling in at Bellbrook, where some acts of barbarity had been committed upon them, *'the mere relation of which makes Humanity shudder.'*[9]

Upon reaching Waterloo Point Jorgen Jorgensen discovered that Captain Hibbert had been transferred. In his stead was a young man named Richard Lane. While he recognised his breeding and manners to be irreproachable he questioned his efficiency, so deciding that he needed the assistance of a clerk of *'sedate manners and of very active disposition'* he enquired if there were such a man in the district. He was recommended to interview Thomas Buxton.

Cursing a road that could scarcely be worse, he travelled to Mayfield to see him. He found him to be industrious and community minded, *'though somewhat of a busybody'*, and on returning to Waterloo Point recommended him for the post. When approached, Thomas Buxton accepted without hesitation, for yet another attack by aborigines had made him eager to do all in his power to stop such activities.

The attack had started while one of his men was shearing. As he was bending over a sheep he had felt a sharp pain in his chin, and thinking that one of his mates was trying to frighten him had growled, 'What did you do that for?', *'But on looking up'*, he said later during an official enquiry into the attack, *'I saw a black fellow.'* In attempting to escape he was wounded in the chest. With spears flying all round him he rushed towards the men's hut, and was helped inside by a fellow convict. The other hut was plundered and, as usual, all the bedding stolen.[10]

It was a great relief to Thomas Buxton and the other inhabitants of the district to learn that a doctor was now available to attend the wounded and the ill in Great Swan Port. The doctor was George Fordyce Story, M.A.; M.D.

He was the son of George Story, a Methodist minister who had counted John Wesley among his close friends. He was sixty years of age when his son was born.

Young George was not an imposing man to look at, being of small build, with dark dank hair and a thin beard. His long face and melancholy eyes belied his quietly happy nature.

In 1824, twenty-four years after his birth, he had taken his diploma in Edinburgh and four years later, following the death of his widowed mother, had signed on as ship's surgeon on the SS *Henry & Mary Jellico* (commonly known as the *Mary*) in which some friends of his, Francis and Anna Maria Cotton, were sailing.

He disembarked when the ship reached Hobart Town on December 16th, 1829 and in April took the only appointment open to him at the time - that of District Assistant Surgeon at the Waterloo Point Military Station. Once there, he found to his dismay that he must attend all floggings of soldiers and prisoners, which was a practice distressing to him. As well, he was expected to look after the health of all personnel, perform post-mortems, give vaccinations, inspect road gangs and issue weather reports. For this he was paid three shillings a day plus expenses. As a means of gaining extra remuneration he was offered the position of storekeeper, or Commissariat, at the station, which he accepted.[12]

At Waterloo Point he moved into a whitewashed stone cottage with a sod roof, and soon the small man on his tall horse was a familiar sight along the sixty miles (96 km) of sparsely settled coastal strip where he plied a private practice as well as performing his military duties. Although there were practically no made roads he never lost his way, for he had an unfailing sense of locality.[13]

Two months after his arrival at Great Swan Port his lifelong friend, Francis Cotton, joined him.

Cotton's ancestors had been people of good standing. One of them, William, was a wealthy linen draper who lived in London in the 1750's. While he was busy amassing a fortune there his brother joined their cousin-by-marriage, Robert Clive, in India in the fight against the French. The son of a cousin in Shropshire was said to have renounced a title on becoming a Quaker. He died young, leaving a son, Thomas, who became an accountant. It was this man's son, Francis, who became the friend of George Story when they were at school together.[14]

They were completely different in appearance. In contrast to George Story's fragility Francis was a broad man over six feet four inches tall (193 cm), and had sandy coloured hair, a high complexion and very blue eyes. Their dispositions were dis-similar also, for Francis was an outgoing person, friendly and demonstrative.

He had completed his education at The Friends' School, Ackworth, and when he left at the age of sixteen was already trained in book-keeping and the rudiments of architecture.[15] After completing his apprenticeship as a carpenter he had set up his own business as a builder.[16] When he was nineteen he had met and married Anna Maria Tilney of Kelvedon, Essex - a short,* dark, plump, plain, capable and managing little person - but because the ceremony had for convenience been conducted in a church of another denomination the Society of Friends temporarily disowned them for 'marrying

---

*Anna Maria was only four feet eleven inches (149 cm) in height.

out'.[17] Within a few years he had contracted rheumatic fever, which the London fogs did nothing to improve, and this, combined with a bleak outlook for the future of his five children, decided him to join his friend George Story when he sailed for the new settlement of Western Port (Victoria).

They had a rough voyage in the *Mary*, which was dismasted in a storm, and were very relieved when, under a jury rig, they reached the Derwent. Anna Maria Cotton found the scenery beautiful and the scent of the wattle reminded her of the hawthorn at home, causing her to take an instant liking to the place. She was only too pleased when they were unable to find a vessel willing to take them through the unchartered waters near Western Port and were forced into the decision to settle in Van Diemen's Land.

Leaving his family in the care of George Story, Francis travelled with a fellow-passenger named Pyke* to the Midlands to look for suitable available land, which he failed to find. Back in Hobart Town he built a house in Campbell Street,# while George Story travelled by whaleboat to Waterloo Point to commence his duties. There he was so taken with the country-side that he persuaded the Cottons to settle in the district. In June 1829, in possession of a location order for a grant of seven hundred and fifty acres (300 ha) on the coast south of Waterloo Point, Francis Cotton and his family set out. Good luck did not go with them. When they reached Maria Island the *Prince Leopold* went ashore in a heavy swell and when they were taken onto the island they found great difficulty in getting food and shelter. As George Meredith's meat boat (at that time a built-up whale boat, partly decked)[18] was leaving for Waterloo Point they boarded her, but halfway to their destination Charles Meredith decided to go back and collect a small boat they had left behind. At this, Francis Cotton's patience broke. With Anna Maria and the three youngest children he climbed into the boat's dinghy and, in spite of an injured hand, rowed the remaining fifteen miles (24 km) to shore.[19]

George Story was there to welcome them and took them to the sod hut he had arranged they should occupy for a while. Anna Maria was a deft worker and by the time the winter night set in had everything in order. As they sat down for their meal George Story, accident-prone all his life, directed his man to hand down a side of bacon from the roof,

---

*Ram Island. at the mouth of the Little Swanport River, was part of the land granted to the Pyke family.
#The house was next to Mathers Domain Stores.

and in holding a candle to assist him set fire to the thatch. The flames spread with amazing rapidity. The children were rushed outside, a few of the doctor's books were rescued, and then the new arrivals could do nothing but stand back and watch as all their furniture, stores and clothing were burned. The fire attracted all the occupants of the military station, and Mrs Lane, the wife of the Police Magistrate, invited the Cotton family to stay with her until more permanent arrangements could be made.

During the days that followed the family was so handicapped by lack of belongings that Francis took advantage of Lieutenant Lane's offer of a government boat and set off for Hobart Town in order to get fresh supplies and clothing. When he reached the half-mile neck of land (Mather's Neck) between Frederick Henry Bay and Ralphs Bay he contacted a nearby friend, Robert Mather of the Lauderdale property,* who used his bullock team to pull the boat across on a wooden railway constructed for such a purpose.[20] Purchases completed in Hobart Town, Francis and his crew set off on their return trip, but wayward winds made it a long journey and so short of rations did they become that at one stage seven of them breakfasted off a single wattle bird.

Back at Great Swan Port he chose his grant. Situated to the east of Rocky Hills, it contained an area of coastal flat land backed by steep forested hills; close to the sea was a stretch of water known as Muddy or Salt Water Lagoon into which ran a small creek. There were many who prophesied that he would do no good there but he took no notice, for he found himself in thrall to the beauty of the place, sheepishly admitting: *'I fell in love with its pretty face.'*[21] He named it Kelvedon.# From his temporary home in a sod hut at Waterloo Point he travelled the six miles daily, and with the help of three assigned servants started clearing land in preparation for the building of a house for his family.

His government men viewed him with mixed feelings. He was a good master who treated them firmly but well, though he would not tolerate slackness and expected them to keep pace with him. Yet he gave them a sense of unease because he refused to carry a gun, for although he had discarded the speech and dress of a Quaker, he still carried out their peaceful precepts. It was a source of comfort to them that he allowed them to be issued with arms, even though, as it happened, they

---

* Robert Mather also owned a store in Hobart Town.
# Kelvedon is still occupied by the Cotton family.

were unable to make use of them on the one occasion they were needed.

This was on a cold spring morning in September 1829, before Francis Cotton had arrived from Waterloo Point. The men went to where they had felled a tree the previous day, and, placing their guns in the butt, had just started to lop off the branches when they saw an aborigine stealing their arms, while behind him were about thirty more blacks. The men managed to escape and one of them, running northwards, later met Francis Cotton near Piermont and gasped out his story. His master returned immediately to Waterloo Point and Lieutenant Lane sent three parties of soldiers to Kelvedon, George Story accompanying them. However, when they arrived the blacks had gone, and so had everything belonging to the men.[22]

Two of the men were ill for some time, suffering from wounds received during the attack. This retarded the work and Francis Cotton carried on as best he could building what was to be a temporary house for the family; but because pressure of work never seemed to ease he was forced to add room to room as the family increased, so that the permanent house he planned never eventuated. As it was, in the initial stages the place was so long in becoming habitable that they left Waterloo Point and occupied the huts the men had built for themselves.[23]

Kelvedon, from a sketch by George Washington Walker in 1833.
(Tasmanian Collection, State Library of Tasmania)

Another settler on the East Coast was Captain Peter Maclaine*, a Scot from Tobermory on the Isle of Mull. Late of the 65th Regiment, he, like many other soldiers, had emigrated under the regulations of 1827, which allowed military officers to become settlers in the colonies on special terms. He, with his twenty-four-year-old wife and his baby daughter, arrived in Van Diemen's Land en route for New South Wales on May 8th, 1829 on the barque *Orelia*, but were so attracted by the scenery and climate of the island that they decided to stay.[24] He brought with him property to the value of £1,488 and goods worth £700.[25]

During an interview with Governor Arthur he stated that he would rather have a government appointment than settle on the land, but as there were no suitable posts available he accepted a location order for 2,560 acres on the East Coast.[26] With an eye for beauty as well as practicality he chose a grant at Spring Bay beside a creek# near Silas Gatehouse's stockyard, at the place where George Meredith and Adam Amos had camped for some days during their exploratory trip eight years before. Peter Maclaine named his grant Woodstock after the native place of his Irish wife,[27] and moved there in July, 1829. Frances, fifteen years his junior, was merry and full of gaeity, loving fashion and company. She stayed in Hobart Town, lightheartedly declining to share his tent at Spring Bay, awaiting the time when he could offer her more permanent accommodation. The convicts were detailed to make bricks, in addition to their other work, but it was two years before she and young Frances installed themselves in the two rooms of the house that were then completed. To her surprise, she found herself quite content in her new surroundings. A son, Hugh Donald, was born in 1831, and another, John Joseph Hone, in 1833.[28]

In April, 1830, Peter Maclaine found that he was to have a neighbour. This was the Commandant of Maria Island. Through the years Major Thomas Daunt Lord had come to know the coast opposite the island very well and chose for the 1,560 acre grant due to him, land lying on the northern side of the entrance to Spring Bay. This area contained mineral springs that were reputed to have healing powers equal to any in Europe.[29] He named it Oakhampton.* *

The building of a house on his grant afforded him some diversion from the troubles he was experiencing at Maria Island. He had been

---

*George Boyes, the Colonial Auditor, described Peter Maclaine as 'by far the ugliest man in the Colony.'
#The Macquarie River.
* *The spelling was later changed to Okehampton. The building was demolished in the 1950's.

Okehampton, Spring Bay
(Courtesy Mrs. S. Lester, Triabunna)

charged by his storekeeper with embezzlement and with taking government property for his own use and it had taken a great deal of ingenuity to prevent the charges being pressed, as well as to arrange for the commissariat officer to be removed.[30]

In June there was a third arrival in the area - a naval gentleman, Captain William Leard. He was a courteous young bachelor who had visited Van Diemen's Land three years before and had taken such a liking to it that he had now returned to settle. He was given a location order for 2,560 acres (1,024 ha)[31] to the north of Peter Maclaine's Woodstock on condition that he went to live there at once, for it was known that he had applied for the position of storeman at Maria Island, and this, should he obtain it, would give him little time to develop his grant, Rostrevor.[32] He gave the required undertaking to live on his land and work it.

In the early summer of 1828, well to the north of the three new arrivals, things were going well at Banwell. In spite of several attacks by the aborigines when they had pillaged his farm and destroyed his sheep,[33] Joseph Castle was in good heart, for the £1,500 he had spent on improvements had been justified. He had completed a few rooms of the freestone house he planned and was almost ready to bring Edith and the two younger children to live in it.* One day, as usual, he was hard at work; his sons, John and Robert, were out of sight. Suddenly he became aware that he was no longer alone. Spinning round, he saw a group of aborigines creeping up on him. Frantically he turned and started to run in the opposite direction from where he knew his sons to be. A spear struck him deep in the middle back.

He tugged at it as he ran, but it broke off. In great pain, but knowing that to stop was death, he ran along the curving beach until he reached the stock hut at Grindstone Bay, five miles away. There he collapsed. The spear was so deeply embedded that the stock-keepers were forced to cut deep to get it out. There was little they could do for his comfort, for before going to Banwell the blacks had plundered the stock hut and there was not so much as a blanket there with which to cover him.

He was taken to Hobart Town, where it took him a long time to recover even a small measure of health, but long before he was in a fit state to do so he returned to Banwell. A short time there was sufficient to convince him that he could never again live the life of a settler, and he was forced to move back to the capital. There for a time he was dependent on whatever Edith and their young daughter could earn by taking in needlework.[34] Then because of his training he was able to obtain a position in the Surveyor-General's office, after which he applied in April 1829 for a secondary grant for an allotment in town so that he could build on it. As nothing suitable was available except in the new township of Kangaroo Point (Bellerive)[35] he settled there, but his health deteriorated to such an extent that he was forced to retire from work.

In January 1835, 'in a most wretched state of health', he applied for a further grant of 1,000 acres in compensation for the aboriginal attack, pointing to it as the cause of his having to leave Banwell.[36] After that, fully aware that he had not long to live, he sent for his 'very dear friend, Mr Edward Bisdee of Hutton Park', and with the help of a solicitor friend made his will.

The thousand-acre compensation grant was approved by both the Surveyor-General and the Colonial Surgeon,[37] but by the time it came through Joseph Castle was dead.[38] Less then five months later, on August 4th, 1835, Edith married Henry Elliott.[39]

---

* Banwell homestead, though long unoccupied, is still standing and has potential for restoration.

John and Robert at twenty and eighteen were of an age to manage for themselves, and returned to Banwell, which they found in a very neglected state; nevertheless, it represented too much for them to abandon so they settled down to the long task of making it a paying proposition.

CHAPTER 10

In an effort to assist the search and capture parties scattered round the colony the government published in the *Gazette* of February 20th, 1830, advice that *'a reward of five pounds shall be given for every adult aboriginal native, and two pounds for any child, who shall be captured and delivered at any Police Station.'* The readers knew that the earnings of such rewards would not be an easy task, for the aborigines had an acute sense of hearing, very keen sight, and were adept at covering their tracks; also, by this time they were exceedingly wary, as well as hostile.

Some months before this notice appeared one of George Meredith's men, John Raynor, had been attacked while on his way back from Hobart Town. After being speared in several places he was brutally beaten into unconsciousness. Recovering his senses some time later he endeavoured to find help, and three days later the stock-keepers at Grindstone Bay saw what they took to be a drunk man staggering, stumbling and crawling towards them. Then, recognising him, they ran to his assistance, and were horrified to find that he was blind in one eye and had had the other knocked out, and that his festering sores were crawling with maggots. They carried him to their hut and did all they could for him before taking him to the hospital at Hobart Town, but he died shortly afterwards.[1]

Such incidents might well have discouraged any new settlers to the area, but a recent arrival, James Radcliff, was not a man to be turned aside easily.

He came from a family of some standing, whose crest showed a crown bestowed when an ancestor married Lady Mary Stuart, one of Charles II's acknowledged daughters by an actress, Mol Davis. This connection with Royalty did them little good, for in 1716 their son, James Radcliffe, the third Earl of Derwentwater, had estates worth £300,000 confiscated and was beheaded, while his brother Charles (said to be the immediate ancestor of the Van Diemen's Land settler) in 1746 paid for his allegiance to his cousin Prince Charles in the same way, being the last man in England to be beheaded.[2] It may have been

Portrait of James Radcliff
(Courtesy Mr. James Radcliff, Devonport)

in an effort to dissociate themselves from this event that the family dropped the 'e' from their name.

James was the son of William and Anne Radcliff of Belfast. A bachelor in his late twenties, he had a great sense of dignity, and as well as being accounted by some as rather eccentric, had the reputation of being frugal.[3] Certain it was that he was well-to-do and had a head for business.[4] Upon arriving in Van Diemen's Land in January 1830 he made extensive enquiries about the prospects awaiting a settler there and then sailed on to Sydney, where he went through the same process. Deciding that the island held more promise he returned, and in July made application for 2,560 acres as a grant. This he located four miles or so east of the Little Swanport River in that beautiful area next to Two Mile Creek which Roderic O'Connor had described as *'picturesque to a degree'.* Fronting on Cumming's side line, it extended south to Boomer Creek.[5] He named it Lisdillon.

Driving his men hard, he started on the initial settling-in process. Finding that he needed more than the amount of capital he had in hand, he authorised his agent in Belfast to sell various houses and warehouses there.[6] Half of the money he handed over to his younger brother Richard, with the recommendation that he join him in Van Diemen's Land.

More and more settlers were heading for the East Coast. Well to the north, the Lyne family was delighted to learn that they had new neighbours. They were Captain Thomas Watson and his two sons, Thomas (22) and Robert (21), and a pregnant lady whom he introduced as his wife.[7]

An erect, openfaced man of fifty, Thomas Watson was the son of Thomas and Ann Watson of Sherbourne Hall near Durham, and was a collateral descendant of the late Marquis of Rockingham. Although married to Elizabeth Blauk, it was a thirty-four-year-old spinster named Mary Burrows who accompanied him to Van Diemen's Land. The *Wave*, square-rigged and three-masted, berthed at Hobart Town on June 25th, 1830, and with military precision the ex-soldier set about establishing himself in his new life. Procuring a location order for 1,280 acres (512 ha), he chose his grant at the north-western end of Moulting Lagoon, not far from where William Lyne's chartered boat had stuck in the mud over four years before.

The head of Moulting Lagoon. Sherbourne Lodge was towards the left of the photograph.

Sherbourne Lodge, from a painting in the 1920's by Miss Trixie Amos.
(Courtesy Mr. J. Fenn-Smith, Coombend.)

Remains of the Watson Cemetary, Sherbourne

Although inured to the rigours of army life, he was too used to a background of civilised living to willingly subject himself and family to life in a hut, so had brought with him a small house in frame.[8] This was erected close to the waters of the lagoon, and, with his English home in mind, he named it Sherbourne Lodge.

There was an element of haste in settling in, for it was almost time for Mary Burrow's child to be born. On August 2nd, 1830 she gave birth to a son, who was named John Percival Watson.[9]

The new settler was not a stranger to farming, for before entering the army he had spent his life on the family property, and now, with the help of his sons and his government men, he set about establishing a farm. So ingrained in him were the niceties of life that no matter how tired he was at the end of a day's toil he always dressed for dinner, as did the other members of the family.

It was the practice of the settlers near the lagoon to transport to the mouth of the Swan any produce they needed to sell, and from there it was rowed out to a local trading ship or a larger craft bound for England. In the spring of 1830 Robert and Thomas Watson had been so engaged, and before returning home allowed some of their men to bathe in the river at a spot opposite Robert Hepburn's Swanwick. Robert's shirt blew off the dinghy while he was sunbathing and upon diving into the water to retrieve it he got into difficulties and sank. At once Thomas stood up in order to dive in, in an attempt to save him, but the convicts, fearful that he would drown and they would be charged with murder, prevented him, and he was forced to watch his brother die.[10] His body was never found, but a headstone was erected not far from Sherbourne Lodge in an area reserved for a private cemetery.*

Not far from Sherbourne Lodge a relative of Thomas Watson, Brereton Watson, had been farming at Bellbrook since August 1829.[11]

In or before 1827 John de Courcy Harte's profligate living, plus the expense attached to building a moderate-sized double-storey stone house and barn at Bellbrook, had affected his finances to such an extent that he had either sold or exchanged the southern half of his property - that part situated across the Wye. At the same time he had acquired in unusual circumstances (which would in later years be questioned) three hundred or so acres of inferior and marshy land close to the southern bank of the Little Swanport River.[12] This property he named the Head of Little Swanport, or Muirlands, and on it grew potatoes and built a hut. Continued wild living further reduced his circumstances to such an extent that in 1830 he was glad to accept the offer of Brereton Watson to buy the remaining three hundred acres of Bellbrook for £800. But before the sale could be finalised he was arrested as an insolvent and in April was taken to Hobart Town and gaoled. Both of his properties were advertised for auction on May 24th, 1830. An amount of £200 was raised on Muirlands but £320 more was required before he was free of debt and able to cancel the auction.[13]

He sent for the Reverend Father Conolly, with whom he had kept in close contact since they had sailed down from Sydney together in 1821[14], and requested him to buy Bellbrook for £320 at the auction on the understanding that he - Paddy Harte - would buy it back from him later. To this the reverend gentleman agreed.

At Great Swan Port the advertised sale occasioned a great deal of interest. Adam Amos remarked to his brother John that except for the

---

*A few headstones are still visible at Sherbourne.

106

fact that he had heard of a private arrangement between Paddy Harte and Father Conolly he would have given £700 for Bellbrook; Alexander Reid, who was living at Cranbrook at the time, went up to attend the auction with the intention of asking whether he could rent or buy it from the priest after the sale; Richard Allen, wishing to extend The Springs Farm by acquiring the adjoining property, engaged James Baynton of Browns River to bid for the property for him; and Brereton Watson, baulked in his first attempt to buy Bellbrook, attended with the firm intention of gaining it. However, during the auction when word was circulated among the bidders that Father Conolly definitely wished to help Paddy Harte by paying only £320 for the property, all the would-be buyers ceased bidding, allowing the priest to become the new owner.[15]

A month later John Harte was released from gaol and returned to Bellbrook, which Brereton Watson was still farming. Within a year, however, Watson found the situation unsatisfactory and left. His overseer, George Kirby, took over the lease for five years, paying £75 per annum to Father Conolly.

In November 1832 John Harte left Bellbrook and settled at Muirlands, where for two years he kept cows. Then he left for New South Wales, taking a position in Sydney.

The spring of 1830 had brought the members of the May tribe back to their old haunts, bitter against their enemies and keen for revenge. They killed a soldier stationed at Boomer Creek and made their way towards Mayfield.[16] In preparation for building a kitchen near the house two sawyers, Wainwright and Gay, were cutting timber at the sawpit near Christmas Island.[17] They proved an easy target for attack. Wounded and terrified, they ran the half mile to the homestead where, although not severely wounded, a few days later Wainwright died of pain and shock.

Within two days of the attack the aborigines had plundered James King's hut at New Grange and then continued on to Apsley where, fired upon, they fled to George Meredith's stock hut. After robbing this they went a few miles further up the Swan from Glen Gala to Brook Lodge, the grant of a small[18] Irishman named Paddy Duffy, and plundered his hut and killed one of his assigned men.

Elusive and wary, they were not to be caught, though each time a report of an attack was received at the military station the new

107

Assistant Police Magistrate, Lieutenant Aubin, sent out parties of soldiers and settlers in search of them.[19]

Francis Aubin*, born in 1802 on the island of Jersey where his half brother was governor, was a fleshy, full-lipped florid gentleman[20] with impeccable manners which showed to advantage while he was A.D.C. to Colonel Arthur in 1828.[21] He was posted to Great Swan Port in May 1830 and had only been in office for four months when he received the following gazetted orders, issued in preparation for the Black Drive.

'Between the 7th and 12th October 1830 Lieutenant Aubin will thoroughly examine the tier extending from the head of the Swan River, north, down to Spring Bay, the southern extremity of his district, in which duty he will be aided in addition to the military parties stationed at Spring Bay and Little Swan Port, by Captains Maclaine and Leard, Messrs Meredith, Hawkins, Gatehouse, Buxton, Harte, Amos, King, Lyne and all settlers in that district.'[22]#

The settlers, remembering that fourteen of their number had been killed in eight years,[23] responded to the call without hesitation. For seven weeks the parties tramped the region, chasing shadows. Then, bearded and longhaired, their boots worn out and their clothes tattered,[24] they returned home, dejected at the news that in the whole island the only captives had been one aboriginal man and a boy.

A builder and lay preacher in Hobart Town, George Augustus Robinson, appeared in the district a few months later, authorised by the government to try to persuade the aborigines to give themselves into his care. Frightened by their recent experience of being hunted a number of them followed him, much to the astonishment of the white people they encountered. When they reached Glen Gala the assigned servants clustered round them, but Adam Amos and his family stayed inside their house, making no acknowledgement of their presence.[25] Arriving at Waterloo Point the following day they received better treatment, George Robinson being invited to lunch by Lieutenant Aubin, after which the party collected a week's supply of food at the commissariat from Dr Story, who then walked with them to Kelvedon. There they demonstrated their unusual physical prowess. While playing a ball game, one gin ran after it up a bare brick wall as easily as a mouse would.[26] Then they gave such a superb display of spear throwing that Dr Story rewarded them with two boxes of apples.

* Francis Aubin married the daughter of Major Thomas Daunt Lord in 1864.
# Because of his pacifist beliefs Francis Cotton was not required to take part in the drive.

Greatly pleased, they all sat down to do justice to them. After choosing the largest of the fruit for themselves the men threw the smaller ones over their shoulders to the women, not realising that they were by far the sweeter and therefore unable to account for the smothered giggles they heard.[27] Watched by the Cotton children, the aborigines appeared to be in very good spirits, with the exception of a young mother who, having recently lost her baby, 'sat apart in quiet sorrow, appreciating the comfort another mother offered her but gently refusing to be comforted.'[28]

The next day the group travelled on to Spring Bay (which the blacks called TRI-UB-BUNNER), and after calling in at the small military post, accepted Captain Maclaine's invitation to spend the night at Woodstock. On leaving the following morning the aborigines told their leader that during the night some of the soldiers stationed nearby had appeared, wanting 'to have liberties' with the females among them.[29] On January 19th, 1831 George Augustus Robinson succeeded in bringing the group safely to Hobart Town.

The year 1831 was marked by the cancellation of the government's practice of giving to settlers free grants of land in proportion to their capital. This formula, in use since the establishment of the colony, had been successful in attracting British migrants, but because of the difficulties of policing it too many settlers had acquired more land than they were entitled to.[30] Now the Home Government issued instructions to Governor Arthur that instead of the land being given away it was to be sold to the highest bidder at public auction, the lowest price to be set at five shillings an acre.

Consternation ruled among the settlers when the new law became known. There was a rush to finalise outstanding applications and extensions to original grants.[31] Alexander Reid, frustrated in his attempt to either buy or lease Bellbrook, chose for himself three hundred and twenty acres (128 ha) in a rockstrewn but attractive area at the junction of the east and west branches of the Swan, calling it Watersmeeting,* while the other ex-convict from Little Swanport, John Radford, free since 1825, chose land beside him, buying half of Paddy Duffy's six hundred and forty acres at Brook Lodge.[32]

John Lyne had applied for land in 1829 and now his request for three hundred and twenty acres was given official sanction, while

---

*The homestead at Watersmeeting has disappeared.

By His Honor George Arthur Esqre
Lieutenant Governor of Van
Diemens Land

These are to certify, that John Radford.
who was tried at Exeter, the 19th March, 1817
and who arrived at Van Diemans Land
in the Ship Lady Castlereagh, Welder
Master, in the year 1818, under Sentence
of Transport for Seven years, and whose
description is hereunto annexed, and
is henceforth restored to Freedom.
Given under my hand Seal, at
Government House, Hobart Town,
this Twenty Second day of August
in the year of our Lord,
One Thousand Eight hundred and
twenty five.

Copy of John Radford's pardon.

110

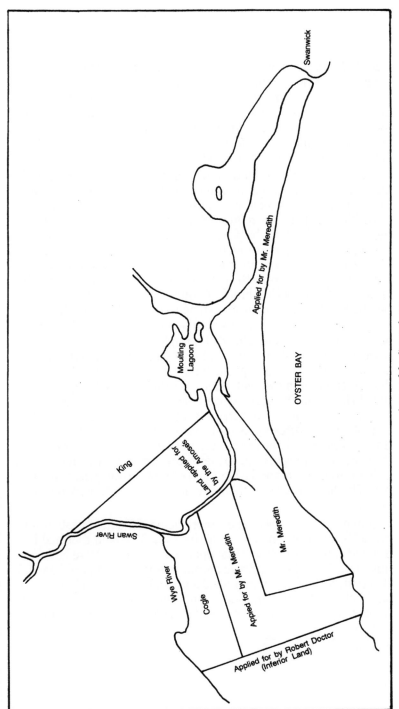

A map of the disputed area

George Meredith[33] was successful in obtaining a further thousand acres. John Amos, granted an additional thousand acres in January because of the improvements he had made to Cranbrook, in June was given a further two hundred acres, while his son James received a location order for three hundred and twenty acres, as did also his cousins, John and Adam, all three grants being taken next to James King's reserve near the mouth of the Wye.

The rush to finalise land grants affected George Story also. He applied to have his seven hundred and fifty acres (300 ha) located at Spring Bay; this was refused because the area was now reserved for a township.[34] Then he requested permission to be granted the neglected land owned by Cumming and located south of Buxton Creek; he was told that this had been promised to James Radcliff. However, his third application was approved and he took possession of that area of land opposite the mouth of the Wye which John Amos had vacated in favour of Cranbrook. At once Adam Amos declared that it belonged to him, and as the government could not decide which of the two claimants owned it he moved to an adjoining block situated at an acute bend of the Swan, already known locally as The Bend, and set his men to work building a hut for him. Again Adam Amos intervened, saying that the land belonged to his son John. Aroused, this time the doctor refused to move, emboldened by the fact that the government upheld his claim.[35] But so belligerent did Adam Amos become[36] that after a few months he withdrew his men and looked elsewhere for a suitable grant. After applying in vain for land behind Apsley and Sherbourne in 1834 he gave in and went to Kelvedon with his friends the Cottons, adding his land to theirs. Welcoming him warmly, Francis built on some rooms and a laboratory for his private use, and for the rest of his life he lived with them as comfortably as if he were one of the family.

Young John Lyne was also experiencing difficulty in establishing himself on territory he could call his own. The land that had been granted to him in 1831 was that upon which George Meredith's stock hut stood.[37]* When he drove his entire flock of a hundred and fifty sheep there they were impounded and Adam Amos told him that the land belonged to his son Adam, who rented it to George Meredith. Impassioned letters were written to the Surveyor-General by both

---

*This was probably Riverslea.

112

men, and relations were strained. They became worse when late in 1831 the aborigines stole guns from Watersmeeting while Alexander Reid was 'at plow'[38] and the Lynes did not carry a warning of armed blacks to the stock hut, later saying that they knew it to be unoccupied at the time.

No sooner did George Meredith hear that forty or so aborigines were in the district than he guessed that they would follow their usual practice and go to the Peninsula. When he found this to be so he sent word to all settlers from William Lyne in the north to Peter Maclaine in the south, requesting that all available men be sent in an all-out effort to capture the blacks.[39] He then wrote a hurried and self-laudatory letter to Governor Arthur describing what he had done - a letter so scribbled and scrawled that His Excellency had to have it deciphered before he could read it.

For a fortnight a party of about a hundred men kept the aborigines penned up on the southern part of the Peninsula. Then one dark night they broke through the cordon of men and fires that stretched from Promise Bay to Wineglass Bay and escaped. All that the weary men had to show for their vigil was a piece of a scalp hanging from the broken stump of a she-oak tree.[40]

Apsley House, with a verandah added.
From a photograph taken in 1900

113

Low in spirits, the settlers and their men disbanded and returned to their homes, not realising that the episode had so alarmed the aborigines that they would never again be a danger to them.

William Lyne, thankful to have his three sons back again to help with the work, continued to supervise the building of Apsley House.* Situated on a hill some hundred and forty yards (128 m) above the log cabin, it was a square double-storey brick place constructed in Flemish bond design. Strong and well built, it offered oceans of room to its occupants after their five years in the cramped quarters of the cabin. Upon its completion a cider house was commenced a little further downhill.# As it rose deep and vast and cool its owner's pride in it became so marked that he spent all of his time supervising its construction. It was a handsome building, and when it was completed it was with satisfaction that William Lyne installed the cider press he had brought from Gloucestershire. Gathering from their stored place in his coffin the first apples the orchard had produced, he set to work

Apsley Cider House, 1987.

* Apsley House, built about 1832, with alterations and additions is still used as the Apslawn residence.
# The cider house, in an excellent state of preservation, is still used for farm purposes.

to do what he had looked forward to for years - making cider as he had made it at Coombe-End.

At the end of 1829 James King of New Grange had received word that his father had died in London. By this time he was insolvent, so after legal complications had been settled he advertised for sale both Betsey Island and his Great Swan Port property.[41] The island and its ten thousand rabbits* sold for £470, New Grange for £675 - this in spite of James King Snr having spent over £1,000 on improvements. It was bought by Charles O. Parsons#[42], who shortly afterwards sold it to Joseph Gellibrand, who had been Attorney-General until dismissed by Governor Arthur in 1825.[43]

About this time the settlers at Great Swan Port had occasion to wish young Thomas Watson every happiness as he left for England to be married. On his return two years later he took Dorothy, his wife, to live at Milton, where she became the one personal friend Mary Meredith had in all the colony.[44] Upon applying for a grant of land young Thomas was dismayed when it was refused, on the grounds that he had delayed too long before making his application.[45] In spite of all he could do officialdom did not relent. At this time - the autumn of 1835 - the one impediment to his father's respectability was removed when, at the Anglican church at Sorell, he married Mary Burrows.

John Allen, too, had temporarily returned to England, his sister having come out from Somerset with a purse full of sovereigns with which to pay his passage home. Sailing on the barque *Science* in 1832, they had a dangerous and eventful voyage when the ship was driven south among icebergs. With damaged masts and tangled rigging and with several seamen lost overboard, the ship seemed to be on the point of capsizing. Spurred on by the danger, several passengers - John Allen among them - climbed the mast and cut away the loose sails and rigging, after which they opened some bales of wool in the hold and plugged up the leaks. In this way they managed to keep afloat for six days until a South Sea whaler took them on board, after which the passengers looked on without regret as someone set fire to the *Science* prior to her sinking. Put ashore at Rio de Janiero, they were taken on board a sloop-of-war, *H.M.S. King William IV*, and conveyed to England, where John Allen received a warm welcome from his family.[46]

---

* The type of silver-grey rabbit bred on Betsey Island has since died out.
# C.O. Parsons later became commandant at Maria Island

Such were the stories he told of his life across the seas that his twenty-two-year-old nephew, Joseph Butler, made up his mind to emigrate. Pointing out that it was too late for him to obtain a grant of land, John Allen suggested that he stay at Egg Farm (his additional grant on Moulting Lagoon), until he himself returned to the island, by which time other arrangements could be made. Joseph Butler agreed, and, accompanied by his sister Agnes, reached Van Diemen's Land in the barque *Ann* in November, 1833. They travelled to Great Swan Port and were at Egg Farm to welcome John Allen when he arrived there the following year.

CHAPTER 11

In January 1831 Lieutenant Aubin heard on good authority that there was some irregularity going on among the government men working for George Meredith, Junior[1]. As a result he passed the information on to the young colonist, telling him that he intended having a strict watch kept on his men. He then posted two constables near the convicts' hut and for two nights from eleven o'clock on they kept a fruitless vigil there. On the third night, realising that the building was empty, they moved to a hut about a quarter of a mile away. There they found that the rumours heard by Lieutenant Aubin were true.

In the enquiry that followed it was established that the constables had raided Gunn's hut at about two o'clock in the morning and in one room found several men drunk and others nearly so. They were insolent to the officers and rebellious, saying the young Master had invited them and they were his guests. It was then disclosed that 'the young Master' was in a back room, from which he did not emerge until so ordered.

His Excellency took the matter seriously, saying that any master who could be found drinking early on a Sunday morning with his servants *'is in my opinion unworthy of the trust reposed in him by the Government.'* Young George was told that if such a thing happened again all his assigned servants would be removed. The men were all given thirty lashes each[2] and their master received a tongue-lashing from his father.

The two Georges did not get on well together. As a property owner the father, it would seem, could well be proud of his son; as well as the original five-hundred-acre grant of Redbanks he also possessed a secondary grant and a great deal of rented ground as well, all of which was well stocked. This made him appear, at twenty-six, a very well-established young settler indeed. But he was deeply in debt to his father, and when in 1832 he told him that he was unable to pay back the money there was a violent quarrel between them.

117

Furious and vindictive,[3] George Meredith Senior went to Hobart Town. A lawyer, T.W. Rowlands, later told what happened during an interview he had with him.[4] *'Some time ago George Meredith called on me, having been previously introduced by Mr Fareday (but who had cautioned me most particularly to have as little to do with him as possible), and after much circumlocution informally asked me whether I knew of a man who would become a Special Bailiff to arrest his eldest son. I told him I only knew one blackguard who was likely to suit him, and his name was___. He was, I believe, employed by this fond parent, but happily without effect! He next called on me stating he had an award against his Son, who was about to quit the Colony ..., that he did not come to me professionally, but would be happy to make a compensation if I would assist his views, which were for me to purchase his Son's Estate, and then say I had done so for him, by which means he would obtain it in part payment of the amount owed to him. I declined lending myself to these 'parental views', and I well know that I was not the only member of the Profession to whom he had made similar applications.'*

Almost at once young George slipped away in the *Defiance,* a schooner he had himself built, and set sail for Sydney, swearing he would never return.[5] It was then that his father, abundant in ownership of land but hardpressed for money, was forced to accept the fact that not only would the debt owed him never be paid but that Redbanks was about to pass out of the family.

By order of the trustees the property was offered for sale. The *Hobart Courier* of September 7th, 1832 gave glowing details of *'that beautiful farm ... of fine mellow land, which affords the only landing and watering-place for the important township of Swansea'* (which name George Meredith was substituting for Waterloo Point). *'The good substantial house,'* the notice continued, *'would be fit for a tavern, which by the way, is much wanted.'*

During a keenly contested auction the property was bought jointly by William Morgan Orr, a prosperous merchant of Hobart Town, and a young clerk in his office, Edward Carr Shaw.*

Edward Shaw had been born in 1813 in Terenure, Dublin. An ancestor, William Shaw, had left Scotland for Ireland in about 1689 with the troops of William III to fight the rebels under the deposed

---

*The Shaw family still lives at Redbanks.

King James II, and when the king rewarded his supporters by giving them land, William Shaw settled down in County Cork. There the family thrived to such an extent that nearly a century later - in 1771 - a descendant, Bernard Shaw, was born into both property and money. A prosperous solicitor, he married Frances Carr, but misfortune struck in 1826 when his business partner absconded with all the firm's money, including £50,000 which belonged to Bernard. Out of the remains of his wealth he made good all debts, but that same year the strain resulted in his death. Frances was left to bring up eleven children, the eldest of whom was only fifteen. One of these children was Edward Carr Shaw.[6]

Leaving home at sixteen he went to England to take up a cadetship for the West Indian service, but after only a week in London he met with his sister Fanny, who, newly-married to Arthur Greene, was about to emigrate to the recently settled state of Western Australia. Fearing that his brother-in-law might be killed out there, so leaving Fanny alone in a strange land, Edward decided to go with them. Accompanied by a servant named Kevin Quin[*] they set sail in January 1830 in the 500-ton ship *Rockingham,* and almost at once ran aground in the Thames - an incident which set the pattern for their voyage.[7] While in the Indian Ocean there was a fire in the cargo; weeks later, far to the south, the ship's rigging became encrusted with ice and snow and the sailors' hands were torn so badly as to imperil the ship's safety. The run of bad luck extended to Edward Shaw when a fellow-passenger gave him some oranges and lemons as an insurance against scurvy: these made him so sick that the ship's doctor was sent for and he, blaming tonsils for the illness, commandeered four sailors to hold him down while he cut them out with a pair of scissors.

It was a relief when, after a voyage of three months, they dropped anchor close to a sandy shore at King George's Sound, Western Australia.[#] However, their troubles were not over, for a hurricane burst upon them, causing the *Rockingham* to settle on the shallow bottom and half keel over, so that the waves broke over her, drowning the stock and forcing out the cargo. Next morning all the drenched and exhausted passengers struggled ashore, where they were thankful to find a small settlement already established.[**] Within a few days they

[*] Descendants of Kevin Quin still live on the East Coast of Tasmania.
[#] King George's Sound is about twenty-eight miles (45 km) south of Perth.
[**] The settlement changed its name from Peel to Rockingham.

119

started to build houses for themselves out of timber from the wrecked ship.

For four months Edward Shaw and Fanny and Arthur Greene survived under perilous conditions, but when a small steamer, the *Eagle,* called in on its way to Van Diemen's Land they boarded her and arrived in Hobart Town a fortnight later, in September 1830.[8]*

Although their stock and implements had been lost they still had the sum of £500 each, and with this Arthur Greene made application for a grant of land for his young brother-in-law and himself.[9] Receiving no reply, after many weeks they took a small farm at Campania.# Five months later they were alarmed by the appearance there of aborigines, who the following day killed a neighbour. This, together with the fact that Fanny was pregnant, caused them to return to Hobart Town, where they found there was still no word from the Surveyor-General.

Upon hearing that a certain sea captain had been trying to get in touch with them, they contacted him and took possession of a heavy box which they found contained one hundred and fifty gold sovereigns, sent by the Shaws' uncle, Sir Robert Shaw. Instead of being delighted Edward looked on it as a bribe to return and would not touch a coin of it, although he encouraged Fanny and Arthur to use it to buy a passage home. Disheartened by all their misfortune and conscious of the responsibility of a newly-born baby, they were not hard to persuade. It was while he was selling his furniture and discharging his servants that Arthur Greene received the long-awaited letter from the Survey Office explaining that the delay had been occasioned by the absence of all the staff during the Black Drive, and appointing a day for examining vouchers, etc., with a view to granting land. Informing them that he was on the point of departure, he and Fanny set sail for Ireland, where within a week of landing he received a position that earned him £1,000 a year.**Fanny was received back with thankfulness by her family, her grandmother, Mrs Carr, writing to *'her dear suffering child'* to welcome her back from her *'banishment',* but giving it as her opinion that her dear Edward was right in remaining,[10] and so *'favouring the colony by giving it the social tone that the Shaw family always associates with itself.'*[11]

*Another passenger on board the Eagle was *'Lippscombe. the seedsman. who has been with us from the start.*

The farm was on the present site of the railway station.

** Arthur Greene eventually became Judge of the Supreme Court in Ireland.

Back in Hobart Town Edward Shaw was busy giving tone to the mercantile office of William Orr. His inclination, though, was for the land, and when his employer suggested that they buy Redbanks in partnership he at once agreed. But even as joint owner he continued working in the office, only going down at intervals to supervise the work at Great Swan Port.[12] He was there often enough, however, to observe a disturbance that arose round the person of the Chief District Constable.

Early in December 1832 Adam Amos and his close friend, Alexander Reid, called in at the police office at Waterloo Point on their way to Hobart Town. There they found Lieutenant Aubin greatly upset because of a notice in the *'True Colonist'* stating that in the next issue a letter from a Swan Port settler would be published, bringing to public notice the disorderly state of the district. Politely assuring him that the district had never been in better order, the two Scots left the police station and continued on their way.

When published, the letter exceeded the worst of Francis Aubin's fears.[13] He was outraged and wrote to the *'True Colonist'* denying in the most vehement fashion that crime in his district existed in anything like the degree claimed in the anonymous letter. Far from clearing his reputation for inefficiency, this served as an opening for the malice of the editor, George Meredith - that hater of Great Swan Port magistrates - who informed his readers that previous complaints had been received about lawlessness in the area; indeed, he wrote, so disturbed had he himself become that he had offered to improve the moral tone generally by conducting divine services if a suitable building were erected and attendance by the convicts made compulsory.[14] Also, he said, by chance a constable from Great Swan Port was at that time in Hobart Town and had confirmed many of the accusations contained in the letter.

This pointed the finger firmly at Adam Amos.

Raging, Lieutenant Aubin charged him with being the man alluded to and the Scot admitted it. The writer of the letter, Alexander Reid, remained outside the furore, identified but unpunished.[15]

Because his term of duty was now expired Lieutenant Aubin's sense of outrage was heightened by the belief that he was leaving under a cloud. Determined to clear his name, he wrote an official report of the matter and demanded an enquiry. As a result, when Adam Amos called in at the police station some weeks later for his usual weekly discussion he was confronted by a court composed of Captain Robert Hepburn, J.P.,* Lieutenant Francis Aubin and the new Police Magistrate, Major Thomas Lord, who had been transferred on December 28th, 1832 following the closure of the penal settlement at Maria Island,[16] as Port Arthur was in course of being established.

Having dismissed the episode of the letter from his mind, Adam Amos was totally unprepared for what followed and listened in bewilderment to the charges brought against him. Confused and hurt, he asked for time in which to prepare his defence[17] and asked for a copy of the charges against him. The case was deferred while his application was referred to Governor Arthur, who recommended a stay in proceedings until May 1833, stating that he considered Mr Amos 'the tool of someone more mischievous than he.'[18]

At this particular time, George Meredith was also in trouble with the law. In January 1833 six convicts escaped from a road gang at Constitution Hill. Making their way to Great Swan Port they contacted John Nicholson, a Belmont government man, who was at the stock hut at Spring Vale. When they told him they intended to steal one of George Meredith's whaleboats the next night and make their escape he agreed to join them. The next day he went to Waterloo Point to get provisions for the trip and, in Major Lord's absence, told a publican and storekeeper, John Ferguson,# of the plan. Together they worked out details whereby the men would be enticed to the inn and captured there that night.

Accompanied by the innkeeper, John Nicholson called in at Belmont to acquaint his master with events. Immediately the arrangements were taken out of their hands, and George Meredith told them that in order to prevent possible bloodshed he would leave the whaleboat and oars afloat in the boathouse that night. He then directed his assigned servant to take the bushrangers to the inn when they had stolen the boat, persuade them to steal something, and then he would see that they were captured - to the mortification of Major Lord, who until then would be quite unaware that there were bushrangers in his district.

The two men then left Belmont, John Nicholson going to Spring Vale and John Ferguson to Waterloo Point. There, finding that the

---

* At this time Adam Amos's son, John, married Elizabeth Hepburn. They settled at Glen Heriot, part of Adam's grant.

John Ferguson was also the first postmaster for Waterloo Point (1833-1837) but was then considered unsuitable for the position because of his drinking habits.

Magistrate had returned, he told him what had happened. At once Major Lord took things into his own hands, and late that night his constables were in hiding both outside and inside the store. Then the escapees entered, stole a revolver, and ordered drinks. They were rushed by the police. In the struggle that followed one of the bushrangers was killed. The others, with the exception of John Nicholson, were marched off to gaol.

A week later, having ignored two summonses and a Magisterial Notification, George Meredith was arrested and taken to Waterloo Point, where, after being charged with leading the bushrangers to commit a felony, he was put in gaol for a short time before being released on bail.[19]

The trial of the men was set to be heard in Hobart Town in May, 1833. Having persuaded Mr Rowlands to defend them out of the goodness of his heart, George Meredith told the lawyer that he wanted him to bring a charge on his behalf against both Major Lord and Captain Hepburn for wrongful imprisonment, saying that in the meantime he intended to get possession of the evidence prepared against him at Waterloo Point. When Mr Rowlands enquired how he intended doing that, *'he tucked his stick under his left arm, at the same time extending it at full length, and tapping the palm of his left hand with the fingers of his right, he said, 'Yes, Sir, my key, Sir, my key is a silver key, and a most efficacious key it is; I have information of everything that transpires in the police station at Swan Port while it is still warm.'* Then, when the lawyer expressed doubts as to the possibility of his being awarded any damages for wrongful imprisonment George Meredith *'bent his fingers like the talons of a hawk and said, 'Oh, but that would not do for me. I would have damages.'*[20] Within a few days he had returned home and by devious means passed silver to the value of five pounds to a convict clerk at the police station, William Hogarth, a previous servant of his who had obtained the position because he could write. In return he received the depositions requested, but the offence was exposed. Hogarth was subsequently sent to Port Arthur and George Meredith was ordered to present himself before Governor Arthur.

He was not abashed; rather, he was coolly insolent. When asked for an explanation as to why neither he nor his son had captured the convicts he replied: *'It would have been very easy to have apprehended them, but neither of us could be expected to render such assistance to the Government.'* Not the man to accept either defiance or impertinence, the governor informed him that in future no more convicts would be assigned to him, although he would permit him to keep those he had, even though this was contrary to the advice of the Executive Council.[21]

In the trial that followed the escapees were all sentenced to death. George Meredith was severely reprimanded,[22] which caused him to return home in a vindictive mood, ready to cross swords with anyone.

He had never relinquished his rancour at William Lyne for settling on land he desired, and had closely followed the development of Apsley. Now, in the autumn of 1833, he was fairly sure that the efforts to drain the northern head of Moulting Lagoon* would be successful, and, owning as he did some fifteen hundred acres (600 ha) adjoining Apsley, he was desirous of sharing in any reclaimed land. Requesting William Lyne to show him their common boundary, he arranged that this should be made clear by a deep ditch, both men sharing the expense of having it dug. After the completion of the work he sent one of his men, Stakely, to fill in this trench and to dig another one some distance further to the west, so encroaching on Apsley land. It happened that William Lyne caught him at it, and, his temper aroused, threatened to throw him in the lagoon if he found him there again. Later, Major Lord told George Meredith that had William Lyne reported the matter and taken out a warrant he, George Meredith, would have been severely punished.[23]

Meanwhile, relations between the Lyne and Amos families were deteriorating in every way. Young Adam Amos and John Lyne each still regarded the three hundred and twenty acres (128 ha) to the north of Apsley as his own, thus cancelling out occupancy by either. But at last John's patience came to an end and he informed Adam Amos, George Meredith and Major Lord that he intended taking possession of the stock hut on May 20th, 1833. Accordingly, on that day Thomas Lord, accompanied by his assistant magistrate, Robert Hepburn, rode there to take official note of whatever might occur.

Within a short space of time a scuffle took place when George Meredith attempted to force John Lyne (a man twice his size) out of the hut. Defeated, he called Adam Amos and a servant to help him. By this time the two magistrates were almost helpless with laughter - a fact that caused George Meredith to lose the last shreds of his temper.

---

* The draining of the lagoon never succeeded, the tidal flow being too strong. The huge pipes are still in position.

Furious, he ordered Adam Amos to arrest John Lyne, which he did, being so aroused himself that he refused to take orders from anyone but George Meredith. But upon the magistrates warning him that he would keep his prisoner at his own peril he regained control of himself enough to release John Lyne.[24]

Upon being released John Lyne returned home, where, on hearing what had taken place, his father became so upset that he wrote to Governor Arthur. As page followed page his beautiful copperplate writing increased in size and decreased in legibility, until it clearly portrayed the state of his emotions. He ended: *'Seeing that the District of Great Swan Port is every Day more and more distracted by the Powerful, overbearing and Tyrannical conduct of our continual oppressor, Mr Meredith, I fear that unless supported by Your Excellency, not only myself and Family, but also every weak Settler in this quarter will severely suffer by him.'* *

Out for vengeance, John Lyne laid a charge of assault against George Meredith, upon receipt of which Major Lord issued a warrant for his apprehension.[25] On receiving this document from the constable (an ex-convict at Belmont) George Meredith ordered him to first handcuff him, and then walk behind him with a loaded musket and take him to the police station. This he did, to the delight of all who saw them. Arriving at Waterloo Point, he was committed to the cells, where he remained a short time only, Thomas Lord realising too late that he should have served a summons for him to appear. After releasing him, the Police Magistrate told him that the charge of assault was dismissed, only to have an action brought against him later for false imprisonment, as a result of which he was forced to pay £200 damages.[26]

The incident at the stock hut had yet wider repercussions, for the official report sent in by Major Lord did not reflect well on Adam Amos. It could not have come at a worse time for him, as Lieutenant Aubin's recommendation that he should be dismissed was in process of being considered, and the Chief Police Magistrate, the half-blind[27], vindictive Matthew Forster (no admirer of the Scot), also advocated his dismissal. (*'When I get my harpoon into a man,'* he was heard to remark in later years, *'I don't take it out again'*[28]). So that when the local court at Waterloo Point met to decide what action to recommend

---

* Governor Arthur's inter-office note read that Mr Meredith seemed to possess a curious ability to create difficulties with his neighbours.

finally to headquarters, they were entirely out of sympathy with their Chief District Constable. Accordingly, Major Lord requested permission from His Excellency to remove him from office, on the grounds that he was totally disqualified by age (59), the distance he lived from Waterloo Point (seven miles), and, above all, his close association with Mr Meredith.[29] Governor Arthur agreed reluctantly. So on June 8th, 1833 Adam Amos received his letter of dismissal.

He was dumbfounded, outraged, hurt to the depths of his being. All his years of faithful service had been ignored, he thought - the distances he had travelled on foot, the dangers he had faced, the resulting interference with his pioneering work.[30] The disgrace was almost more than he could live with. Determined to clear his name, he wrote to the *True Colonist*. Making reference to the letter vilifying Lieutenant Aubin's administration, he stated that because he had overheard discussion in the house of a friend of the possibility of its being published, he had through honour been unable to pass on information, and because sly grog-running had been discussed with Mr Meredith in a private capacity the editor should never have published what he had told him. As for keeping the magistrate in the dark about the happenings in the district, that was nonsense, for he and Lieutenant Aubin had often discussed those problems in detail. He concluded: *'My offence, I suppose, is that I am not quite enough of a government man, according to Lieutenant Aubin's idea of duty; and if to act either as a spy or an informer amongst my neighbours is to be part of that duty, anyone else is welcome to the situation.'* Inserted in the paper immediately after this was a most laudatory letter testifying to his character and behaviour in both his private and official capacity. This was signed by all the settlers in the Great Swan Port district with the exception of the Lynes.

Although the publication of the letter and the support of his friends eased his hurt, he remained deeply wounded, and, resigning as poundkeeper, he retired from public life.

CHAPTER 12

Finality had yet to be reached as to the ownership of the three hundred and twenty acres of land contested by John Lyne and Adam Amos, Jnr. As both young men held proof that the grant belonged to them the Surveys Department was in a quandary, finding it one of the most difficult cases they had ever encountered.[1] In the end they wrote to John Lyne offering him twice as much land of his own choosing if he would relinquish his claim to the disputed area. Their offer was accepted by return post.

He chose for his square mile of territory an area adjoining the north-west boundary of Apsley, naming it Apslawn.* There, with a stretch of good land watered by Apslawn Creek, the thought of young Adam Amos being in possession of the other land caused him no distress at all.

Seeking diversion from the monotony of life in the country, he went to Hobart Town to attend the Regatta, having arranged to go there with Michael Steel.

After ten years in the colony Michael - known as 'Dollar' Steel because of his constant use of Spanish dollars for currency - was a wealthy man, owning property both in country and town. He and Jane, together with a financier, Richard Cooke, lived on the ground floor of one of his town houses while letting the top storey to a widow, Mrs Hawthorn, and her seventeen-year-old daughter. The girl was almost engaged to be married, but her mother, realising what matrimonial potential there was on the ground floor, ordered her to concentrate on their landlord instead. From then on they found so many excuses to linger before they mounted the stairs that Jane, who was not easygoing by nature, lost patience with them, and Richard Cooke, nearly blind though he was, remarked that he could well see what they were up to. Michael was the only one who enjoyed the encounters. A veteran at avoiding matrimony, he took delight in encouraging their efforts. To spur them on a little, when John Lyne arrived he suggested that little Miss Hawthorn should come to the Regatta too. The outing gave

---

* This is now known as Old Apslawn.

mother and daughter such obvious satisfaction that he tried his luck too far, foolishly writing a note to the girl saying how much he had enjoyed the day and expressing the hope that one day he might perhaps marry her. The ink was barely dry before the two clattered down the stairs and accepted his offer. Alarmed, their forty-year-old landlord protested that it was a joke - surely they could see it was a joke? They could not. Miss Hawthorn's heart was broken and he must pay for her suffering. On May 20th, 1833 he was tried for breach of promise. Under interrogation he stood firm: the whole thing had been *'a lark'*; he was not *'a marrying man'*; she *'had got one leg in but he meant to take care of the other'*. In the end he retained his freedom but was the poorer by £200, plus costs. Miss Hawthorn found the money useful in setting up house shortly afterwards when she married her previous suitor.[2]

Less than a year later Michael was visited by his brother William, who had come down from Thomsonville on the East Coast to collect the machinery he had imported for a flour mill. After supervising its loading onto his vessel *Jean* he set off, in company with a millwright, for home.[3] About a fortnight later Michael received the following letter:

'Georges River.
Dear Sir,
I am sorry to relate the melancholy account of the loss of your unfortunate Brother which was drowned with Capt. Murgrime and Mr Dunn, they were all drowned in going ashore (in the dinghy) with the Boat on the Bar. I was in the Boat myself going ashore with them a sea broke on the Boat and (it) filled when we was half way to shore. Me and two sailors swam back to the vessel, the three unfortunate people tried to get ashore but the tide swept them away. I swam out to them but they did not hear me. The vessel is on the Bar, and full of water with the stern part, but I expect to get her off; I expect we shall get the greater part of the cargo ashore, I have been up three days and nights trying to get the vessel off, but the crew are wearied of that so we cannot move. I managed to reach the Military Station, where I now relate the melancholy affair. If you please to write and let me know what I am to do.
I remain Your Humble Servant,
Will Green

I wanted to stop at Falmouth but Mr Steel stopped me. He particularly requested me to go on over the Bar or else I should not have gone. I should not have gone and all the Sailors know this, to which they have signed to that effect.

Joseph   X   Cook
John   X   Gard
William   X   Taskar   their mark[4]
Thos.   X   Earle

The death of William affected Michael and Jane deeply, for they were a devoted family. For many years they spent a great deal of time and money in administering the estate, now known as Thompson Villa,* in preparation for the time when William's nephew and heir, Michael - then only three years old - should come out from England to claim it. It was not until the forty-seven-year-old Jane was safely settled as Mrs Richard Cooke in 1838 and the property leased three years afterwards that Michael felt free to return to England for a holiday. He stayed there for four years, during which time, to everyone's surprise, he married. Returning with his bride, formerly Martha Moore, in 1854, he lived in Glenorchy for nine years and then returned to England with their two daughters. When he died in 1865 he was a very rich man.

Two men whose wealth lay in the spiritual rather than the material realm were the Quaker missionaries, George Washington Walker and James Backhouse. In April 1833 they walked from Hobart Town to the East Coast, and near Prossers Plains were met by Francis Cotton, who guided them to Kelvedon, calling in at each settler's dwelling on the way. Among these was the home of that son of Ireland, Paddy Harte. Of him James Backhouse wrote, *'We visited a free man living in a miserable hut near the Little Swan Port, who had been notorious for the use of profane language and for cursing his eyes; and had become nearly blind, but seemed far from having profited by this judgment.'* Once settled in at Kelvedon, they held the first Quaker meeting in Australia.[5] For a fortnight they made the homestead their base, visiting many settlers' homes and at each receiving a welcome. They were greeted with special warmth when, with Francis Cotton still leading them, they reached Apsley. There they held a religious meeting,[6] and their guide at this meeting found himself for the first

---

* The name was later changed to Williams Wood. It was when the present house was built later in the century that it was named Enstone Park.

time in his life in touch with God. From then on he was actively engaged in evangelical work, reading religious books and filling his bookshelves with tomes carrying such titles as *Satan's Snares* and *Don't go to the Gin Shop*. Whenever he went to Hobart Town he handed out edifying tracts - sometimes with disappointing results, as when he passed one to a sailor who promised to read it but shortly afterwards was seen lighting his pipe with it.[7] So genuine and persuasive was he in his new life that his friend George Story was also led to become a believer and joined the Society of Friends, openly adopting their ways of dress and speech.

George Meredith thought little of Quakers, considering them to be shrewd worldly men, and was often heard to say that a Jew slept with one eye shut but a Quaker slept with both eyes open. Deriding gentle little George Story for *'turning to religion',* behind his back he sneered about his Quaker's coat and broad brimmed hat and remarked that he *'thee'd and thou'd it like a thoroughbred broadbrim'.* Once when the doctor went into the drawingroom at Belmont with his hat on *'to prove himself a converted Quaker'* his host was so irritated that he told him he hoped that *'in changing his religion he had not forgotten the manners of a gentleman',* whereupon the doctor immediately removed his hat.[8]

At this time John Radford was also concerned with a religious matter - or, rather, with a religious ceremony, for he hoped to get married. Before Paddy Harte had left the colony in 1832 he had leased Muirlands to the Devonshire ex-convict, who had sold his land at Brook Lodge to Messrs J. McDowell and W. Lindsay,[9] being anxious to return to the area that was more familiar to him. There was also another reason. Through his years of servitude he had first known Mary Ann Buxton as a girl, and as a ticket-of-leave man had watched her grow into a young woman. Now, a free man, his interest in her had deepened and he began to seek her company. Her father, however, would have none of it and they were forbidden to meet. Since there was no possibility of consent to a marriage Mary Ann and he eloped and on March 13th, 1833 were married at St David's Church, Hobart Town.[10] Then, first building a small place between Ravensdale and Little Swanport River for their temporary accommodation, Radford started on the construction of a much larger building on the southern bank of the river. This he named the *Swan Inn,* and in 1840 paid for it to be licensed as a public house.*[11]

---

* *The Swan Inn* was situated about 150 yards (137 m) below the present bridge.

It was about this time that a neighbour to the south of them, Captain Leard, was waiting in Hobart Town for a chance to get some iron and blacksmiths' tools taken to Rostrevor.[12] Upon hearing that George Meredith had chartered a small coastal vessel to take supplies to his whaling bases he contacted the ship's captain and quietly passed him a sum of money in exchange for taking his goods on as deck cargo. As soon as they had been stowed aboard the *Amelia* set sail, but almost at once while crossing Storm Bay ran into foul weather and sprang a leak. Heading for shore, those on board found instead of shelter only a rocky outcrop and high cliffs, against which they seemed about to be driven by the galeforce winds. In desperation they decided to abandon ship, but while they were trying to launch a row boat the *Amelia* drifted broadside on to the weather and immediately overturned, drowning two of the crew. William Leard, floundering among the waves in the darkness, managed to cling to the keel of the small vessel. This, newly-coated with tar, stuck to his trousers, and there he remained, a willing prisoner.[13] Eighteen hours later the crew of one of Captain Kelly's whaling boats, pulling strongly towards what they thought was a whale, came instead upon the freezing and exhausted man. Cutting him loose from his trousers, they warmed him as best they could and rowed him to Wedge Bay, with the upturned *Amelia* in tow. It was George Meredith's stated opinion that it had been William Leard's unauthorised deck cargo which had caused his chartered vessel to capsize. It was not long before that gentleman left Rostrevor and settled in Victoria, where he kept the *Ship Inn* at Williamstown.[14]

Through the years George Meredith had constantly planned and prepared for the time when he would build his permanent home. Sandstone was the material he favoured, and as this abounded on the small island beyond the mouth of the Swan River, he had instructed his whalers at The Fisheries some years previously to use their spare time in quarrying and cutting uniform blocks and stacking them there in readiness for removal. Enraged at this high-handed action the owner of the island, Robert Hepburn, had ordered them off and had then inserted a notice in the press[15] warning all unauthorised persons to cease quarrying stone on Rabbit Island. He then informed George Meredith that he would prosecute him for felony if he had the blocks removed. Seething, there was nothing he could do but obey, but was quick to point out to everyone that it was extremely fortunate that he had had the foresight not to use those blocks, saying that air and weather had caused them to disintegrate into heaps of sand, and *'Hepburn's malignant cunning in securing the fruits of another man's labour proved in the end to be a favour to the man he sought to injure.'*[16]*

Nemesis was descending on one of George Meredith's hated enemies - Thomas Daunt Lord. Always less than scrupulous when it came to the appropriation of government stores, in spite of his earlier scare he had continued to take things from Maria Island and have them sent across the water to his home. But the Commissariat Officer was on the alert. As each item disappeared from store it was noted by him: each item was found at Okehampton by Constable Morgan in a raid in February 1834.[17]

Major Lord was arrested at his office at Waterloo Point and charged with larceny and embezzlement. He appeared in the Supreme Court in Hobart Town in May. The case against him had been prepared meticulously. Evidence was produced of misappropriation of government property extending back over five years,and a watertight case was made against him by procuring statements from prisoners who had actually conveyed the goods across the water to Okehampton. But Mr Justice Montagu and seven commissioned officers, with Attorney-General Stephen assisting, returned a verdict of not guilty. So great a public outcry arose that His Excellency queried the decision and referred the case to the Executive Council. The members gave it as their opinion that a further prosecution should have been brought against Major Lord, following which he must of necessity have been convicted. His acquittal, however, was upheld and his position as Police Magistrate at Great Swan Port unaffected, though his rather outrageous application to be relieved of the expenses of the case was rejected out of hand.[18]

By now the population of the district had increased to such an extent that three hundred and forty one people were living there - one hundred and eight free males, sixty five free females, and one hundred and fifty eight male and ten female convicts. As a result the administration of Great Swan Port involved so much work that in 1834 the district was divided into two. The district south of the Little Swanport River was renamed Spring Bay[19] and was placed under the

---

*The original part of Swanwick is built of sandstone and is still in good condition.

supervision of Captain Peter Maclaine, J.P.,*[20] and the northern part remained under the same name and administration as before.

During Major Lord's enforced absence James Radcliff had been appointed a Justice of the Peace, which office enabled him to act as the Major's deputy.[21] His duties made him very unpopular with the convicts, for he proved to be a severe magistrate. Efficient and conscientious to a degree, his time was fully taken up, for as well as supervising Lisdillon[22] and the nearby Salt Works (an enterprise he had started because of the scarcity of salt both in the colony and New South Wales), he was overseeing the erection of a watermill and working on a plan for supplying Launceston with water - a proposal that was never endorsed.[23] At this time, too, his younger brother, Richard, arrived from Ireland. Wishing to be within the same part of

Rheban (formerly Omoroe) in the 1890's, showing the Gill family in residence.
(Courtesy Mrs. Frances Travers)

* Captain Maclaine was promoted to Assistant Police Magistrate three years later.

the island as James, he bought land a few miles south of the entrance to the Prosser River. He named the lonely and beautiful place Omoroe* and, settling there, began the life of a pioneer.

Some of the pioneers who had arrived at the East Coast many years before him - those who had come out with their parents - were now of an age to set up establishments of their own. John Castle of Banwell, the eldest son of Joseph and Edith, in the winter of 1837 married Maria Antonet Luttrell, grand-daughter of Dr Edward Luttrell of Dunster Castle.#[24] After the wedding she went with her young husband to join his brothers at Banwell,** where they were all labouring to restore and improve the farm. Adam Amos's eldest son, James, had married his cousin, Ellen, while his sister, Helen, was now Mrs Henry von Stieglitz, the double wedding being conducted at Campbell Town by the Reverend Mr William Bedford. James took his bride to a quaint four-roomed cottage he had built directly behind the Glen Gala homestead+, within easy waving distance of her old home, Cranbrook House.

Someone who would dearly have loved to have been within waving distance of his parents was Henry Tingley, a convict lad from Sussex who was assigned to the Lynes. In a burst of homesickness he wrote to them in 1835: *'I have a place at a farm house, and I have got a good master, which I am a great deal more comfortable than I expected.... We have as much to eat as we like, as some masters are a good deal better than others. All a man has got to mind is to keep a still tongue in his head and do his master's duty, then he is looked upon as if he was at home; but if he don't he may as well be hanged at once, for they would take you to the magistrates and get a hundred of lashes, and then get sent to a place called Port Arthur to work in irons for two or three years, and then he is disliked by everyone.... This country is far beyond England in everything, both for work and for money. Of a night after I have done my work I have a chance to make a few shillings. I can go out hunting ... I have dogs and a gun of my own, thank God for it, to get a few shillings, anything that I want. Thank God I am away from all beer shops, there is ne'er a one within twenty miles of where I live. I have a fellow prisoner living with me, which he is a shoemaker, and he is learning me to make shoes; which will be a*

---

*A quarry on Omoroe later supplied stone used in the construction of the Melbourne Law Courts.
The present-day Castle family is descended from this line.
** Banwell remained in the possession of the family for many years.
+ The cottage is still there in original outline but is crumbling badly. It was occupied briefly by Robert Wardlaw and family in 1843 when Adam Amos encouraged them to emigrate from Scotland.

great help to me, in about two years I will be able to make a pair of shoes myself. Then, thank God, I am doing a great deal better than ever I was at home, only for the wanting you with me, that is all, my uncomfortableness is in being away from you.'[25]

Young Henry Tingley was not the only one desirous of having his own people with him. George Meredith, too, wrote home. The letter

Louisa Anne Meredith
(Allport Library & Museum of Fine Arts)

135

was to his niece, Louisa Anne Twamley, and in it he offered her a position as governess at Belmont. Since arriving in Van Diemen's Land, he wrote, he and her Aunt Mary had been blessed with six children, and it would be pleasant to have a member of the family give them their schooling. At the same time, he added, it was a great opportunity to experience what a new land could offer.

At the age of twenty three, George Meredith's niece was tall, dark, attractive and distinguished-looking, in spite of what her detractors might term a wall eye. Assured and ambitious, she was already becoming recognised as a portrait painter of merit as well as a poet and writer, and had just published *'An Autumn Ramble on the Wye'*. When she read her uncle's letter she could hardly credit that he had made the offer seriously. She had heard from his cousin, John Meredith, his impressions of life in Van Diemen's Land, with particular emphasis on the social entertainment available at Great Swan Port, and had no intention of leaving her delightful existence in Birmingham to teach children out in the wilds. She said as much in her answering letter. *'Where would my literature be in Van Diemen's Land?'*, she asked, *'Writing sonnets to whales and porpoises, canzonets to kangaroos, madrigals to prime merinos and dirges to black swans?'* As for the £100 per year he offered, she added, she could get that in England any time she liked and still be with her family and her friends, without sacrificing her interests. She ended by thanking him for the offer and firmly declining it.[26]

Back in the wilds, far from the comfort of her home and friends, Mary Meredith continued to give her children some schooling before they were to be sent away for their formal education. By now all her step-children had left Belmont. Nothing had been heard of young George since his departure two years before, and his sisters, thanks to their father's shepherding, were all settled satisfactorily, Sarah having married James Poynter, Louisa, Captain John Bell of Belle Vue, and Sabrina, John Boyes.

Earlier in 1834 Charles, deciding to strike out for himself, had also left. It so happened that at that particular time he was in his father's good books, having punched an ex-convict, Robert Lathrop Murray, after he had published uncomplimentary things about him in his *Tasmanian Austral-Asiatic Review.*[27] George Meredith, wishing him well, gave him £2,000[28] and with this he set off for Sydney, where he passed up the opportunity of buying any amount of land on the North Shore for five shillings an acre and instead bought stock to the value of £1,200 and ran them on Crown land on the Murrumbidgee.

At Red Banks, the wattle and daub cottage once owned by young George Meredith was in process of being enlarged prior to the marriage of its new part-owner, Edward Carr Shaw. In Ireland his grandmother, Mrs Carr, rested content in the knowledge that he was upholding the 'social tone' of the family, for he was marrying dark-haired, quiet-eyed Anne Fenton. Her great grandfather was Earl Spencer and several of her mother's brothers were peers of the realm, while the Countess of Shaftesbury was a close relative and the late Prime Minister, Spencer Perceval, was her mother's cousin.[29] The three years which Mrs Fenton and her three sons and three daughters had spent in the colony had not been easy ones, for on the voyage out James Fenton had died, leaving a great burden of responsibility on his widow. Upon her daughter Anne forming a friendship with young Edward Shaw, she was pleased to approve of him as a future son-in-law, and the two were married at St David's Church on December 22nd, 1835. Edward had walked to Hobart Town for the wedding but he hired a lugger to take Anne and her belongings to Great Swan Port.

The original Red Banks building in the 1920's

137

Once there, she settled in happily at Red Banks, determined to be a good wife. Her experience with assigned domestic girls had made her wise to their ways and she kept a close eye on personal and household goods, listing *'five calico shifts and five linen ditto, five new pairs of stockings and five old ditto, two linen bolster covers',* etc. in her day book. Watching over the contents of the cellar was an easier matter, for Edward drank only two bottles of port a month; prior to the birth of their son Bernard in October, however, they laid in a stock of three bottles of port, three of cape, one of porter, seven of sherry, five of brandy and two of whisky.[30]

Also listed were the cooks and the maids as they came and went - the Marys, the Susans, the Kittys, the Sarahs. Twenty-seven of them passed through their hands in seven years, and twenty-seven of them had to be outfitted with caps and neck handkerchiefs, with stockings and stays and dresses. Because of this the Shaws were much the poorer for introducing into the male-dominated district a flow of eligible females.

Such newly-found comfort of married life was welcomed by many a member of George Meredith's sealing and whaling crews when they returned home from their trips, for their work was extremely hard and hazardous. The truth of this was emphasised when a seal broke the leg of James Amos of Cranbrook, who had been pressed into service. Badly set, it resulted in a permanent limp, so that from then on he was universally known as 'Hopping Jimmy'.[31] On another occasion a crew member was jerked overboard and drowned when he became entangled in a line attached to a harpooned whale, and once during a violent storm the onlookers at Waterloo Point watched in helpless horror as the entire crew of a whaleboat was drowned while attempting to cross from The Fisheries for their week's rations.[32]

In the early spring of 1836 when the whales came to give birth to their young in the waters round Great Swan Port - or Glamorgan, as George Meredith was beginning to call it[33] - a total of sixty-nine was taken, making the owners of the thirteen boats involved richer by £7,706.[34] That the number of whales was decreasing, however, was obvious to George Meredith, and so, taking into consideration the four vessels he had lost over the years,[35] he took stock of the situation. Including Richard Radcliff, there were seven or eight newcomers to the industry, all with larger boats and better equipment than his, so, congratulating himself on having done remarkably well overall out of the venture, he decided to withdraw, estimating that he now had sufficient money with which to complete his house.

High above the Meredith river, almost opposite Red Banks, preparations for this house had started ten years before with the establishment of flower and vegetable gardens close to the now flourishing orchard, and every day Mary's tall form could be seen stooping over the beds, lovingly tending the plants.[36] Already the place had been given the name of Cambria and now all that was lacking was the house.

The terrain was difficult, for it was very steep. No less difficult was the problem of fitting a large building onto it, and in this George Meredith displayed a great deal of skill, drawing plans that accommodated the structure to the slope in such a fashion that the single-storey front graded to three floors at the back. Stacked near the site for years before building started had been piles of quarried stone gathered to replace the forbidden blocks on Rabbit Island. Also close at hand had been the right man to fit them together into the house that his master had designed. He was known as Old Bull.

Cambria. Drawing by Louisa Anne Meredith.
(My Home in Tasmania)

Old Bull was a blacksmith, a stonemason and a builder. First transported to New South Wales, he had been sent to Moreton Bay (Brisbane), and, rebelling against the barbarous discipline there, had joined a group of escapees determined to return to Sydney. As they were forcing their way through the almost impenetrable rainforest his companions were captured and murdered by aborigines. Old Bull - a small man who weighed less than nine stone (57 kg) - had remained hidden under a log within sight of the camp for three days. Incredibly, he did eventually arrive in Sydney,* where he was recaptured, flogged and returned to Moreton Bay. Again he escaped, again he found his way to Sydney and again he was flogged. Then, instead of being hanged, as he feared, he was sent to Van Diemen's Land, where he was assigned to George Meredith, in whose employ he remained for years, valued highly.[37] As his skills as a builder became known he was 'borrowed' by so many of the settlers that the greater number of houses in the district were built by him.# This experience with local conditions proved invaluable in building Cambria, which was the most ambitious building he had ever attempted.**

The verandah with its simple colonnade and balustrade of wood conveyed no idea of the architectural complexity of the building. Following the contours of the land, time and again the roof and the verandah merged into one to accommodate the size and placing of the twenty-six rooms contained in the house.[38] When it was finished in 1836 and the rooms furnished with carefully selected furniture it proved to be a charming and inviting dwelling into which the family was proud to move. Of a gossipy and gregarious nature,[39] George Meredith now made it his custom to invite the officers and local gentry to dine, the evenings usually ending with a dance.[40]

A good hater, he had actively worked in association with others of a like mind for the recall of Governor Arthur, so that when news reached him that he was to leave the island in October 1836 he was openly jubilant that he would be free of someone he termed *'one of the most tyrannical, vindictive and unscrupulous men who had every wielded power.'*[41]

During the final construction of Cambria it had become obvious to its owner that even more money was needed. He wrote to John Amos.

* Old Bull claimed to be the only escapee from Moreton Bay to find his way back to Sydney.
# After Old Bull helped Francis Cotton with the brickwork of extensions to Kelvedon he said he had never worked with a better carpenter.
** Cambria is still in use as a residence.

140

Referring to the agreement entered into on the *Emerald* he explained to him that because of financial stress it had become imperative that the terms stated in it should now be applied. Quoting from the document, he wrote: *'... every grant or grants of land which may be made ... to the said John Amos ... shall be conveyed to the said George Meredith as his property and possession ... and all papers and deeds ... of the same given to him...'*[42] He then claimed all the land as his under the terms of the agreement.

With the bitterness of what had been forced upon him during the past fifteen years welling up within him - of the uncertainty of his future, of having to work for George Meredith whenever required, of having to pass over two-thirds of all profits resulting from his and his family's industry, of the humiliation of having his son, James, clean shoes and wait on tables[43] at Creek Hut and Redbanks, John Amos rebelled.

In the ensuing battle the matter came under the scrutiny of the government, so that on October 12, 1836 - a fortnight or so before Governor Arthur left - the Solicitor-General wrote to the Colonial Secretary, sending a copy of the agreement. In it he noted that he had spoken to Mr John Amos, who admitted to having been betrayed into the most dishonest act he had ever committed in his life when he allowed Mr George Meredith to claim on his behalf that he owned capital to the value of four hundred pounds. The letter continued, *'... it is difficult to see how the corruption of this simple and industrious old man can enable his wily opponent to possess himself of the fruits of his laborious life, because he himself suggested the fraud of which he seeks to make Amos the victim.'*[44]

The case was referred to private arbitration where, although sympathy was wholly with John Amos, the fact that he had received land while holding no capital could not be denied. Therefore, because no flaws could be found in the agreement, a large award had to be made in George Meredith's favour, of which £2,160 had to be paid within two years.[45]

Although he was assured of his title to Cranbrook, John Amos, half dazed at his near ruin, was forced to mortgage the property. It was apparent to his sons that more sacrifices would have to be made and they gave what little money they had and mortgaged their own properties in order to help their father. Year followed year, decade followed decade, and still money had to be paid to the Merediths, so that it was not until the early years of the twentieth century that they were free of their debt.[46]

CHAPTER 13

In 1837, the year of Queen Victoria's coronation, Sir John Franklin and his fascinating wife had arrived in Van Diemen's Land in time to experience the hottest summer since the white men had settled there. So hot was it that at Great Swan Port the fruit baked on the trees.[1] To Dr. Story, riding the sixty miles of his district, it was a wearisome time. As well as the heat, other things depressed him - the amount of spirits supplied to the military station, the effect it had on the soldiers, the dilapidated state of the gaol. Of this he had written to the government, pointing out in vain that the building was in such a state of disrepair that *'should prisoners of opposite sexes be imprisoned at the same time it could not be supposed that conversation of the correct character would be carried on between them.'*

He was soon to inspect buildings more substantial than the gaol, for early in 1838 James Radcliff had requested a grant deed for land allocated to him three years before but not formally granted until evidence should be provided that certain specified improvements had been made to the property.[2] So in April he invited Francis Cotton, Edward Shaw, Francis Aubin, George Story and James Hobbs (the new owner of Ravensdale) to accompany him on a tour of inspection. They were very favourably impressed by what they found. Standing on slightly raised ground at the mouth of Two Mile Creek was the house,[*] with only a narrow paddock of grass separating it from the sea, so that the loveliness of the view was unobstructed. Valued at £400 the previous year, it was a medium-sized, sturdy building of eight rooms, with a symmetrical front of stone relieved with a trim of brick, with the solid door overtopped with a fanlight and flanked by sidelights.[3] At the back the stables and coach house harmonised with the house, the whole group of buildings forming an unexpectedly pleasing and friendly scene.

Taking them further south on his property, James Radcliff pointed out to the party the stone cottages and the long storage building which

---

[*] Lisdillon is still in use as a residence.

143

Lisdillon
(Achives Office of Tasmania, State Library)

Old Coach House, Lisdillon

144

comprised the Salt Works,# the produce of which was so necessary to the settlers for brine and pickling.[4]

Full of admiration for all they had seen, the men had no hesitation in certifying that James Radcliff had spent £4,500[5] -more money than any other settler on the coast - in improvements, and that the clearing,

Portrait of Richard Radcliff, showing slug holes
(Mitchell Library, Sydney)

Samuel Lapham managed the Salt Works until 1838, when he moved across the river to Wybellina (Seaford). His wife was the sister of Frances Maclaine.

the fencing and the substantial way in which his buildings had been erected could not be bettered in the district.

South of the Prosser River, Richard Radcliff was now a Justice of the Peace, and was proving to be just as unpopular with the convicts as was his brother James. After he had broken up some of their stills in the bush they swore revenge and several of them set off to Omoroe to settle with him. As they approached the house they saw him at one of the windows and as soon as they were within range they levelled their guns, fired, and then vanished into the bush. Later it was with mixed feelings that Richard Radcliff surveyed the slug holes in the oil painting of

Piermont, built in 1838
(Courtesy Mrs. Frances Tavers)

himself that the servants had propped up in a chair during spring cleaning.*

In 1839 business affairs took him to the newly-formed township of Melbourne, and the following year, in company with Charles Gatehouse, Silas's son, he set sail for home in the barque *Britomart*. Neither he nor the other ten passengers or crew were ever seen again, and subsequent discoveries on Preservation Island# led to the belief that sealers had lured the vessel ashore and killed all on board, for she was rumoured to be carrying bullion.[6] In his will, Richard Radcliff, having neither wife nor children, had left Omoroe to his brother.

To the north, Robert Webber of Piermont was, like James Radcliff, spending a considerable amount of money on his property. With the first rush of pioneering work behind him he had now turned his attention to building a permanent home - a project he and Mary had looked forward to but which he had to undertake without her involvement, for she had died in 1830, leaving Elizabeth and Jane to take over the management of the home and the care of the younger

Riversdale Mill, built by John Amos

---

* During recent restoration of the portrait of Richard Radcliff it was necessary for its preservation that the bullet holes should be covered in.
# Preservation Island is slightly south of Flinders Island.

children. With the help of his men and his two eldest sons, William (33) and Robert (31), he built a large stone house of simple design next to the existing one.* The double-storey house dominated its surroundings, and in 1838 when the family moved in they set about softening its severity by extending the existing garden, so that soon Piermont was said to have the largest of its kind in the island.[7]

Early in the same year Old Bull finished building a house on the Riversdale property.# A plain stone building, its two storeys reached higher than the flour mill built nearby by John Amos some years before. George Meredith found tenants for the house at once. As John Allen had let Milton to other tenants, young Thomas Watson and Dorothy, his wife, were only too pleased to move into Riversdale, even though they had to pay £1,500 a year for it and all the Meredith land surrounding it.[8] However, after staying at Riversdale for about two years[9] they moved to Belmont, which, besides being more suited to their means, also brought Dorothy closer to her friend, Mary Meredith.

Riversdale, with southern wall protected by weatherboards (1987)

---

* The present kitchen at Peirmont is on the site of the original building.
# Riversdale homestead is still in use as a residence.

The person to whom John Allen had leased Milton was the ex-convict George Raynor, who agreed to pay rent of £70 per annum for the rest of his life.[10] John Allen then leased Egg Farm to tenants for seven years and made application for the secondary grant of land that Governor Arthur had promised him after the aborigines had burnt his first homestead in 1828.

The location he chose for his two hundred and seventy acres (120 ha) was an area of good land on the Douglas River, some miles up from Waubs Harbour.[11] His application approved, it made him the owner of eleven hundred and fifty acres (460 ha) altogether.[12] Spurred on by his success, he had a small inn, the *Morning Star,* built at Spring Bay in 1839.[13]

His sister, Hannah, had been staying with him for some time and when she returned to England her other brother, Joseph, accompanied her, leaving his property near Campbell Town in the care of his nephew, Joseph Butler. Left without Hannah to look after him and hampered by domestic duties, John Allen overcame his fierce independence to the extent of asking his niece, Agnes Butler, to come to Allen-Grove and keep house for him. When she chose instead to stay with her brother he was deeply hurt, expressing his feelings to Hannah by writing: *'I do not intend to request Miss Butler's attendance again if Providence will permit me to pass through this World without any female attendance.'*[14]

In December 1838 while he was busy building a stone storehouse* at Allen-Grove he was approached by three strangers whom he suspected from their bearing to be bushrangers, and though they swore they were free men in search of work they nevertheless found themselves unable to undertake any task he offered them. Because he was short of ammunition and his men were not within call he was forced to let them go, but next day when his neighbour, James Hume of Templestowe, found them killing one of his sheep he wrote to the Police Magistrate at Waterloo Point, Lieutenant Bayly#, pointing out that the nearest constable was thirty-eight miles (61 km) away at the military station and requesting police protection. It was refused.

A few months later in April 1839 eight bushrangers descended on Swanwick and plundered it. Furnished with boats, two search parties were despatched, one under the command of Robert Webber, and the

---

* The storehouse, together with the homestead, was demolished earlier this century.
#Benjamin Bayly was a nephew of Lord Dunalley, after whom the township was named, and a cousin of Smith O'Brien.

other, the recently appointed Police Magistrate, Lieutenant Bagot; but although they searched for six days they were unable to trace the men.[15]

The days were gone when search parties automatically looked to the Amos families for their leaders. Age, rheumatism and wounded feelings had rendered Adam no longer available, while his crooked leg held back his nephew James - although this disability did not prevent him in 1838 from limping down the aisle with Mary Collins Jackson, the daughter of a well-to-do early settler in New South Wales. James

Cranbrook House
(Courtesy Mr. James Amos, Cranbrook)

took his bride to Cranbrook House, a fine stone residence built five years before, which they shared with the rest of his family. This arrangement did not particularly appeal to Mary, so when in 1842 an aunt died and her uncle sent her £500 with which to buy herself a mourning ring, she decided instead to put the money towards the building of a house.[16] On top of a sudden little hill near a high rock known as the Aborigines Lookout Stone, Craigie Knowe* was located nearly opposite Glen Gala homestead, and was a staunch and interesting little dwelling.

Hopping Jimmy was not the only Amos in 1838 whose thoughts were set on matrimony. His cousin Adam - no beauty, with his long face, his grim mouth and bleak, black, slitted eyes inherited from his mother - was causing consternation in his family by courting pretty blond Susan Lyne, the seventeen-year-old sister of his ex-rival for land, John Lyne. Realising at length that his son was serious in his intentions, Adam Amos Senior made plans to vacate Glen Gala,

Craigie Knowe, 1976

* Craigie Knowe is still used as a residence.

leaving it free for his son to take over. To the surprise of everyone in the district he retired to Hobart Town. There he bought a house in New Town formerly belonging to the ex-Colonial Architect and Civil Engineer, John Lee Archer.[17] On the last day of 1838 Adam Amos bought it subject to the mortgage, paying £420, the purchase price amounting to £640 altogether.[18]

Early in 1839 he and Mary, accompanied by their daughters Margaret and Jessie, moved into their new house. It was here soon afterwards that William Lyne and Susan and her prospective husband stayed prior to the wedding, having ridden over the bridle track via the Bogs to Campbell Town and then to Hobart. Dressed in a tailor-made riding habit of pale green cloth, Susan was married to young Adam Amos at St Andrew's Presbyterian Church,* a building designed by John Addison of Coswell who, with his brother and his partner, John Jackson, had built it some five years earlier.[19] After spending their honeymoon in the capital the couple rode back to their future home, Glen Gala.

The Amos Properties - Glen Gala and Gala on the right of the Swan, Cranbrook House and Craigie Knowe on the left. (Courtesy Mrs. Ruth Amos)

* Now Scots Uniting Church, Bathurst Street.

152

Gala Mill
(University of Tasmania Archives)

Mayfield Mill, built 1836.
(University of Tasmania Archives)

153

James, the eldest of Adam's sons, now decided that the time had come for him to build a permanent home and for the site he chose a position - still on his father's original grant - about a quarter of a mile to the south of the Glen Gala homestead. It was near the bank of the Swan and nearly opposite Cranbrook House. The building he erected on it contained eight rooms, with three more in the attic. In 1840 he and Ellen removed their belongings from the sturdy little cottage where they had lived for five years and settled into their permanent home.* Two years later, realising that with the growth of population in the district the flour mill at Glen Gala was too small, and the one Thomas Buxton had built at Mayfield in 1836 was too far away, James built a larger one downstream from his house.# This was constructed of red brick, as was the Miller's Cottage which was built at the same time.* * Because of the association James Amos's new home became known as The Mill, then Gala Mill, and finally Gala,[20] while James himself was referred to as James the Miller.

Early photograph of Gala
(Courtesy Mrs. Ruth Amos)

* The original Gala homestead forms part of the present 17-roomed house, which is still the residence of a member of the Amos family.
# A large portion of this mill was washed away in the 1929 flood but the rest is still standing and is used as a granary.
* * The Millers's Cottage and a workman's cottage built in 1843 are still in use.

Two months after Adam and Susan were married there was another Amos/Lyne wedding when Adam's sister, Mary, married the red-headed Henry. Fortunately for them a house was available, because in April 1839 George Raynor had unexpectedly died, leaving Milton without a tenant, so they moved in on a four-year lease.[21] However, in 1841 Henry learned that a square mile of good land adjoining the southern boundary of Apslawn was available and he bought it.[22] In the sheltered valley where so long ago the aborigines had murdered one of George Meredith's shepherds he built a long, pleasant brick house which he named Coombe End.* Half way through his four-year lease of Milton he moved into it[23] and three months later John Allen exchanged the property for five hundred and thirty acres (212 ha) near Allen-Grove that was owned by his brother, Joseph, this being subject to a cash adjustment.

Further up the coast at Falmouth[24] William Busby was the temporary manager of Thomsonville, or Thompson Villa, as it had been called ever since William Steel's death. Upon meeting John Allen one day in 1840 he told him that a man named Archibald McIntyre from the adjoining property, Glencoe,# together with a person named Steward, was branding the young unmarked stock on the place and selling them under another brand. With his own stock running wild and Falmouth within ranging distance of the Douglas, John Allen became alarmed. Happening to meet Jane Cooke in Hobart Town one day he passed the information on to her. Within a short time he received a letter from a Launceston solicitor warning him that unless he wrote to Mrs Cooke and told her he had been mistaken in what he had said Mr McIntyre would enter an action against him for defamation of character. Stunned, he wrote an immediate reply. *'By the hand of Mr Busby I have received your note of the 29th ulto. With the utmost Astonishment and Sorrow I have read it over and over again. It is a very hard case for me...'* And so it was. As an honest man, composing a letter to Jane Cooke proved almost impossible and resulted in a jumble of truth, propriety and outrage, his half-retractions being interspersed with such phrases as: *'It now seems to me that your Overseer Wm Busby is an Infamous Liar,'* and *'There appears to be some Mystery in the Proceedings at Falmouth. Your Overseer will, I believe, say or swear anything.'*

---

* Coombe means a valley or sheltered place.
# There were two properties named Glencoe.

The contents of the letter failed to satisfy Archibald McIntyre, and John Allen was brought before the local court, where he was treated more harshly than he anticipated or relished. So incensed was he that the following week when he passed the magistrate, W.T. Noyes, in the street he cut him. Included in the treatment was Edward Shaw, who was with him. A few days later conscience broke through his brooding and he wrote to Edward Shaw apologising for not having bowed to him and pointing out that it was because he was ill-disposed towards his companion.[25]

Vitally interested in such items of news but far removed from the district, in Hobart Town Adam Amos employed much of his spare time in acting as agent for his sons - discerning the market trends and advising them what crops to plant, meeting boats that carried their produce and selling it for them, buying seeds or implements they needed and taking them to the wharf. There he enjoyed talking to any Great Swan Port settler he happened to meet. But there was one man he avoided - George Meredith. The ties that had existed between them for a quarter of a century had snapped when he had almost caused the ruin of Adam's brother. Occasionally in his letters to Glen Gala he mentioned him. *'Meredith, I see, is still at the catch,'* ... *'I fear Meredith - keep you all clear of him.'*[26]

Grief had come to Cambria in 1837 in the form of the death of Henry, the son who had been the result of the dalliance between George Meredith and Mary Evans in Wales twenty years before. He had never been brought before the public gaze as had his half-brothers and sisters and was never fully accepted by them, for they were contemptuous of his illegitimacy and would not admit even to themselves that he was a blood relation;[27] his full brothers and sisters, however, adored him and felt his death deeply. Handsome and tall, capable and athletic, it was he who had managed the lands on the Apsley. It had been while riding between there and Cambria that he had been thrown from his horse and seriously injured. For weeks after the accident he lingered between life and death, but the damage to his brain was too severe to permit his recovery. Because there was no Anglican church and graveyard at Waterloo Point his body was taken to Campbell Town - carried the forty miles on men's shoulders - and buried in the Anglican burial ground under the name of Henry Meredith, the name by which he had been known ever since his arrival in Van Diemen's Land.[28]

It was some time after this that a letter arrived from Charles, who had gone to England in an unsuccessful effort to persuade the government there to allot him the grant of land promised so long ago. The news contained in the letter lifted their spirits, for he had become engaged to his cousin, Louisa Anne Twamley. His next letter informed them that they had been married in Birmingham in April 1839, and were about to sail for New South Wales[29] It was while the couple were in Sydney that their first son, George Campbell Meredith, was born. Their joy, however, was dimmed when not long afterwards they received news that their holdings on the Murrumbidgee had failed. Faced with financial disaster, Charles disposed of his assets and turned his thoughts to home. Louisa, experiencing the difficulties of managing a house under colonial conditions and upset by the news of her mother's death, was quick to agree to his returning there,[30] so in October 1940 they set sail in the *Sir George Arthur.*

Like so many others, Louisa took an instant liking to Van Diemen's Land, the sight of hawthorn trees in bloom almost making her feel she was *'on the right side of the earth again',*[31] Louisa Bell, Charles's sister, welcomed them to Belle Vue, from where they were caught up in the social life of Hobart Town, attending concerts at the Theatre Royal and watching the laying of the foundation stone of the new Government House on the Domain, little realising that it would be almost eighteen more years before it would be finished.

As they were anxious to arrive at Great Swan Port they set off within a fortnight, John Meredith, Charles's half brother, having ridden up so as to assist them over the atrocious roads. To Louisa, the hazards of the trip were almost unbelievable as, parasol askew, kid gloves stained, she clung to the seat of their conveyance, terrified lest she and the nurse and baby George would be tipped out. And so, walking sometimes, clinging sometimes, nervous always, she was in a state of fatigue by the end of the third day when they reached the *Swan Inn* at Little Swanport. In a small room that doubled as both dining room and sleeping quarters, Mary Ann Radford, somewhat in awe of the gentry, served them an enormous meal, after which they bedded down for the night, John sleeping in the loft and the maid in the kitchen.

'The cottage,' Louisa wrote later, *'was built in a somewhat singular fashion, a portion of it being continued over a sudden slope in the bank, at the same level as the other parts, and merely supported on its elbows to look into the river below. It was also old enough to have*

157

Radford's Inn at Little Swanport River
(Museum, Morris's Store, Swansea)

acquired a nice mellow colour, with patches of moss and creeping plants about on it. A garden, not very neat, lay between the cottage and the river' [33]

Next morning they continued their journey, coming at last to Waterloo Point, where Louisa saw with interest the whitewashed military buildings on the Point, the three inns that were little more than houses, the two stores and the scattering of cottages. In their turn the residents looked with curiosity at Master Charles's wife, with no knowledge that they were witnessing the coming to the district of a writer and painter whose fame was to go far beyond their region. Soon they reached Cambria, and Louisa, tired beyond telling, tumbled into the arms of her favourite uncle, whom she had not seen since she was a small child.

For half a year they stayed at Cambria, George Meredith and Louisa delighting in each other's company, but by the end of that time she and Charles were anxious to set up their own establishment. Spring Vale, well watered and fertile, appealed to them, so, not without misgivings

158

on his father's part, Charles bought it from him. As there was no building on the place but the tumbledown old stock hut, for fifteen months they lived at Riversdale. There Louisa started her first Australian book, *Notes and Sketches of New South Wales,* while Charles set about taming the wilderness that was Spring Vale and supervising Old Bull when he started building their house.

Facing the junction of the Swan and Cygnet rivers across a paddock to the south-east, the building was no Cambria in size.* As modest as its owner's purse, it was made of ironstone, quarried on the spot, and Oyster Bay pines and other timber grown on the property. The thick walls enclosed a few large rooms and the low-hung verandah looked out onto a newly-planted orchard and garden, filled with an ever-increasing number of plants. '*Dear Mamma*,' wrote Louisa to her step-mother-in-law, '*Could you please let me have some strawberry runners, and anything else from a snow-drop to an oaktree.*'[34] But within a few months of their moving into Spring Vale, Mary was in no condition to send Louisa plants from her beautiful garden, for she was very ill - so ill that all the members of the family were sent for, and in

SPRING VALE COTTAGE.

Spring Vale. Drawing by Louisa Anne Meredith (My Home in Tasmania)

* Spring Vale homestead was partly burnt in 1862, but the present house incorporates the old.

spite of all Dr Story could do she died in November 1842. The funeral was conducted by the Reverend Mr Joseph Mayson,* who had been resident minister for the past three years, and she was buried in the newly-formed Anglican cemetery on Waterloo Point. George Meredith was greatly affected by his loss, and from that time onwards seemed to lose interest in the larger world that had meant so much to him.

Well to the south, death had also claimed Peter Maclaine. Towards the end of the 1830's he had become ill, and went with his family to Hobart Town. There after a long illness he died in July 1840. In an obituary notice the *Hobart Town Courier* reported that *'he possessed in an eminent degree the respect and esteem of his companions in arms ... During his residence in this colony his life has been passed in unobtrusive exercise of every social and domestic virtue, and if in his intercourse with the world he may have offended any, yet of him we believe it may be truly said that few men have lived more generally respected, or have died more universally lamented.'* His widow, Frances, did not return to her Spring Bay home again. Less than a month after her husband's death, Woodstock was advertised for lease and early in 1842, eighteen months after Peter Maclaine's death, she also died, leaving their three children orphaned. Woodstock remained in the hands of Hugh and John Maclaine until John sold it in 1882 to Samuel Salmon.#[36]

The winter of 1842 was a time of heavy and continuous rain. The ground became sodden and the rivers swollen. At Glen Gala the ford over the Swan was impassable and communication with those at Cranbrook cut off. Whenever a shouted conversation was attempted from the opposite bank the honking of the geese and the rushing of the waters blocked out all words, and it was not until later that they learned the actual extent of the flood.

At Spring Vale, Charles and Louisa Meredith woke one day to look out on a vast sheet of water from the overflow of the two rivers. Charles, clad in an overcoat made by Louisa from calico and waterproofed with boiled linseed oil,[37] set off to find out what damage had been done. Returning drenched, he reported that the orchard and the wheatfield had been washed away and most of the sheep swept into the river. The margin of the flood, he said, extended from sixty to a hundred

---

* Mr Mayson remained at Swansea for 38 years, very highly esteemed by everyone.

#.Woodstock has remained in the Salmon family ever since.

yards (54 to 91 m) beyond each bank and the bridges were broken. They immediately printed warning notices and placed them at the approaches, but in spite of this a lad from Watersmeeting tried to cross the Cygnet, and had his horse swept from under him. Frantic, he caught hold of the branch of an overhanging tree and pulled himself up, and there he stayed for two days, the waters thundering away beneath him. To keep his spirits up some of the neighbours stayed as close as possible all night, lighting fires for his comfort and theirs, and calling out encouragement to him. Finally, late on the second day he was able to catch hold of a line Charles Meredith shot to him from a gun, and this he tied round his waist; even so, he could not bring himself to drop in the turmoil below and it was not until the branch he was on broke and he tumbled in by accident that he was able to be rescued. After recovering in a nearby shepherd's hut he returned to Watersmeeting, though without the bottle of gin for which his mother had sent him.

His mother was servant to Eliza Reid, for Alexander Reid was now a married man, having wed Eliza Boothman[38] in Hobart Town three years before. He was then aged forty-six.

Another marriage had taken place in the spring of 1841 when Will Lyne, the popular second son of William and Sarah, married Caroline Amos of Cranbrook House, and took her to live at Aspley.* It was left to John Lyne, that bombastic young man, to break clear of the family habit of marrying members of the Amos family.[39] He owned an acre of land between Waubs Harbour and the Douglas, and on his trips there often called in at Templestowe,# the property below Allen-Grove which Dr Millington leased to James Hume in 1838.[40]

James was of proud Scottish descent, and had established some kind of record in the colony for the number of times he had become insolvent. Since arriving in the island in January 1822 with his brothers-in-law, Hugh and David Murray, he had failed at merchandising, brewing, tanning, auctioneering and farming. His outstanding success, however, was his young daughter, Lillias. Fine-featured and erect, with beauty and dignity inherited from her literary mother, she would have been a social success anywhere, and John Lyne could hardly wait for her to become of marriageable age. When he bought six hundred and forty acres (256 ha) of land two miles south

---

* Caroline Lyne was drowned while at a picnic at Bicheno in 1870, after which Will married her sister, Martha.
# Templestowe homestead has disappeared.

of Waubs Harbour in 1841 he made a play on her name by calling it Lil-la Villa. About the same time he started to build a fine sandstone house at Apslawn.* In 1843 he married the seventeen-year-old girl and took her to live in the home he had prepared for her.#

Apslawn from a photograph taken about 1900

* Part of Old Apslawn still stands in a semi-ruined state.
# John Lyne later became M.H.A. for Glamorgan, and his eldest son, William, married Pattie Shaw and later became Premier of N.S.W. He was knighted and was a member of the first Commonwealth Federal ministry.

CHAPTER 14

In 1841 a probation station to accommodate several hundred convicts was established at Rocky Hills, slightly to the north of Mayfield.* Under the supervision of William Lavender, the first superintendent, discipline was very lax, nor did it improve from 1844 to 1848 - a year before its closure - when Major de Gillern took charge. A strange old German, he had come from Prussia in 1823 and was fond of recounting various military experiences, particularly the battle of Jena, *'de first battle in which I did smell powder.'*[1] Under his kindly reign the escape bell at Rocky Hills rang far too often[2] and there were many complaints about bushrangers from the disturbed settlers. They visited Glen Gala one Sunday in December 1842 just as divine service was about to commence in the granary. News was passed to the congregation that six runaways were hiding in a barn close by and men immediately left the service and stealthily advanced on the building. But they were seen, and, fleet of foot, the bushrangers were away. After searching all day the settlers were elated to discover them hiding in some scrub. They went towards them, calling on them to surrender, which they did, but only after one showed such resistance that John Amos of Cranbrook had to frighten him with a charge of shot.[3] Then followed a series of raids by other bushrangers. Bellbrook, The Springs, Watersmeeting[4]- all were robbed by the starving men and always they escaped. But when the hut of young John Ferguson, between Cranbrook and The Grange, was attacked, Alexander Reid led a party against them and captured four. They spent the night under guard at Glen Gala[5] and were then taken to the gaol at Waterloo Point in a farm cart.

Edward Shaw had been held up by them. He had been riding back from Campbell Town when he was confronted by three men (all mounted on better horses than his, he noted), who levelled pistols and guns at him. Not being a man to panic easily, he had reined in his horse and calmly waited.# For a while, bond and free, they had talked, but

---

* Many of the probation station buildings are still to be seen.
# His nephew, George Bernard Shaw, said of him: 'There is that about him which made you pause before speaking and that would daunt any confidence trickster in the world. He reminded me rather of one of those American sheriffs in the bad old days, stern and God-fearing, hating injustice but swift to inflict the fullest punishment for crime.'

Major de Gillern

when they discovered his name they had let him go, saying that his reputation for treating his convicts justly was well known to them.[6]

Edward Shaw was a friend of Major de Gillern, with whom he often played picquet, sometimes at Red Banks and sometimes at Tirzah*, the Superintendent's home at Rocky Hills. The road, usually made by rolling aside the largest rocks and leaving anything less than a large cannon ball in size,[7] had shown but little improvement under the ministrations of the road gangs and was particularly bad where it traversed a steep gully some five miles south of Waterloo Point - a spot that both riders and vehicles always took cautiously. Tiring of hearing promises to have it improved, the Irishman decided to bring matters to a head, so one night while driving the Major home in his gig he took the gully at full gallop. The resulting discomfort to his portly passenger was so great that the Major lost no time in setting his men to work building a bridge to span the sharp dip. Made of drystone, the parapet of the bridge was so curiously ornamented with jagged bits of rock that it became known as Spiky Bridge.[8]

At the Douglas, John Allen continued to fill all his working hours with toil. At night or on wet days he attended to his correspondence. His communications were varied. He wrote to the Police Magistrate at Waterloo Point requesting that convict musters be held closer to the Douglas, as so much time was lost in travelling that once in his absence and that of his men, the cows had not been milked for three days; he wrote to his financier, Richard Cooke, begging that his bill, now due, be extended at the same twenty per cent per annum, as he had not the ready cash in his pocket at present; he sent a letter to his tenants at Egg Farm notifying them that as they had been before the court for harbouring bushrangers they must leave the farm, first paying the eighteen months' rent they owed him. Early in 1842 he wrote to England, to the parents of one of his assigned servants, saying that their son's spirit failed in the attempt to write to them but he had asked him to say he was sorry for having 'hurted' their feelings; and in April 1842 he wrote to his mother, beginning with a flourish of religious platitudes and ending by telling her that he sometimes had as many as twenty-seven men working at the one time at Allen-Grove.

Each time he wrote he made a copy of the letter in his daybook. Sometimes the spelling was amiss, sometimes the sentences were un-

---

* The original Tirzah, near Mayfield Beach, was destroyed by fire.

165

grammatical, always the writing was scrawled. But once, in June 1842, between a letter to Mr Amos the Miller and one to 'Captn. Heypburn of Swan Wyke' he wrote in perfect copperplate, *'To My Mistress'*. Of that letter there was no copy.

Not for long was this development in his personal life undiscovered. Soon the people of Great Swan Port were intrigued to learn that John Allen had stopped work long enough to go courting. During the sixteen years he had spent in the district he had shown no interest in girls and they were full of curiosity to find out who had taken his fancy. Gradually word came through that the girl was from Browns River, that she was seventeen years younger than he, that her name was Ann Eliza Baynton and that her father was a prosperous man who had a butcher's business in Hobart Town and that he had also been acting as John Allen's agent for some years. When the engagement was announced it was generally agreed that it was a good match for each of them and everyone wished them well. The marriage took place in August 1842 and soon afterwards John Allen brought his forceful and independent young bride to the Douglas and led her into the sandstone house he had worked so hard to build.[9] It was not long before he gave her the farm.

Allen Grove, from a painting by an unknown artist (Courtesy Mrs. C. Gray, Bicheno)

Providence having not permitted him to pass through the world without any female attendance, he was no longer in need of the domestic assistance denied him a few years earlier by his niece, Agnes Butler,[10] who now lived about ten miles south of Allen Grove, acting as housekeeper and companion to Joseph '(Old-Bang-o'Day)', who had purchased a six-hundred-and-forty acre (256 ha) area of land on the coast below Waubs Harbour. On this he built a modest stone house, which he named Courland.*

They were not the only Butlers to live on the East Coast, for in October 1843, Anna Maria Butler of Victoria became Mrs James Radcliff. The daughter of Mr J.L. Butler, late of Rheban Castle, Ireland, she was a resolute woman with a firm jaw who was not one to enter into matrimony lightly; neither, indeed, was the forty-two-year-old James. A marriage settlement was arranged between their solicitors. After the wedding they remained in Victoria for some months, returning in 1844 - not, however, to Lisdillon, which had been leased, but to Omoroe, the name of which was changed to Rheban.[11]

Their satisfaction with life at this time was in stark contrast to the feelings of Adam and Mary Amos. It was in May 1842 when John Addison of Coswell had delivered a letter from young Adam to his father at New Town complaining that the twenty-year-old Robert was behaving as no Amos should. This roused his father to write: *'We are Very Much Vexed about Robert, I fear he will do no Good untill he geat a Checke of the bridle and come to his Sences.'* But this was forgotten when almost a year later another letter from Glen Gala gave him sad news of his youngest son. It told how Robert had been driving a mob of cattle to Traycoon# and when approaching Coombe End had been thrown from his horse. He was found lying unconscious on the road and was taken to Sherbourne Lodge, where, without regaining consciousness, he died the next day. His body had been taken to Glen Gala and two days later buried in the Amos cemetery.[12]

His parents were devastated. A few hours after receiving the news, Adam, seated at his desk, wrote: *'I this day Received the letter containing the Mellancholy Newes of the death of Robert, My Youngest Son, Your Brother - I need not Say how we felt the Shock. It is possible that it may bring down My Gray Hairs with Sorrow to the Grave, as well as your Disconsolate Mothers. May the Stroke be rightly Improved by us*

---

* Courland homestead is now only a heap of stones.

Traycoon was an Amos property beyond Bicheno. It was previously named Traquhoun, and later, Ferndale.

Dr. George F. Story (Courtesy Tas Museum & Art Gallery)

all to Seek a Saving Interest in the Lord our Redeemer, so that Living or Dying we may be within the Bounds of the New Covenant.'[13]

The accident had occurred during one of those periods when Dr Story was still practising his profession, for it was in the early forties that he had temporarily turned to the land for a living. It came about through his dissatisfaction with his income. He had written to headquarters requesting a rise in pay, pointing out that the local magistrate's clerk and the district constable were each paid more highly than he. *'On entering the duties of my situation in April 1829,'* he wrote, *'the District of Great Swan Port was scarcely known and did not even possess footpaths through it and was frequently infested with a very ferocious tribe of Aborigines known by the name of May tribe, in whose excursions through the District some either Soldiers or Convicts were sure to be attacked or injured, and these persons I was called upon to attend at the hazard of my life, having to travel alone.'* He continued by stating that after twelve years' service he considered he was entitled to more than the three shillings a day plus allowances that he was paid. He requested five shillings. It was the refusal to pay this that caused him to resign.

Moving to The Grange, which Henry Cotton was managing for his father,[14]* he threw himself wholeheartedly into farming. After purchasing eighty 'wedders' from James Amos of Gala Mill for twelve shillings each[15] he put them out to graze and then set to work to learn the art of ploughing. Here his strength could not keep pace with his will. It was a sorrow to him and a fond joy to the onlookers to view a furrow after he had ploughed it.[16] It wavered, weaved and collapsed, until he was forced to admit that he could wield a scalpel better than a ploughshare. Other less than successful experiences reinforced his suspicion that he would never make a farmer, and six months after he had resigned he was re-appointed District Assistant Surgeon.[17] But he was still dissatisfied and restless, and in May 1844 he resigned again. Being passionately interested in botany,[18] for the past ten years he had been importing plants and seeds from Kew Gardens and had been growing them at Kelvedon,# keeping abreast all the time with the latest botanical developments abroad, so that when a secretary was required to supervise the Botanical Gardens he applied for the position. He was appointed at a salary of £200 per annum, and moved into a cottage in

---

• Francis Cotton had bought the original grant of James King from the executors of J.T. Gellibrand's estate.
Some of these specimens still grow at Kelvedon.

the Gardens.*[19] For eighteen months he stayed there; then the government let it be known that it would in all probability not be able to renew its grant, and he returned to his medical work at Great Swan Port.[20]

In March 1843, during his previous period in practice, he had been called in to attend Robert Webber. So ill did he find him that it was decided that Dr Frederick Teuch, the medical officer at Rocky Hills, should also examine him. Agreeing in their diagnosis, together the two medicos advised their patient that his condition was critical and

John Perkins King and his wife, nee Elizabeth Webber (Courtesy Mrs. Frances Travers)

* Now the Museum, built in 1829.

170

that he should make his will. This he did. To his son William, who had angered him some years before by leaving Piermont, he left five shillings; to John - who, though he had also deserted him, was still in the district - he left £100; his property he left to Walter and the girls, but Jane, the dark-eyed beauty, was excluded from this inheritance and bequeathed only £5 a year, for in 1840 she had gone to Hobart Town and married a carpenter and wheelwright, Thomas Travers, who had helped build Piermont two years before.[21] .

A week after making his will Robert Webber died *'of dyssentry'* and was buried next to his wife. It was left to eighteen-year-old Walter, with some assistance from his brother, John,[22] to manage the property. But within six months as he was bringing up a load of kelp from the beach the dray hit a stump and overturned, the wheels running over his head.

Some time before her father's death Elizabeth had met a sailor, John Perkins King, who had called in at Piermont while his ship, *Susan* (of which he was master), was in the area. Since the cutter was a trader on

First School at Swansea on the Point. It was used as a church in 1845.
(From photograph at School Library. Swansea)

171

the East Coast run there was opportunity for their friendship to develop, and seven months after Walter's death, she married her master mariner at the little schoolhouse which had been erected on the Point to serve the military establishment. Forsaking the sail for the plough, John King then commenced farming at Piermont, where his help was sorely needed.*

In the isolated area of the East Coast of Van Diemen's Land it was difficult for settlers to give their children more than an elementary education. By 1836 there were thirty-three publicly supported schools in the colony[23] but these were established in centres with a large enough population to support them. The rural community of Great Swan Port was too scattered to warrant one so the children had the choice of being taught by their parents, attending a boarding school, or being educated by a tutor. At Kelvedon the Cottons decided in 1839 to employ a tutor to instruct those of their fourteen children who were still at home. The man they chose was Robert Mather, a brother of their agent in Hobart Town. An extremely satisfactory arrangement, it lasted only until he fell in love with a friend of one of the Cotton girls, and was terminated by his marriage.

Then followed a succession of teachers, the first two of whom drank to excess; the third, a French convict, proved to be excellent for three years, but was dismissed when Anna Maria's sharp eyes observed that Mary Cotton was becoming too interested in him.[24] After that the children attended school mostly in Hobart, travelling in George Meredith's top-sail vessel, the *Independent*, or the *Susan*, or the *Breeze*.

Because visits to Hobart Town were infrequent, goods were mainly ordered from Kelvedon by mail, the task of writing to Joseph Mather# often falling to the boys. The joyous sense of humour they had inherited from their father showed in these letters. Bonnets were returned, not suiting 'the sensible Kelvedon faces'; young Robert's trousers were sent back, being so tight that he complained that he could not close his eyes when he had them on; bed sheets must be strong, only a little inferior to iron. Often, too, their father wrote. Once he asked for a high hat, white, for the doctor's use, as his had blown off into the sea near Swansea causing him to borrow a cap from Mr King of Piermont. He

---

* In 1855 Coswell, 'the late Addisons' estate', was advertised for sale and John King bought it. Later he retired there. He died in 1882.

ordered a suit for himself. *'When making my clothes,'* he wrote, *'remember I am very stout and weigh nearly 15 stone. The clothes I am wearing will hardly last me into town.'*[25] He was not above becoming testy in his letters, as when he commented on the quality of flannel Joseph Mather had sent. *'It is quite rotten,'* he wrote, *'thou should'st use it for padding coats. I put on a new pair of drawers, and in a week they were worn to shreds.'*[26]

Often Anna Maria herself wrote the orders. Never robust, her temper plagued by inefficient maids, she informed the agent, *'I tell thee then, I intend to put all the girls and boys from George to little Teddy into tartan, with the intention of sparing washing this coming winter, so wilt thou oblige me by procuring the needful thing.'*[27] When goods were inferior she said so, as in the case of musty and rotten tobacco for the workers. *'Though smokers might manage it, the chewers certainly would not,'* she wrote tartly, *'so it will have to be used for sheepwash.'* Equally put out on finding maggots in the fat she had ordered for the making of candles, she complained that they had been forced to use it, and were still suffering under it, the smell being unendurable.[28]

Careful in all her details, she was particularly specific when ordering clothes for George Story, pointing out that his shoes were size four and that his stockings must be women's size and of lambswool, for he was very fidgety about his feet.

The attention of the inhabitants of the East Coast was directed to matters of higher concern than their domestic interests when in August 1843, amidst a web of malicious intrigue, Sir John Franklin was recalled.* Sir John Eardley Eardley-Wilmot was appointed in his place, and four months after arriving in the colony travelled through Great Swan Port. Calling in at Spring Vale, he was immediately attracted to the Merediths. From Charles he learned that in establishing his property he had overspent and was close to bankruptcy,[29] so, impressed by his manner and address, he offered him the position of Assistant Police Magistrate at Port Sorell. This offer Charles accepted at once, relieved at the prospect of receiving £300 per year.

For long after the governor had left he and Louisa excitedly discussed their change of fortune, and had hardly fallen asleep that night before they were awakened by a neighbouring farmer who told them that his cottage had been ransacked by bushrangers and his servants

---

* Sir John Franklin met his death a few years later in the Arctic regions.

173

held up. Inured through the years to the warnings about escapees, Charles checked the locks and returned to bed, but the next day he rode over to his father's lands to the north-east to see that the bushrangers were not there and on the way back called in at Apsley to warn the Lynes. Upon knocking at the door he saw a window open and Will Lyne, gun in hand, cautiously look out. Amid hearty apologies he was ushered inside, to be reminded that it was the Sabbath by the sight of William and Sarah, with their sons, daughters and grandchildren seated around them, bibles and prayerbooks in hand and guns and an old yeomanry sword on the table before them.* That they had already been warned was obvious, so he was not surprised when he heard that they had seen a notorious bushranger on the property early that morning but that he had eluded them.[30] That was the last reported sighting of the runaways.

Charles Meredith went to Port Sorell in April after his second son was born, and returned again in the spring when the country had dried enough for the family to travel. In a special carriage made partly by their carpenter and partly by John Amos, and with a servant clad in a velveteen suit and a high glossy black hat, they set off past The Springs and over the Tiers to start a new phase of their lives at Port Sorell.[31]

In the month of their departure a Presbyterian minister, the Reverend Mr Thomas Dove, M.A., was appointed to the parish. So heartened was Adam Amos by this that he immediately offered an area of five acres of land across the paddocks from Glen Gala as a site for a church and burial ground, an offer which was accepted.[32] Plans for the building were drawn up in the capital by the Reverend Mr Lillie and a building committee was formed. On this the Amos family was represented by James the Miller of Gala, who was the secretary, his uncle, John Amos of Cranbrook, who was the successful tenderer, and James Amos of Craigie Knowe (Hopping Jimmy), the treasurer. Alexander Reid was also a member of the committee.

Lime for the building was obtained by burning oyster shells bought for sixpence a bushel at Swansea, where they had been conveyed by coastal vessels from forty-foot-high (12 m) banks of them on the Schouten Mountains and Little Swanport.[33] Brick by brick the building rose, but it soon became obvious that the money needed for its completion could not be supplied locally, so the treasurer volunteered to travel round and collect funds for the project in other districts.

---

* The sword is now at the Bark Mill, Swansea.

Despite his best efforts only £464 was raised,[34] part of it being donated by the government, so John Amos and his son James offered to finish the church for that sum. With the help of other members of the family the building was completed less than a year after it had been commenced.[35] With the addition of pews and a pulpit of carved cedar and with the bell* hung above the thatched roof, Glen Gala Church was opened on November 25th 1845.#[36]

Adam Amos did not live to see the building completed, though he watched its construction at the beginning. Seventy years old and slowed down by rheumatism, in New Town he had welcomed visits from family members as a breath of his old life. In between those visits he kept the links strong with letters. His last, written on March 10th, 1844, concluded with:

'I hear the Queen has got a young Prince of Wales - Edward the Seventh.'[37] From then on his mind was occupied with less happy thoughts, for catastrophe struck. Driving back to his home, Jutland,

Gala Kirk (University of Tasmania Archives)

* Years later in 1862 when the line of road was altered and the section between Milton and the church was being surveyed, the bush was so dense that the bell had to be rung at intervals in order to indicate the right direction.

#The name was later altered to its present one of Gala Kirk.

after seeing one of his daughters off in a boat, he suffered a stroke. So severe was it that he was never able to walk again.[38] A carrying-chair was made for him, and, after renting out Jutland, he and Mary returned to Gala, where he wanted to be. On January 16th, 1845 he died. He was buried in the Amos cemetery.

His son James wrote the sad news of his passing to William Pringle, his father's lifelong friend in Scotland. He wrote back, saying, *'It was to me and my brothers sorrow of heart to know that your father was gone - a man above all men, whom we loved and esteemed.'*[39]

CHAPTER 15

On July 1st 1845 Alexander Reid rode into Swansea where, as usual, he headed for the *Rose and Crown*.* Six hours later, at a little after ten o'clock, he left, having declined George Kirby's advice that he should spend the night there. Then, remembering that he owed Fred Lewis some money, he rode along to his inn, where he settled his account and stayed drinking for another hour. Although he talked sensibly and appeared to be in command of himself, Esther Lewis twice suggested that he stay the night. This he declined to do, and mounting his horse, walked it slowly down the road and out of their sight.

The next day his grey horse was seen wandering about without its owner. A search party was formed, and for an afternoon, a day and a morning unsuccessful efforts were made to find him. Finally, opposite Cambria homestead they found the tracks of a horse leading down to a waterhole - a waterhole with a hat floating on it and a body lying about five feet below the surface. The body was that of Alexander Reid, with his riding whip still grasped firmly in his hand.[1]

Later that day at an inquest at the *Swan Inn*# the finding of William Hepburn, John Amos, jnr., John King and others was that he had missed the road before he reached the ford and had tried to cross the river in the wrong place. A verdict of accidental death by drowning was brought in. His was the first body to be buried in the graveyard of Glen Gala Church.

Through the years there had been a considerable amount of concern and speculation at Great Swan Port as to what had become of young George Meredith after he had left so suddenly in 1832. Rumours there were in plenty - that he was in Sydney, that he was in New Zealand, that he was shipwrecked, even that he was dead. But it was not until official notification came from the Mounted Police of South Australia that his family finally learned the truth, and that truth appalled and horrified them. Evidence had shown that in 1836 George had been living on Kangaroo Island with a black girl named Sal

---

*Llanstinnan is the site of the *Rose and Crown*, which was licensed in 1839.
#The name was later changed to Resthaven, and is now Oyster Bay Guest House.

when a would-be suitor in a jealous rage attacked him with a tomahawk and then clubbed him to death.[2] George Meredith decided at once that on no account should these details become public, and shortly afterwards, unpopular though he was in the district, general sympathy was felt for him when he let it be known that young George, while on a sailing trip off South Australia, had been staying at Kangaroo Island and one day was reading his bible on the beach when some blacks, suspecting him of being about to decoy one of their wives (for one of them worked for him as a wallaby hunter) had crept up behind him and murdered him.

John Radford (Courtesy Mr. Bob Poole, Victoria)

In the same year that Adam Amos died William Talbot, the man with whom he had exchanged, *'mighty words'* in 1824, also reached the end of his life. Through the years he had developed and extended Malahide so successfully that at the time of his death it was considered one of the principal properties in the island.* He was buried at Fingal, and on his tombstone was engraved the Talbot arms and the words: *'To the memory of the Hon^hle. William Talbot, sixth son of Baroness Talbot de Malahide and brother of Lord Talbot de Malahide, in Ireland..'* His obituary notice read: *'A man of the first rank, not more distinguished by noble lineage than by individual high and honourable principles. He possessed an innate love of justice.'*

That fellow-countryman whom in 1821 he had helped settle at Great Swan Port, John de Courcy Harte,[3] in 1839 had left the position he held in Sydney and had travelled overland to Port Phillip. There he stayed for two years; then, hearing that Father Conolly had died in 1839 and that his brother in Ireland, Patrick Conolly, was claiming Bellbrook, he wrote to George Kirby requesting money so that he could return to Van Diemen's Land.[4] On arrival he officially contested Patrick Conolly's claim. Knowing that the legal fight ahead would be long and expensive, he offered to sell Muirlands to its tenant, John Radford, completely ignoring the fact that there was doubt as to whether it actually belonged to him. Radford, with a huge hunger for land,[5] agreed to give £800 for it, half of which was to be paid on receipt of the deeds and the rest within two years.# When time passed without the relevant deeds being produced he became suspicious and made enquiries at the Surveys Office, where it was found that not only were all the Muirlands documents prior to 1844 missing, but that the property had never been chartered to anyone by the name of John de Courcy Harte. In the flurry that followed representations were made on behalf of the one who *'through extravagance and prodigality has lost his money',*[6] and in the end the officials decided that the only possible course to follow was to allow the sale to proceed. Mary Ann Radford was listed as the owner, the first instalment was passed over and the law suit as to the ownership of Bellbrook proceeded.

It was in 1846 that the Surveyor-General, J.E. Calder, by chance met Paddy Harte, and having met him never forgot him. Of the incident he wrote: *'It has never been my fortune to meet with anyone who, after a score of years' association with such men as one was formerly to meet*

---

* William Talbot left Malahide to a nephew in Ireland. who also managed the estate in an expert manner. A member of the family still lives there.
# Muirlands was not paid off entirely until 1871.

with in the backwoods of Tasmania, namely, half-lawless stock-riders and professional hunters, convict constables and bolters, who had made so complete a descent, as Mr Harte had done, from the status of a gentleman of high birth, etc., to that of an absolute lout. His conversation, peculiar mode of expression, habits and demeanour were at the time of my making a brief acquaintance with him those of a man who had completely degenerated from the position he was entitled to in society and of the family from which he claims descent.   My personal acquaintance with 'Paddy' Harte, as he was universally known, began and ended on the same day. I was travelling, on foot as usual, from Hobart Town to the Rocky Hills, and stopped a minute at Radford's Inn at Little Swan Port to enquire the road thither, and was informed that there was a 'gentleman' within who was riding that way who would start directly. The gentleman in question proved to be the subject of this notice; who, having before 'got into funds' by the sale of some pigs to a hawker, had been indulging in a fortnight's debauch at the local hotel, but being 'cleaned out', or in other words, penniless again, he was on the wing homewards, wherever that might be. By very good luck, my guide was very nearly sober at the time of introduction, but the occasion of a stranger soliciting his acquaintance was immediately seized upon as a good opportunity for another glass 'just to do honour to a new acquaintance'. Wishing to ingratiate myself with my guide, and not knowing that he had been drunk for a fortnight before, I ordered in a bottle of ale to commence our acquaintance upon, instead of a glass of vulgar she-oak, and which Mr Harte, that no time might be lost, knocked the neck off by some process known only to professional goodfellows, without spilling a drop. At this moment I was called out of the parlour, and upon my return in a few minutes I found that my friend had made the best use of my absence and had finished the contents of No 1 without my assistance. Of course I looked a little blank at this state of doing things at Swanport; but was revived by Mr Harte insisting on it that it was now his turn to call for a bottle - his uniform practice, he said, when in company that he liked; and which he did with all the airs of a man whose credit was as good as the bank. Knocking out the cork in some curious way with the back of a knife, he helped me to a glass - a very frothy one - and made short work with the rest himself. His thirst being now slaked by three rapid libations, he went out - for a moment only, he said - to look after his horse, leaving me, as he expressed it, to finish the bottle myself, and in which I found about a thimbleful undisposed of. As my guide seemed in no hurry to *return to me, I enquired what had become of him and received the comforting intelligence that he had gone off at a hand-gallop about ten minutes before, leaving me to pay for both bottles, and a message to overtake him as soon as I could. After this I saw no more of Mr Harte.'* [8]*

It was April of 1847 - a year after this encounter - before the slow processes of the law culminated in Patrick Conolly being declared the owner of Bellbrook. At this, Paddy Harte's friends and acquaintances rallied round and sent a petition to Governor Denison, who ordered that the case be re-opened. During the ensuing investigations a letter in Father Conolly's handwriting was discovered in the Registrar's Office. It supported what Paddy Harte had maintained all the time - that the transaction had been undertaken on behalf of the owner, who was to have it back on paying the purchase price and interest. Since the amount received by the priest in rent had more than repaid the amount owing, the former decision was reversed and Bellbrook was returned to its original owner. [9]

John Allen (Courtesy Mr. J. S. Allen, Dysart)

---

* Mr Calder continued: *'It may be added, that it is to the refined tastes of this settler that we are indebted for many of the silly names that disgrace our maps of the East Coast. It was he who first called the odious ravine through which the Prosser River flows to the sea, 'Paradise': Hell's Gates, somewhere near Buxtons; the Devil's Royals and Thunderbolt. The Burst-My-Gall and Breakneck Hills are also said to be of his coinage.'*

Thomas Watson, who had taken a great interest in Bellbrook when Brereton Watson had been its tenant, did not live to see the outcome of the dispute. Towards the end of 1846 he died, leaving Mary to rear six children, all under the age of ten. Fourteen months later in a ceremony held at Sherbourne Lodge* she married Richard Allen of The Springs.[10] This marriage was of short duration,# for in June 1851, after a long illness, he died. His body was conveyed from Hobart Town to The Springs, where it was buried within sight of the homestead.** The following year his son Edwin advertised the thousand-acre property for sale.[11]

Edwin's cousin-by-marriage, Ann Eliza Allen, frequently proved herself to be quite different from the wives of the other Great Swan Port settlers. Armed with a pistol for defence and always alone, in the early days of her marriage she often walked the one hundred and twenty miles (193 km) from Allen Grove to her father's house, Huntingfield, at Browns River. Nothing her husband could do or say could prevent her. With the passing of years her ungovernable temper and

The Guest House, Picnic Point, Bicheno (Courtesy Mrs. C. Gray, Bicheno)

---

* Sherbourne Lodge remained in the possession of the Watson family until early this century.

Dr Story's casebook records that Mary Allen lost her grip on reality as a result of her troubles, but had periods of lucidity.

** In later years it was found that the grave interfered with ploughing, so the heavy gravestone was moved to a more convenient place nearby.

increasingly violent ways caused John Allen great concern, and he was often forced to call upon Dr Story to sedate her. In 1852, ten years after their marriage, she had ordered him out of the house, so, leaving his four children behind*, he moved to Picnic Point, a one-hundred-and-three-acre (53 ha) property[12] which he had acquired at Bicheno. With him went a nineteen-year-old girl named Ann Bell. Their first child, Alfred Australian Allen, (the first of many) was born the following year. Initially they lived in a shanty while the new homestead, a simple weatherboard cottage,# was built opposite Diamond Island - an ideal position with uninterrupted views of white beaches, lovely granite headlands and a wide stretch of ocean.

William Lyne (Archives Office of Tasmania, State Library of Tasmania)

---

* John Allen's children by Ann Eliza were Amy Amelia, John Elijah, James Baynton and Joseph Adam.
# The house was later known as The Guest House, and is now Homestead Holiday Estate, a motel two miles north of Bicheno.

Several years after John Allen had settled at Bicheno, (as it was officially named in 1851), he was concerned to hear that William Lyne had suffered a stroke. William adapted bravely to his restricted life style, writing to a friend in a crabbed script that he considered that the Almighty had dealt gently with him in thus sending him a warning. Two years later, in 1854, while eating a meal, a bone lodged in his throat and in spite of frantic efforts to help him he choked to death. A large crowd attended his funeral and watched as his body was laid to rest in the nearby Llandaff cemetery, surrounded by the gums and black wattle of his adopted land - trees so different from the beeches and elms of the land where he had been born 72 years earlier.

By that time death had twice visited Cranbrook House. In January 1848 Hannah Amos had died, followed eight months later by her husband John - that tireless worker and clever artisan who had been of such use to Great Swan Port since its turbulent start. Their son James, who in spite of his deformed leg had been the mainstay of the farm for some years, inherited the property, so he and Mary left Craigie Knowe and moved back into the homestead,[13] where, as mistress, Mary was much more contented than in her early married life.

It was twenty-five years since Hannah Amos and Ellen Buxton had assisted Mary Meredith during her first confinement in Van Diemen's Land. Two were dead now, but the baby, John, whom they had delivered, was very much alive. Now that his half-brother Charles was at Port Sorell and Henry and George were dead, it fell to him to manage the Meredith lands. With so much responsibility and insufficient incentive for someone as ambitious as he, he made an offer to buy part of the Cambria estate. This offer was refused, his father pointing out that it would cause trouble in the family should he accept it. To John's mind, he was experiencing enough trouble with his family already, for, living alone at Riversdale as he was and denied many of the social activities enjoyed by other young bachelors of his standing, he had made what he could of life. When his family became aware of his mode of living he was accused by Charles of being intemperate, by Sabina of *'associating with a class of being calculated to have .. injurious influence upon his habits and manners'*, and his father for his habit of smoking.[14] Disgruntled, he decided to leave Great Swan Port and try his luck in South Australia, where Crown leases were being offered.

Realising that at twenty his youngest son Edwin was too inexperienced to take on the position abdicated by his brother, George

George Meredith. A portrait by or after Thomas Bock. (The Institute, Swansea)

Meredith wrote to Charles and suggested that he come back to Riversdale and work in partnership with the lad. The idea appealed to Charles, who had been content to sit out his term of office as police magistrate rather than make it his career.[15] Accepting his father's invitation, he moved back in 1847.

He found his father much changed. No trace remained of the personable young man who had stormed into the life of Sarah Hicks and later swept Mary Evans off her feet in Wales. Never one to deny his appetites, his years of good living had caught up with him, so that now he was bloated and overweight. Jowls distorted the shape of his large face, his lips protruded in a pout, while his complexion had coarsened and deepened in colour, in distinct contrast to his eyes which, though as arrogant as ever, had paled.

Through the weeks that Charles and Louisa spent at Cambria they found that he had changed within himself also. His interests had narrowed and become localised and, critical and intolerant, he was no longer good company. When a steamer eventually arrived with their belongings they were happy to move to Riversdale and exchange his companionship for that of Edwin. Unfortunately, the strong-minded Louisa soon took a dislike to the young man, besides which the thirty-six year-old Charles had little in common with him. Within a year the partnership was dissolved. Edwin moved back to Cambria and rented some of the Belmont, Apsley and Cambria lands, while Charles leased what remained of the 12,163 acres (4865 ha) owned by his father.[16]

In 1851 John returned briefly from his property in the Mount Gambia district and earned the approval of his family when he married Maria Hammond, the niece and adopted daughter of James and Caroline Grant of Tullochgorum, St Pauls Plains.

A gentle and well-mannered girl, she delighted George Meredith, who much preferred her to Louisa, now seldom seen by him and consequently quite out of favour.

Shortly after their departure for South Australia George Meredith, finding that the new arrangement with his sons was working no better than the previous one, in 1852 offered £4000 to either of them if he would make a new start in New Zealand. Edwin accepted the offer, leaving Charles to lease for twenty-one years all the land excepting Cambria and its farmlands.[17]

By this time many of the younger generation of settlers were leaving home. Already several of the Cotton family had married, and in 1846 Lavinia Amos, one of the twins Hannah had found so difficult to wean twenty-three years before, became Mrs Henry Cotton. Seven years later Francis Cotton transferred his land on the eastern bank of the Swan to Henry, James and Tilney, The Grange becoming the home of Henry and Lavinia.[18]* It was with the intention of visiting them there that one day in 1855 Dr Story and Anna Maria Cotton set off from Kelvedon in a gig, with the thirteen-year-old Rachel# on horseback.

They dined at Red Banks, and soon after resuming their journey were held up by two bushrangers. In farcical circumstances these two (one of whom was Dido, one-time cook at The Grange), were captured, and each was subsequently sentenced to seven years' imprisonment. [19]

---

* Henry did not inherit The Grange.
# Rachel Cotton later became the second wife of Samuel Salmon of Woodstock. Spring Bay.

CHAPTER 16

At Rheban, James Radcliff was concerned about Lisdillon. During the years various managers had lived there, running the estate under the watchful eye of Edward Shaw, but there was no denying that the property was deteriorating.[1] As it was too far away for him to give it his personal attention he decided to sell before further value was lost, so in March 1850 the *Courier* carried an advertisement offering the seven-thousand-acre (2800 ha) property for sale. It was occupied for two years by Lieutenant William Champ, a Cambridge and Sandhurst man who had been Surveyor-General in 1840 and then Civil Commandant at Port Arthur.* While he was at Lisdillon he became Colonial Secretary and soon found that pressure of work made it impossible for him to run the estate at a profit, so in 1852 it was sold to a godly man named John Mitchell, a Cornish surveyor who had arrived in the island in 1837 and was appointed superintendent at Point Puer, from which position he resigned in 1849 and moved to Villeneuve, (now Twamley) Prossers Plains.[2]

Although James Radcliff was a frugal man[3] he was also a speculator, and in 1851 when a small company in Hobarton offered £15,000 to anyone who could find a workable goldfield he arranged to support two prospectors for three months while they searched the North-East Coast for such a find - a venture which proved a failure.[4]

Another promising business prospect lured him to England in 1856. Before leaving he settled Anna Maria Radcliff and his children into Lyle Cottage, New Town, and leased Rheban to Stephen Grueber, who, as well as being given a detailed inventory, received two small booklets of conditions governing his tenancy. His Tasmanian affairs in order, he sailed in May 1856. The voyage was unpleasant. Blown far to the south, the *Mercia* soon became coated with ice and encountered icebergs. The ship's doctor died. So did all the livestock that had been taken on board for fresh meat.

Upon reaching London one hundred and twenty three days after leaving Van Diemen's Land James Radcliff lost no time in making his

---

* William Champ later became the first Premier of Tasmania.

business contacts. In October, heartened by the way his negotiations were proceeding, he sent a letter home. '*The outcome.*' he wrote to Anna Maria, '*should be of great benefit to us all.*' That was the last letter she received from him.

As the months passed without further word she became alarmed and made enquiries. Their bank in London reported that early in October James Radcliff had cashed £1500 in Tasmanian debentures; John Degraves, back in Hobart after a voyage to England, told her he had met her husband, also in early October, on Waterloo Bridge, and had learned that he was staying in lodgings in Waterloo Road kept by an ex-convict named Wolfe. But when she followed this lead she found that Wolfe had disappeared without leaving an address and that nothing was known of her husband. She reported his disappearance to the London police, giving his description and his last address. The receipt of this information caused them to re-open a case which they had been unable to solve. On the 9th of October a boy in a coal boat, while passing below Waterloo Bridge had noticed a carpet bag lodged on one of the buttresses. Using his long pole he had hooked it down, and, finding it locked, had taken it to the police. It was found to contain dissected human remains, clothing, and a small sharp saw. They made enquiries and were told by the tollkeeper that at 11.30 the night before a female had carried the carpet bag on to the bridge.[5] No further information could be found. However, when Anna Maria's letter arrived they sought to identify the remains in the bag as those of her husband - a task made difficult because the head was missing. The height corresponded - 5'8" (172 cm); the complexion matched - dark; the hair was similar - snow white; even the clothing fitted the description, but final identification could not be given official sanction. The police informed Anna Maria of this and she, distraught and unable to accept what all the evidence pointed to, sent a friend to England to make further enquiries.[6] These led nowhere. Before long it was generally accepted that James Radcliff had been the murder victim. Anna Maria refused to believe this, and for years continued to meet every ship that arrived at Hobart.[7]

Lisdillon was not the only original grant on the East Coast to change hands about this time. Since Brereton Watson and George Kirby had left Bellbrook it had been leased for some years to Edward Shaw and later to Charles Willis. Willis proved to be an unsatisfactory tenant. He was often absent for a week at a time on a drinking bout, and many a

189

night Edward Shaw (now appointed trustee of the estate by Paddy Harte), would hear him singing as he passed Red Banks, lolling in the saddle and enjoying the sound of his undoubtedly fine voice.[8] Finally in 1847 after four men at Bellbrook had murdered their overseer, Willis was dismissed. Following this, Paddy Harte, now older than his fifty years and lacking the health that had been his when he had received his grant twenty-five years before, sold the property.[9] It was bought by another hard-drinking Irishman, William O'Connor,* who held it for a few years; then, learning that his close relative Paddy Duffy was bankrupt, he sold it and with the money bought Brook Lodge, which he then leased back to Paddy Duffy.[10] The new owner of Bellbrook then gave it to his daughter, Margaret Cameron, as a wedding gift when she married Robert Hepburn, junior. It was there

Robert Hepburn junior
(Courtesy Mrs. Rhoda Prestidge, Latrobe)

* William O'Connor was the natural son of Roderic, the ex-land commissioner.

that she died in 1857 as the result of burns received in a house fire, and soon afterwards Bellbrook was offered for sale by the assignees of her husband's estate.

Robert Hepburn married again the following year. This time his bride was Matilda Amos of Gala, and their home was the Hepburn store* next to a new school (now the Institute or Museum) which had been built at Swansea.

It had become quite obvious to George Meredith that at farming and financial matters Charles was a failure but in the face of no alternative he had been forced to watch the Belmont, Riversdale and Apsley lands deteriorate under his management. Cambria, too, caused him concern, for most of his convicts had by now worked out their time, and so many of his paid employees had left for the Victorian goldfields that a four-roomed workman's cottage opposite Cambria# was deserted and conjoined cottages near the ford** housed too few men to attend the crops and the stock. When John came home from South Australia on a visit in 1853 his father poured out his troubles to him, and was amazed and delighted when he offered to buy the estate and all his other lands for £40,000, saying that he had done exceptionally well during his six years at Mount Gambier. He accepted the offer without hesitation, quite ignoring his former statement that to sell any of his property would mean trouble within the family. Aware that trouble was inevitable, however, he wrote to each of his sons and daughters explaining what he had done and why. To Charles he was careful to say that now that he had the money he could set him up in New Zealand, where he would in all probability in time become a wealthier man than his father.[11]

When Charles and Louisa received the letter they were appalled. Although Charles had recently been shown his father's will and was aware that he was not to be the sole inheritor of Cambria as he had assumed, he now felt shocked and betrayed. Louisa, who had expected to live out her life in the homestead, was so affected by what

---

* The store, now the Swansea Cottage Home, was later bought by John Alexander Graham, and in about 1884 James Morris removed the upper storey and converted the building into a private residence. The material removed, with the addition of bricks from a brewery behind Schouten House, served in the construction of a second storey for the old Swan Inn, now known as the Oyster Bay Guest House.
# Enlarged and altered, this is now Redcliffe.
** The cottages, similar to those later built by John Mitchell at Mayfield, were prone to flooding, and were demolished in the 1920's.

she termed treason that she never again visited Cambria; neither did she ever again speak to her father-in-law.

They made no secret of their animosity towards both George and John Meredith. Gossip rippled through the island and even surfaced in the newspapers, so that the former owner of Cambria spent his days justifying the sale in lengthy letters to everyone remotely concerned with the matter. To help clear his conscience he also detailed for Charles' information each occasion on which Louisa had offended him. She had not visited Cambria for months, even when Rosina had been very ill; although frequently passing his gates on her way to visit at Red Banks she had never taken the trouble to call in to see him; often when driving with Miss Fenton she had merely bowed upon meeting his carriage and had driven straight by - all of which was true, but did nothing to heal the rift.

With the passing of time Charles, having inherited his mother's gentle nature, became reconciled, but Louisa, a Meredith to the backbone, never relented. Nor would she allow Charles to drop the feud with John, to whom, however, he once wrote: *'Matters over which I have not had control compel me to be distant, but I am nevertheless, you affectionate brother...'*[12]

In December 1855 Charles sold his lease of the Meredith lands to John for £6500* and with part of this money purchased a house in Swansea. This was a small stone cottage named 'Plas Newydd'# which had been erected in 1834 by the then police magistrate, Lieutenant Alexander McKenzie. After adding two large rooms he and Louisa moved in and made it their home for the next three years.

It was during this period that Charles discovered his true vocation. In 1856 he became the first member for Glamorgan in the new Tasmanian Parliament,[13]** the press saying of him *'His large mind, his sterling worth, his power of debate, and his fearless independence singled him out as the candidate above all others to whom the interests of the Colony could be most safely confided.'* Gifted with his father's oratory and with a ready wit of his own,[14] he made a success of his new life, holding office after office, in time becoming Colonial Treasurer.

---

*The Apsley lands had by this time been sold to William Lyne.
#Plas Newydd later became the Rectory, and is now privately owned.

** Charles died in 1880. Louisa in 1895. John Meredith later became an MHA: he died at Cambria in 1909. After Maria's death in 1912 Cambria was sold.

George Meredith, happy to live on at Cambria with John and Maria, now made a new will, of which Bishop Nixon and Thomas Gregson were executors. In this he left £2000 to each of his children, thus disposing of the £20,000 which was all that was left of the £40,000 he had received for his estates.

By now his health had deteriorated to such an extent that it was necessary to have a nurse living in the house. Grossly overweight and ordered to exercise, he took a daily drive in his carriage, but the time came when he could no longer manage this and he was confined entirely to his room.[15] Within three years of having sold his estates to John he died, and in June 1856 was buried next to his beloved Mary in the family vault on Waterloo Point, close to the waters through which he and Adam Amos had rowed on their voyage of discovery thirty-four years before.

To the man who had been his neighbour for most of that time, Edward Shaw, three important events had happened in three years. In 1857 Anne had died, the following year he had married a distant relative of the Merediths, Emma Cope, and in 1858 Mrs Fenton had died. The family, now living in the big Red Banks homestead, suffered a great loss in 1862 when it was burnt down, the fire starting in the roof and spreading so quickly that the furniture was all that could be saved.

Red Banks, from painting by Frederick Shaw. (Courtesy Mr. Charles Shaw, Swansea)

Only the walls were left, but from that shell the present house was built, the cost amounting to £845.[16]

In 1860 Edward Shaw presented himself as one of the candidates in the first election of councillors when it was held in the Pier Hotel* in February. In an atmosphere of great excitement and tension those chosen by the people were John Graham of Llanstinnan, John King of Piermont, John Amos of Glen Heriot, Francis Cotton of Kelvedon, James Amos of Cranbrook and John Meredith of Cambria. Edward Shaw, together with John and Will Lyne, John Mitchell and Henry Cotton, were later included in order to form a composite council.

Uninterested in elections and living a life of her own within herself, Ann Eliza Allen continued at Allen Grove with her four children. With the passing of years her wild eccentricity increased, until in her early forties she became quite dangerous -so dangerous, indeed, that in September 1863 Dr Story was forced to have her locked up in the Swansea gaol. There she told him she was determined to kill John Allen who, she said, was living on a farm that rightly belonged to her. When the doctor pointed out the enormity of such a course she replied, *'Ah, but the commandment to kill him came from God and therefore can't be considered a sin.'*

Taking the only course open to him, he certified her as deranged and she was admitted to the Asylum at New Norfolk, where the doctor in charge reported that she had been a patient of his even before she was married. Year after year passed by, and in 1876 her brother visited her with a view to taking her away, but after talking with her for only a few minutes he left, observing that there was a wildness in her look and expression and her energy of manner and that she had no command over her temper. She remained in the Asylum, her condition unchanged, until her death.[17]

Another person who was in need of medical attention was Ellen Buxton, but for purely physical reasons. The passing years robbed her of her once exuberant energy, bringing ill-health in its place, so that Dr Story was often called in to attend her. The time came, however, when he could no longer help her. She contracted an illness when she was seventy-four and although he exercised all his considerable skill and visited her frequently there was no improvement, for she had cancer of the throat and it was obvious that the end was near. All her life she had been a splendid cook and she retained her interest in culinary matters

---

* The Pier Hotel was built by James Hurst in the mid-fifties at a cost of £3500 and was burned down at the turn of the century.

until the end. Her last words were, *'Look, you girls, don't forget that lard you've got to cut up.'*[18]

With the passing of years she and Thomas, both quick-tempered, had quarrelled more and more, so that in the end there was a deep bitterness between them. Her death did nothing to soften his attitude. A grave was dug in the family cemetery near the house and many of the early settlers attended her funeral. As the ropes were placed under her coffin and the pallbearers were about to lower it into the ground Thomas Buxton called out to them, *'Turn her round.'* They paused, and the undertaker quietly explained to him that people were always buried with their feet to the east so that they would be facing in the right direction on Resurrection Day - a fact of which Thomas was fully aware. The pallbearers were about to proceed with their task when he again called out, *'Turn her round.'* At this John Meredith went over and spoke to him, but it made no difference: Ellen Buxton was buried facing the west.

After a decent interval George Story sent in his account for attendance on her and also on Miss Woollet, a relative of Thomas Buxton, but this he refused to pay, his bitterness still needing an outlet. The account was sent again, and when no money was received the doctor called in person. Upon meeting with a blank refusal to pay he took the matter to court, and there Thomas Buxton was ordered to pay the £22 owing, plus expenses.[19]

Two of Ellen Buxton's sons had not been present at her funeral, for some years before George, after building a vessel at Mayfield, had sailed her to California, where he stayed, and Thomas, the eldest son, had settled in New Zealand. Neither were they at their father's funeral when he died the following year, 1865. But the year after, when John Mitchell of Lisdillon bought Mayfield and there was a sale of stock and implements, Thomas was there, having sailed his boat, the *Dancing Wave,* across the Tasman to attend. Upset at seeing his old home pass out of the family and the familiar belongings change hands, he set out on his homeward journey. His departure was noted by a young lad named Fred Rapp. *'When he started to return to New Zealand',* he wrote later, *'he sailed up from Mayfield one dark night. As he turned Waterloo Point and got a clear view of the light over the Pier Hotel door he fired about six or seven shots at the light. Bullets went whizzing along the road. One struck the terrace under the steps, one knocked out a piece of brick near the light and brickdust and crumbs* fell on Mr P. Miller's head, who lost no time in getting to a place of safety. He declared it was not safe on the terrace. Other bullets went over the house. Next morning Thomas Buxton sailed for New Zealand. As the vessel started to lead off he fired five or six shots into the cottage at the corner.* He must have been drunk.'[20]

Three months after the death of Thomas Buxton Captain Robert Hepburn died, having reached the age of eighty-four. His will was somewhat unusual. It read in part: 'This is the last will and testament of me, Robert Hepburn of Roys Hill in the district of Fingal, Tasmania, Esquire. Lineal descendant by my Father, Captain Hepburn, of the family of Hepburn of Leith, East Lothian; and by my Mother, Mary Ann Roy, Great Grandson of Rob Roy McGregor, and by my Grandmother, Isabella, Princess of Diabenti. Lineal descendant of the King of that nation of Africa. First, I direct that upon my decease my

Mayfield House, probably built in the late 1830's. The small conjoined room, is earlier, c1830.
(Archives Office of Tasmania, State Library of Tasmania)

* The cottage used to be where the cafe is now opposite the Swan Motor Inn.

body be buried beside my Honeysuckle Tree, marked and situated in the gathering Paddock on the North side of the old road about twenty yards from the road and towards the river; and in case of my decease at a distance from Roys Hill, then I direct my body to be buried in the nearest Scottish Burial Ground at any place at which I may die in Tasmania.'

He died at Swanwick and was buried in the Gala Kirk graveyard.

At Kelvedon Francis Cotton, now a distinctly well-to-do man, was able to spend more time following his own interests, secure in the knowledge that the property was well looked after by James* and Edward Octavius, the eighth son. With the increasing need for roads, his help was called upon in surveying better routes to Avoca, Campbell Town and Spring Bay.[21] These became of personal benefit to him, for as a truly devout member of the Society of Friends he travelled the roads in his ministry of faith; nor were his activities confined to the island alone, for in 1867 he journeyed 'under concern' to Melbourne, Adelaide and Sydney.[22]#

By now most of his children were married, most of them outside the denomination in which they had been raised. Francis had married Margaret McLeod in 1850 and had moved to Old Belmont; Joseph, the youngest son, had married Isabella Jackson and was living in a house his father had built at The Bend, the property adjoining The Grange which Dr Story had owned temporarily; and in 1860 Tilney, then living at Glencoe (or 'Hard Scrabble', as he called it), had chosen Anne Allen** as his bride and taken her to live in South Australia.[23]

Joseph Allen had retired form The Plains and had spent his last years in Hobart, where he died in 1868+, but his brother John continued to live on at Picnic Point. In 1874 he and Ann Bell experienced great sadness when one of their young sons was drowned while he and his brother were fishing.[24] John remained healthy and active all his life. When he was over seventy he went with one of his daughters to the Campbell Town Show, and when his horse and gig failed to arrive afterwards as arranged, walked the forty miles (64 km) home, insisting on arrival that he was not very tired. In 1879 at the age of seventy-three he died after a short illness and was buried at

---

* James Cotton later became a Friends' Missioner in the U.S.A.
# Dr Story also travelled to these places.
** This Anne Allen was not related to John Allen.
+ Joseph Allen adopted a sister of Joseph and Agnes Butler. On his death she had a large stained glass window in St Davids Cathedral dedicated to his memory.

Edward Carr Shaw (Council Chambers, Swansea)

Bicheno.[25]* Three of his pallbearers were grandsons of William Lyne, through whose influence he had settled on the East Coast.

The remaining pioneers who had come to Great Swan Port in its early days were now feeling their age. Edward Shaw had lived a full life. In the 1850s he had built a store# in Swansea, letting it to a man named Webster, and as well as acting as trustee to Lisdillon and Bellbrook estates had gradually acquired land of his own until Red Banks extended far beyond the five hundred acres (200 ha) on which Adam Amos had first settled in 1821. Many public offices had been his - those of churchwarden, magistrate, coroner and councillor, but in 1883, saddened by the loss of his wife Emma the previous year, he resigned from those positions he still held, left Red Banks for his son Frederick** to manage, and went to live with Bernard in Launceston. Shortly afterwards Bernard's position as Commissioner of Mines was changed to that of Commissioner of Police and the family moved to Hobart, where after a long illness Edward Carr Shaw died on December 16th, 1885.[26] In accordance with his wish his body was taken by train to Campbell Town and from there conveyed by cart to Red Banks. Later, a large crowd gathered on Waterloo Point to pay honour to one of the finest men who had lived on the East Coast. His obituary notice said of him: *'He was kindhearted to an extreme, affable and agreeable, unostentatious, yet always commanding respect.'*

Another obituary notice appeared in the press in February 1883. It read: *DEATH OF AN AGED COUPLE: The name of John Radford is as familiar as a household word on the East Coast, but after more than 70+ years' residence in Tasmania, he died on one of his own estates at Swanport, in the 92nd## year of his age. He began the world with nothing, and left it with 9000 acres (3600 ha) of land and its belongings behind him. His life was devoted to one object, and till the last he succeeded in adding house to house, and farm to farm. In his wife he had indeed a helper who was even more intent than her husband in heaping up riches. She was a power at Swanport in the money market; she has not, however, lived long after her husband to hold their united gains, for she died yesterday in this city at the residence of her sister, Mrs Mitchelmore, in the 73rd year of her age,*

---

* Anne died in 1926 at the age of ninety-two.
# Shaws Buildings, now Moreys Store, were built by Fogarty, the Red Banks carpenter.
** Frederick Shaw was a Member of the House of Assembly for Glamorgan from 1899 to 1903.
 + The notice should read: 'after 64 years residence in Tasmania'
This should read: 'the 83rd year of his age.'

leaving all behind amongst their six surviving children. Poor Radford and his wife had no weakness for dress or show, but their death, within a fortnight of each other, will leave a blank at Swansea.'[27]

Both were buried by the side of the Little Swanport River, beside the Swan Inn and on the land they had bought with such difficulty from John de Courcy Harte so long ago.[28]

News of Paddy Harte had been brought to Great Swan Port some time before by Charles Meredith, who, while attending a function at the Brickfields Invalid Depot in North Hobart* had encountered him there among the paupers; some time later it was learned that he had died there.[29]

At Courland Agnes Butler, still unmarried, continued to keep house for Joseph. They never addressed each other by their christian names but always as *'Brother'* or *'Sister',* and as a result were always referred to as Brother or Sister Butler.[30] The bond between them remained strong and she was devastated when he died in 1888. He was buried in the Gala Kirk graveyard and later she had a large headstone erected on his grave. After the main inscription were added, in italics, the words: *'O Brother: Brother.'*

At Kelvedon through the years George Story continued to derive a great deal of simple enjoyment out of life. He wrote in his journal: *'The swallows have come, but no-one but I has noticed them.'* Whenever he set out on a case he took small parcels of crumbs with which to feed the fish as they swam round his horse's mouth while he drank at the fords. But the time came when cataracts so affected his vision that he could no longer see either the swallows or the fish, yet he continued to ride about the country attending those patients who called for his help, for even with impaired eyesight his skill at diagnosis was remarkable.[31] However, he was forced to tell people he could no longer attend them after he was one day unable to find his hat when he knocked it off as he rode into a tree.

His eyesight was not needed when it came to diagnosing Anna Maria's trouble after she had suffered a stroke. Half paralysed, she was carried to her bed, and there she remained for the rest of her life. Even so, for a while she contrived to rule as much as possible, issuing her orders and thumping with her stick on the floor if she considered there was too much noise or laughter downstairs,[32] but in the end her mind

---

* The Invalid Depot was near the present football ground.

200

Francis Cotton
(Courtesy Mr. James Amos, Cranbrook)

Anna Maria Cotton
(Courtesy Mr. James Amos, Cranbrook)

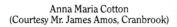

became clouded and when she died in 1882 her family accepted her passing as a kindness from their Lord.

By now Francis Cotton was very ill indeed. The 'mild indigestion' he had dismissed as nothing years before had turned to an ulcerated stomach and finally to cancer. In the end he found it impossible to retain even a spoonful of liquid, so that he starved to death. He outlived his beloved Anna Maria by only six months.[33]

George Story lived on at the homestead, busy in his now sightless world, gardening still. Two years passed, and on his eighty-fifth birthday he caught a chill. As independent as ever, he refused to go to bed until it became obvious even to him that he must, for by this time he had contracted pneumonia. Nursed by Edward and his wife, (the former Helen Grueber of Spring Bay), he took a professional interest in his illness, but from the outset it was obvious what the end would be. He died on March 6th 1885 and was buried beside his two friends in the Kelvedon cemetery. His obituary notice read: *'His benevolence was so large and active that he was ever more ready to give than to receive, and so he went about doing good, loving every living thing and loved by all.'*

ABBREVIATIONS

ADB	Australian Dictionary of Biography
AOT	Archives Office of Tasmania, State Library of Tasmania, Hobart
CON	Convict Department, AOT
CSO	Colonial Secretary's Office, AOT
CSD	Colonial Secretary's Department, AOT
DO	Deeds office, AOT
GO	Governor's Office, AOT
HRA	Historical Records of Australia, AOT
LSD	Land, Survey Department, AOT
NS	Non State Records, AOT
RGD	Registrar-General's Department, Hobart
SLV	State Library of Victoria
SC	Select Committee
TC	Tasmanian Collection, State Library of Tasmania, Hobart
THRA	Tasmanian Historical Research Association
UTA	University of Tasmania Archives
VDL	Van Diemen's Land

ARCHIVES OF TASMANIA REFERENCE NUMBERS

Amos Papers:

Amos, Adam	Diary, 1822-1825	NS323/1
" "	Letters to George Meredith, Wales, 1819	NS123/1
" "	Letters, 1834-1844	NS323/4
" "	Letter to W. Pringle, Scotland	NS323/3
Amos, James (Gala)	Diary, 1840-1844	NS323/2
Letters from W. Pringle, Scotland	1833-1850	NS323/5
Gala Kirk		NS977/1-6
List of Convicts,	Swan Port, 1828 in back of Diary of Adam Amos	NS323/1

Lyne Papers:

Lyne, John	Journal (1896)	NS854
Lyne, Marjorie	Family papers	NS913/1-28

Meredith Papers:

Meredith, George	Diary, 1821	NS123/1
" "	Letters from A. Amos, 1819	NS123/1
" "	Letters to wife, 1823-1837	NS123/1
Archer Taylor, F.R.	Notes on the Meredith Family	NS123/157

Steel Papers:

Steel, Michael		Letter to his brother in England, 1826	NS174
"	Percy Wm.	Some Early History of Falmouth and Surrounding Districts	NS41/1
"	Bessie	Family Notes	NS174
Green, Will		Letter re Death of W. Steel	NS174

PRIVATE COLLECTIONS

Amos Family Papers:
Diaries, historical notes, typescripts, reminiscences, records held by Mrs Ruth Amos, Swansea and Mr Bruce Amos, Cranbrook.

Allen Family Papers:
Family records, photographs held by Mrs C. Gray, Bicheno. John Allen's Day Book; letters from 1835-1844: Mrs Ruth Amos, Swansea. Letters from Mr Jack Allen, Dysart, Mrs L. Nyman, Hobart.

Buxton Family Papers:
Biographical notes and information held by Mrs M. Martin, Rocherlea, Launceston.

Castle Family Papers:
Personal communication, notes and information: Mrs G. Freeman, Wynyard. Records and information: Miss Jess Castle, Lenah Valley, Hobart.

Cotton Family Papers:
Letters, family records, photographs, diaries and typescripts: Mrs Frances Cotton, Swansea and UTA.

Hepburn Family Papers:
Personal communication with Mrs Peg Davis, Elderslie, Tasmania.

Lyne Family Papers:
Biographical notes, family papers, photographs held by Mrs L. Nyman, South Hobart, and Mr W.G. Lyne, Wahroonga, Sydney.

Maclaine Family Papers:
'The Life, Times and Family of Captain Peter Maclaine of Scotland and Van Diemen's Land', by Peter C. Sims, Quoiba, Tasmania.

Radford Family Papers:
Records, information, biographical notes, photographs: Mr Bob Poole, Attwood, Victoria.

Radcliff Family Papers:
Family records, papers, letters, photographs and biographical notes: Mr James Radcliff, Devonport.

Story Papers:
Papers, photographs and records of Dr Story held by Mrs Frances Cotton, Swansea.

Steel Family Papers:
Letters, typescripts, photographs and records: Mrs Christine Logan, Sandy Bay.

Shaw Family Papers:
Bernard's Brethren (C.M. Shaw), held by Mr Edward Shaw, Howrah, Hobart. Notes, records, photographs and Anne Shaw's Day Book: Mr Charles Shaw, Red Banks, Swansea.

Watson Family Papers:
Records, historical data, typescripts: Mr Reg Watson, Kingston Beach.

MANUSCRIPT MATERIAL

Archives Office of Tasmania
Amos diaries and letters (NS323); Meredith papers and photographs (NS123); Lyne journal and papers (NS854); (NS913) Steel letters and typescripts (NS41); (NS174)

University of Melbourne
Calder Papers: Letters and history of John de Courcy Harte (O/N 50215)

University of Tasmania Archives
'Some records of Great Swan Port and the Municipality of Glamorgan, 1820-1920' by Dr G. Musgrave Parker, c 1950. Parker Papers. 'The Story of Great Swan Port and its People, 1821-1908' (P1/6).

Tasmanian Collection, State Library of Tasmania
'Memoir of the late George Meredith by his son Edwin', Masterton (N.Z.), 1873 (TC 920 MER); *Amos and Lyne Family History (C. Amos); The Homestead, Bicheno (J. Allen);* 'Reminiscences and Experiences of an Early Colonist' (Edwin Meredith). Masterton (NZ), 1898.

Royal Society of Tasmania
Diary notes of Charles Meredith

G.H. Crawford. THRAP, *PP*
'The Steel Family of Enstone Park, Falmouth'

Tasmanian Historical Research Association
'The Ralphs Bay Neck Railway', J. Thwaites; Vol. 20, no. 4 (Dec. 1973); 'Home Life in V.D.L.', Frances Cotton; Vol. 21, no. 4 (Dec. 1974); 'Excursion to Swansea', Geoffrey Stilwell and Eric Reed (proposed but not held unpublished) April 1960.

Correspondence, State Library of Tasmania
'Nomenclature on Freycinet Peninsula', Stilwell, G.T.

PAMPHLETS AND PAPERS

'A Short History of All Saints' Church, Swansea', F.C. Shaw; 'Parish of Buckland, Tasmania; Church of St John the Baptist', Reverend R.N. Fox; 'Glamorgan, 125 Years of Local Government, 1860-1985'; Glamorgan Council; 'Lets Talk about Swansea', Tasmanian Tourist Council; 'Lets Talk about Swansea and Coles Bay'; second edition 1972-73 'About Swansea'; Glamorgan Council.

REFERENCE NOTES

Allen, J.: *The Homestead, Bicheno* (Hobart, 1976)

Amos, Clarendon: *The Amos and Lyne Family History* (Hobart, 1963)

Backhouse, James: *A Narrative of a Visit to the Australian Colonies* (London, 1843)

Bassett, M.: *The Henties* (London, 1954)

Bolger, Peter: *Hobart Town* (Canberra, 1973)

Bonwick, James: *The Last of the Tasmanians* (London, 1870)

Briggs, Asa: *How they Lived* (London, 1956)

Calder, J.E.: Notes on John de Courcy Harte. SLF. O/N 50215

Calder, J.E.: Rambles on Betsey's Island, Tasmans Peninsula and Forestiers Peninsula in February 1848

Chapman, P. (ed.): The Diaries and Letters of G. T. W. B. Boyes, Vol. 1, 1820-32. (Melb. 1985)

Clune, F. and Stephenson, P.R.: *The Viking of Van Diemen's Land* (Sydney, 1954)

Cotton, Frances: *Kettle on the Hob: A Family in Van Diemen's Land 1828-1885* (Latrobe, 1986)

Craig, E.N. and Robertson, E.G.: *Early Houses of Northern Tasmania, Vol. 2* (Melbourne, 1964)

Curr, E.: *An Account of the Colony of Van Diemen's Land, principally designed for the use of Emigrants* (London, 1824)

Ellis, V.R.: *Louisa Anne Meredith: A Tigress in Exile* (Hobart, 1979)

Evans, George W.: *A Description of Van Diemen's Land, 1822* (Paris, 1823)

Forsyth, W.D.: *Governor Arthur's Convict System: Van Diemen's Land 1824-1836* (Sydney, 1970)

Godwin, B.: *Emigrants' Guide to Van Diemen's land, 1823* (London, 1823)

Goodrick, Joan: *Life in Old Van Diemen's Land* (Adelaide, 1977)

Hartwell, R.M.: *The Economic Development of Van Diemen's Land 1820-1850* (Melbourne, 1954)

Heyer, J.: *The Presbyterian Pioneers of Van Diemen's Land* (Launceston, 1935)

Hughes, Robert: *The Fatal Shore* (London, 1987)

Hurburgh, Marcus: *The Royal Tasmanian Botanical Gardens, 1818-1986: A History in Stone and Soil and Superintendents* (Hobart, 1986)

Levy, M.C.I.: *Governor George Arthur: A Colonial Benevolent Despot* (Melbourne, 1953)

McKay, A. (ed.): *Journals of the Land Commissioners for Van Diemen's Land 1826-1828* (Hobart, 1962)

Melville, H.: (ed. G. Mackaness): *Australian Historic Monographs: The History of Van Diemen's Land* (Sydney c1947)

Melville, H.: *The Van Diemen's Land Almanac, 1832* (Hobart, 1832)

Meredith, L.A.: *My Home in Tasmania, during a residence of Nine Years (two volumes)* (London, 1853)

Meredith, L.A.: *My Home in Tasmania, or, Nine Years in Australia* (New York, 1853)

Meredith, L.A.: *Tasmanian Friends and Foes, Feathered, Furred and Finned* (London, 1880)

Moore-Robinson, J.: *Tasmanian Nomenclature* (Hobart, 1911)

National Trust of Australia (Tasmania): *Priceless Heritage* (Hobart, 1964)

Nyman, L.: *The Lyne Family History* (Hobart, 1976)

O'May, H.: *Wrecks in Tasmanian Waters* (Hobart, 1971)

Plomley, N.J.B. *(ed.): Friendly Mission - the Tasmanian Journals and Papers of George Augustus Robinson, 1829-1834* (Hobart, 1966)

Ramsay, C.: *With the Pioneers* (Hobart, 1979)

Reid, O.: *The East Coast* (Hobart, 1978)

Reinits, R. and T.: *A Pictorial History of Australia* (New York, 1977)

Reynolds, J.: *Launceston - History of an Australian City* (Melb., 1969)

Robson, L.L.: *A History of Tasmania, Volume 1 - Van Diemen's Land from the Earliest Times to 1855* (Melbourne, 1983)

Rudge, T.: *History of the County of Gloucestershire* (London, -)

Ryan, L.: *The Aboriginal Tasmanians* (Brisbane, 1981)

Shaw, C.J.: *A History of Clan Shaw* (Sussex, 1983)

Sims, P.: *The Life, Times and Family of Captain Peter Maclaine of Scotland and Van Diemen's Land.*

Smith, R.: *John Lee Archer, Tasmanian Architect and Engineer* (Hobart, 1962)

Solomon, R.J.: *Urbanisation* (Sydney, 1976)

Stancombe, G.H.: *Highway in Van Diemen's Land* (Launceston, 1968)

Syme, J.: *Nine Years in Van Diemen's Land* (Dundee, 1848)

Travers, F.: *Pioneers at Piermont: Robert Webber and Family (Hobart, 1986)*

von Stieglitz, K.R.: *Pioneers of the East Coast from 1642: Swansea, Bicheno* (Launceston, 1955)

Wettenhall, R.L.: *A Guide to Tasmanian Government Administration* (Hobart, 1968)

Walker, J.B.: *Early Tasmania. Papers read before the Royal Society of Tasmania during the years 1888-1899* (Tas., 1973)

Walker, P. B.: *Prelude to Federation 1884-1898* (Hobart, 1976)

Walker, P.B.: *All that we Inherit* (Hobart, 1968)
West, J. *(ed. A.G.L. Shaw): The History of Tasmania* (Launceston, 1852)
Dictionary of Australian Biography (Melbourne, 1969)
Register of Admissions and Treatment of Female Patients at Lachlan Park,   (New Norfolk 1863-1879)

LIST OF CONVICTS, NORTH DIVISION OF SWAN PORT, 1828

No.	Name	Ship	Assigned to
12	Aspinal, Abel	*Atlas*	J. Amos
24	Anderson, William	*Minerva*	J. Harte
90	Ambrook, John	*Caledonia*	J. King
216	Allen, John	*Medway*	G. Meredith
236	Aldridge, Peter	*Andromeda*	G. Meredith
242	Atkinson, Thomas	*Andromeda*	G.Meredith
116	Breatt, Stephen	*Lady Castlereagh*	Government employ
536	Brinkworth, Sampson	*Prince of Orange*	J. Harte
574	Barton, Richard	*Arab*	Government employ
624	Buff, Thomas	*Competitor*	G. Meredith, jnr.
817	Bailey, Benjamin	*Lady East*	G. Meredith
825	Baird, Robert	*Lady East*	G. Meredith
916	Barber, John	*Chapman*	J. King
991	Brearsley, Robert	*Layton*	G. Meredith
1007	Basket, Joseph	*Asia*	R. Webber
1069	Best, George	*Bengal Merchant*	J. Amos
1073	Bryant, Henry	*Bengal Merchant*	A. Amos
353	Close, John	*Medway*	G. Meredith
759	Currie, John	*Chapman*	Government employ
844	Crawly, Charles	*Asia*	W. Lyne
282	Dagg, Joseph	*Caledonia*	G. Meredith
333	Duncan, William	*Asia*	Field Police
430	Davies, James	*Governor Ready*	--
440	Day, James	*Layton*	J. King
129	Flack, John	*Julie Anne*	Field Police
170	Frost, Jack	*Lord Hungerford*	--
183	Flack, Henry	*Phoenix*	J. Harte
318	Flashman, Charles	*Layton*	J. King
288	Godbolt, William	*Phoenix*	G. Meredith
428	Gray, Frederick	*Sir Castle Forbes*	--
117	Holland, William	*Surrey*	Field Police
257	Jackson, John	*Chapman*	J. King
260	Jones, Robert	*Princess Charlotte*	G. Meredith
336	Lilley, James	*Lady East*	G. Meredith, jnr.

357	Linton, John	*Woodman*	G. Meredith
414	Lewis, Edward	*Bengali Merchant*	John Amos
494	Munson, James	*Chapman*	--
146	Nicholas, William	*Layton*	Mr Allen
148	Nash, James	*Layton*	Mr Allen
205	Pugh, George	*Lord Hungerford*	J. Amos
236	Pratt, Thomas	*Prince of Orange*	Government employ
343	Packham, James	*Chapman*	J. Harte
355	Priest, Evan	*Princess Charlotte*	G. Meredith
221	Richardson, William	*County Harcourt*	Government employ
382	Raper, John	*Phoenix*	J. Harte
309	Sans, James	*Medway*	Ticket of Leave
476	Smith, Benjamin	*E. Henrietta*	J. King
547	Sewell, John	Commodore Hays	--
771	Smith, William	*Chapman*	A. Amos
814	Schilenake, Riche	*Governor Ready*	G. Meredith
881	Smith, William	*Marmion*	J. King
889	Sullivan, Thomas	*Marmion*	J. King
212	Taylor, William	*Prince of Orange*	G. Meredith
273	Taylor, James	*Phoenix*	Captain Hibbert
326	Tilley, Edward	*Medway*	G. Meredith
551	Worsley, William	*Godfrey Webster*	G. Meredith
553	Walker, John	*Godfrey Webster*	G. Meredith
563	Whitbread, James	*Asia*	G. Meredith
646	Woodcock, Edward	*Charles Forbes*	Government employ
676	Wrien, William	*Medway*	G. Meredith
730	Westgate, Robert	*Chapman*	J. King
36	Maiton, Mary	*Brothers*	G. Meredith
61	Doyle, Elizabeth	*Providence*	John Bickerton

REFERENCE NOTES

CHAPTER 1

1. Ellis, *Louisa Anne Meredith*, p. 17.
2. *ADB*.
3. Meredith, 'Memoir of the late George Meredith'. (TC 920 MER)
4. Dyfed Council, Haverfordwest, Wales. Letter to author, 1984
5. Meredith papers, AOT. George Meredith to Mary, May 1833. (NS123/1)
6. Ellis, *Louisa Anne Meredith*, p. 25.
7. Dyfed Council, Haverfordwest, Wales. Letter to author, 1984

8.   Amos family papers; Heriot Farm Rent Book, 1776. Mrs Ruth
        Amos, Swansea
9.   Meredith papers, AOT. C. Pringle to Adam Amos. (NS123/1)
10.   Amos family papers; Mrs Ruth Amos, Swansea
11.   Amos, *Amos and Lyne Family History*, p. 3.
12.   Amos family papers; Mrs Ruth Amos, Swansea
13.   McKay (ed.) *Land Commissioners' Journal*, p. 91.
14.   Amos papers; Details of sale, Wales, 1816. (NS123/2)
15.   Dyfed Library, Haverfordwest, Wales. Letter to author, 1984
16.   Meredith papers; Adam Amos to George Meredith,
        1819.(NS123/2)
17.   ibid.
18.   Ellis, *Louisa Anne Meredith*, p. 26.
19.   ibid., p. 25.
20.   ibid., p. 26.
21.   ibid., p. 26.
22.   ibid., p. 27.
23.   CO201/147/149, 155.
24.   Robson, *A History of Tasmania*, p. 114.
25.   Amos family papers; Notes by Margaret Amos. Mrs Ruth
        Amos, Swansea
26.   Ellis, *Louisa Anne Meredith*, p. 27.

CHAPTER 2

1.   CO201/11/463
2.   Diary notes of Charles Meredith; Royal Society of Tasmania
3.   Amos family papers; Notes by Margaret Amos. Mrs Ruth
        Amos, Swansea
4.   Bassett, *The Henties*, p. 33.
5.   CS01/884/18, 765
6.   Amos family papers; 'The Amos Family, Cranbrook', M.B.
        Amos; Mrs Ruth Amos, Swansea. Meredith papers; George
        Meredith to his brother, 2nd Apr. 1821. (RS34/2, AOT)
7.   *The Sydney Gazette*, Apr. 6, 1821
8.   Solomon, *Urbanisation*
9.   Diary notes of Charles Meredith; Royal Society of Tasmania
10.   von Stieglitz, *Pioneers of the East Coast*, p. 12.
11.   Robson, *A History of Tasmania*, p. 132.
12.   ibid.
13.   CON67/23
14.   ibid.
15.   Amos, *Amos and Lyne Family History*, p. 7.

16. Meredith papers, Diary of George Meredith. (NS123/157)
17. SC285/320; CS01/79/1746, 310; CS01/79/1746, 319
18. *HRA III, IV*, p. 54.
19. SC01/1746/310
20. *HRA III, IV*, p. 94.
21. ibid., p. 55.
22. *ADB.*
23. Robson, *A History of Tasmania*, p. 73.
24. Calder papers (SLV); Notes on John de Courcy Harte. O/N 50215
25. *HRA III, IV*, p. 97.
26. ibid., p. 95.
27. ibid., p. 498.
28. ibid., p. 497.
29. Police report: Jorgensen to T. Anstey, Oatlands, 1828
30. CS01/150/3649
31. *HRA III, IV*, p. 503.
32. ibid., p. 508.
33. CON13/2, p. 199.
34. Meredith, 'Memoir of the late George Meredith' (TC 920 MER)
35. CO201/111/463 (plan)
36. *HRA III, IV*, p. 450.
37. ibid., p. 446.
38. Meredith papers; Diary of George Meredith (NS123/157)
39. Photograph of Creek Hut
40. CO201/111/463 (plan)
41. *HRA III, IV*, p. 442.
42. CO201/147
43. Meredith papers; George Meredith to Mary, 2/3/1823 (NS123/157)
44. Meredith papers; Diary of George Meredith (NS123/157)
45. Robson, *A History of Tasmania*, p. 194.
46. SC285/320
47. CS01/79/146, 311
48. *HRA III, IV*, p. 455.
49. ibid., p. 504.
50. ibid., p. 528.
51. ibid., p. 517.
52. ibid., p. 515.
53. Robson, A History of Tasmania, p. 116.
54. CS01/79/1746, 311
55. *HRA III, IV*, p. 528.

56.   ibid., p. 99.
57.   ibid., p. 444.
58.   ibid., p. 509.
59.   ibid., p. 511.

CHAPTER 3

1.   Ellis, *Louisa Anne Meredith*, p. 27.
2.   Meredith, 'Memoir of the late George Meredith'; (TC 920 MER)
3.   CS01/79/1746, 319
4.   'Excursion to Swansea, 1960', Geoffrey Stilwell and Eric Reed, THRA *PP*
5.   McKay (ed.), *Land Commissioners' Journal*, p. 92.
6.   *HRA III, V*, p. 341.
7.   Meredith, 'Memoir of the late George Meredith'; (TC 920 MER)
8.   *HRA III, IV*, p. 451.
9.   Meredith, 'Memoir of the late George Meredith'; (TC 920 MER)
10.   *HRA III, IV*, p. 456.
11.   Meredith, *My Home in Tasmania*, p. 136.
12.   Ellis, *Louisa Anne Meredith*, p. 55.
13.   Curr, *An Account of Van Diemen's Land*.
14.   von Stieglitz, *Pioneers of the East Coast*, p. 32.
15.   Amos papers; Diary of Adam Amos, Aug. 1822. (NS323/1)
16.   Amos family papers; 'An Autobiography of the Amos Family'; J.C. Amos; Mr Bruce Amos, Cranbrook
17.   Ellis, *Louisa Anne Meredith*, p. 27.
18.   CON76/899
19.   West, *The History of Tasmania*, p. 652.
20.   *Hobart Town Gazette*, Dec. 3, 1824
21.   Amos papers; Diary of Adam Amos (NS323/1)
22.   CO201/147/149, 155
23.   Ellis, *Louisa Anne Meredith*, p. 57.
24.   Amos papers; Adam Amos to W. Pringle, Scotland, 1826. (NS323/3)
25.   *HRA III, IV*, p. 528.
26.   *HRA III, V*, p. 342.
27.   McKay (ed.), *Land Commissioners' Journal*, p. 95.
28.   Bolger, *Hobart Town*, p. 20
29.   Parker papers, UTA; (P1/6, App. B)
30.   Amos papers; Diary of Adam Amos. (NS323/1)
31.   Parker papers, UTA; (P1/6, B12)

CHAPTER 4

1. Meredith, *My Home in Tasmania*, p. 79
2. Parker papers, UTA; Mrs Eliza Johnston to Dr G.M. Parker, 1924. (P1/6, P1/1)
3. ibid., (P1/6, App. B)
4. Ellis, Louisa Anne Meredith, p. 56
5. Ships Department, AOT
6. *Tasmanian Mail*, Sep. 30, 1893. Notes by E.O. Cotton
7. Parker papers, UTA (P1/6, H6)
8. Robson, *A History of Tasmania*, p. 133
9. Amos papers; Diary of Adam Amos (NS323/1)
10. ibid., Aug. 3, 1824
11. Amos family papers; 'An Autobiography of the Amos Family', J.C. Amos, Mr Bruce Amos, Cranbrook p.18.
12. Meredith papers; Notes on the Meredith Family, Mrs Archer Taylor (NS123/157)
13. Parker papers (P1/6, H12)
14. Meredith, 'Memoir of the late George Meredith', p. 40

CHAPTER 5

1. Robson, *A History of Tasmania*, p. 138
2. Reinits, *A Pictorial History of Australia*, p. 113
3. *HRA III, iv*, p. 92
4. Meredith, 'Memoir of the late George Meredith', p. 16
5. *HRA III, v*, p. 339
6. ibid., p. 160
7. ibid., p. 340
8. ibid., p. 340
9. ibid., p. 339
10. McKay (ed.), *Land Commissioners' Journal*, p. 69
11. Amos papers; Diary of Adam Amos. (NS323/1)
12. CS01/884/765
13. CS01/79/1746, 311
14. *HRA III, V*, p. 160
15. CS01/79/1746, 311
16. Robson, *A History of Tasmania*, p. 145
17. Reid, *The East Coast*
18. ADB
19. McKay (ed.); *Land Commissioners' Journal*, p. 93
20. Meredith, 'Memoir of the late George Meredith'; (TC 920 MER)
21. CS01/141/3495, 241

22. Meredith papers; Notes on the Meredith Family, Mrs Archer Taylor (NS123/157)
23. ibid.
24. ibid.
25. Robson, *A History of Tasmania*, p. 142
26. Ramsay, *With the Pioneers*, p.39
27. *Priceless Heritage*, National Trust of Tasmania, p. 129
28. *ADB*
29. CS01/141/2493, 56
30. Robson, *A History of Tasmania*, p. 141
31. Goodrick, *Life in Old Van Diemen's Land*, p.60
32. Robson, *A History of Tasmania*, p. 143

CHAPTER 6

1. Amos papers, Letters to W. Pringle, Scotland. (NS323/3)
2. Parker papers, UTA; Letter from Mrs Eliza Johnston to Dr Parker, 1928. (P1/6, P1/1)
3. CS01/316/839
4. *HRA III, V*, p. 341
5. CS01/79/1746, 255
6. *HRA III, V*, p. 584
7. ibid., p. 18.
8. CS01/79/1746, 255
9. *HRA III, V*, p. 338
10. ibid., p. 584
11. McKay (ed.), *Land Commissioners' Journal*, p. 92
12. Parker papers, UTA; (P1/6, F9)
13. ibid., Mr Fred Rapp to Dr Parker, 1926. (P1/6, P1/1)
14. Briggs, *How they Lived*
15. Rudge, *History of the County of Gloucestershire*
16. Lyne papers; John Lyne's Journal. (NS854)
17. ibid., Family papers, (NS913)
18. ibid., John Lyne's Journal. (NS854)
19. Steel papers; M. Steel to his brother, 1826. (NS174)
20. *HRA III, V*, p. 435
21. *Meredith*, 'Memoir of the late George Meredith'; (TC 920 MER)
22. ibid.
23. Letter from W. Lyne to Governor Arthur, 1833; (L. Nyman, Sth. Hobart)
24. CS01/380/8623
25. Scott's Map of V.D.L., 1824.
26. Parker papers, UTA. (P1/6, B17)

27. Lyne papers; John Lyne's Journal. (NS854)
28. ibid.
29. McKay (ed.), *Land Commissioners' Journal*, p. 94
30. Personal communication with the late Miss Kate Lyne, Swansea
31. Lyne papers; John Lyne's Journal. (NS854)
32. Personal communication with the late Mr Jack Allen, Dysart
33. Parker papers, UTA; (P1/6, B17)
34. DO4/5747
35. Swansea Institute: Lyne and Amos clothing
36. CS01/79/1746, 344
37. Lyne papers; John Lyne's Journal, p. 19; (NS854)
38. Dorset and Somerset County Record Office
39. Parker papers, UTA; (P1/6, C18)
40. CS01/133/3198
41. Travers, *Pioneers at Piermont*, p. 15
42. McKay (ed.), *Land Commissioners' Journal*, p. 94

CHAPTER 7
1. McKay (ed.), *Land Commissioners' Journal*, p. 94
2. GO2/1, vol. 2/98
3. Calder, Rambles on Betsey's Island
4. *Hobart Town Courier*, Dec. 21, 1831
5. Parker Papers, UTA. (P1/6, B10)
6. McKay (ed.), *Land Commissioners' Journal*, p. 98
7. CS01/79/1764, 271
8. CS01/79/1764, 320
9. CS01/79/1764, 316
10. Briggs, *How they Lived*
11. Lyne papers; John Lyne's Journal. (NS854)
12. ibid.
13. Meredith papers; Notes on the Meredith Family, Mrs Archer Taylor; (NS123/157)
14. ibid., George Meredith to Mary Meredith. (NS123/1)
15. ibid.

CHAPTER 8
1. McKay (ed.), *Land Commissioners' Journal*, p. 96
2. Castle family papers; Miss Jess Castle, Hobart
3. CS01/216/5202
4. McGregor Family Tree (Dr John Ward, Sydney)
5. Hepburn family papers; Mrs Peg Davis, Ellerslie
6. Parker papers, UTA; (P1/6, App. B); and Robson, *A History of Tasmania*, p. 196

7.   GO33/27/909
8.   CS01/229/5606, 129
9.   LSD1/6/89
10.   CS01/316/839
11.   Lyne papers; John Lyne's Journal. (NS854, p. 21)
12.   CS01/316/840
13.   Parker papers, UTA; (P1/6, E6)
14.   Allen family papers; Mrs Ruth Amos, Swansea
15.   *Hobart Town Gazette,* Nov. 26, 1828
16.   Parker papers, UTA; (P1/6; App. B)
17.   Ryan, *The Aboriginal Tasmania,* p. 102
18.   Lyne papers; John Lyne's Journal. (NS854, p. 22)
19.   Parker papers, UTA; (P1/6, App. B)
20.   Robson, *A History of Tasmania,* p. 211
21.   Parker papers, UTA; (P1/6, App. B)
22.   McKay (ed.); *Land Commissioners' Journal,* p. 93
23.   Meredith, 'Memoir of the late George Meredith'; (TC 920 MER)
24.   CS01/79/1746, 344
25.   Amos, *Amos and Lyne Family History,* p. 1
26.   Robson, *A History of Tasmania,* p. 195
27.   ibid., p. 111
28.   McKay (ed.), *Land Commissioners' Journal,* Introduction
29.   ibid., p. 97
30.   ibid., p. 97
31.   *Hobart Town Courier,* Nov. 1828
32.   McKay (ed.), *Land Commissioners' Journal,* p. 95
33.   Calder papers, SLV. John Harte to Police Magistrate, Hobart, 1827
34.   McKay (ed.), *Land Commissioners' Journal,* p. 96

CHAPTER 9

1.   Steel papers; Notes from Bessie Steel. (NS174)
2.   *Hobart Town Courier,* Mar. 3, 1832
3.   Lyne papers; John Lyne's Journal. (NS854)
4.   ibid.,
5.   Parker papers, UTA. (P1/6, App. B)
6.   Clune and Stephenson, *The Viking of V.D.L.,* p. 338
7.   Jorgen Jorgensen's report to Police Magistrate, Oatlands, 1829
8.   CS01/315/244
9.   CS01/331/7578, 119

10.   CS01/315, 242
11.   Hurburgh, *The Royal Tasmanian Botanical Gardens,* 1818-1986
12.   *ADB*
13.   ibid.
14.   Parker papers, UTA; (P1/6, App. B)
15.   Cotton, *Kettle on the Hob,* p. 13
16.   *ADB*
17.   Cotton, *Kettle on the Hob,* p. 13
18.   *The Mercury,* Apr. 23, 1883. Obituary, Francis Cotton
19.   Robertson and Craig, *Early Homes of Northern Tasmania,* Vol. 2
20.   'The Ralphs Bay Neck Railway', Jack Thwaites; THRA PP
21.   Cotton, *Kettle on the Hob,* p. 14
22.   Bonwick, *The Last of the Tasmanians*
23.   Robertson and Craig, *Early Homes of Northern Tasmania,* Vol. 2
24.   *The Colonial Times,* May 15, 1829
25.   CS01/395/8929
26.   C033/16/199
27.   Chapman, P. (ed.); *The Diaries and Letters of G. T. W. B. Boyes,* p.328.
28.   Sims, *'The Life, Times and Family of Captain Peter Maclaine of Scotland and Van Diemen's Land'*
29.   Reid, *The East Coast,* p. 29
30.   GO33/21
31.   LSD1/74/285
32.   Parker papers, UTA; (P1/6, App. B)
33.   G033/19/48
34.   G033/19/48-57
35.   LSD1/92/61
36.   G033/19/48-57
37.   CS01/216/5202
38.   RGD 1835/2362
39.   ibid.

CHAPTER 10

1.   Meredith, *My Home in Tasmania,* p. 84
2.   Radcliff family papers; Mr James Radcliff, Devonport
3.   Parker papers, UTA; (P1/6, App. B)
4.   CS01/467/10342, 86
5.   LSD1/110/190

6.   LSD1/90/50
7.   Watson family papers; 'The Watson Family History in Tasmania from 1830', Mollie Coker; Mr Reg Watson, Kingston Beach
8.   Parker papers, UTA; (P1/6, App. B)
9.   Watson family papers; 'The Watson Family History in Tasmania from 1830', Mollie Coker; Mr Reg Watson, Kingston Beach
10.   Parker papers, UTA; (P1/6, App. B)
11.   SC285/320/987
12.   LSD/SLTX/AO/5
13.   SC285/320/987
14.   Robson, *A History of Tasmania,* p. 271
15.   SC285/320/987
16.   CS01/316/839
17.   Parker papers, UTA; (P1/6, P1/1). Mr Fred Rapp to Dr Parker, 1929
18.   ibid.
19.   CS01/315/839, 840
20.   Portrait of Frances Aubin at Narryna Folk Museum, Hobart
21.   Parker papers, UTA; (P1/6, App. B)
22.   Melville, *The History of V.D.L.,* p. 27
23.   Parker papers, UTA; (P1/6, F28)
24.   West, *The History of Tasmania*
25.   Plomley, *Friendly Mission,* p. 310
26.   The Mercury, Apr. 24, 1883; obituary, Francis Cotton
27.   Attributed to Miss Sarah Mitchell by Mrs Frances Cotton, Swansea
28.   *Tasmanian Mail,* Sep. 30, 1893; Article by E.O. Cotton
29.   Plomley, *Friendly Mission,* p. 312
30.   Robson, *A History of Tasmania,* p. 199
31.   West, *The History of Tasmania,* p. 585
32.   *Melville's Almanac,* 1833
33.   *ADB*
34.   LSD1/60/290
35.   LSD1/60/293
36.   LSD1/1/298
37.   LSD1/91/171
38.   CS01/315/990
39.   CS01/316/1001
40.   Lyne papers; Letter from Kate Lyne to Howard Amos, c 1920. Mrs Ruth Amos, Swansea
41.   *Hobart Town Courier,* Dec. 21, 1831

42.   ibid., Jan. 7, 1832
43.   Parker papers, UTA; (P1/6, App. B)
44.   Ellis, *Louisa Anne Meredith,* p. 56
45.   Watson family papers; 'The Watson Family in Tasmania after 1830', Mollie Coker; Mr Reg Watson, Kingston Beach
46.   Allen, *The Homestead, Bicheno*

CHAPTER 11

1.   CS01/227/3495, 155
2.   CS01/3493/227
3.   C0257/280/46, 109
4.   *Colonial Times,* Jan. 4, 1834
5.   Ellis, *Louisa Anne Meredith,* p. 53
6.   Shaw, *Bernard's Brethren,* p. 68; Mr Edward Shaw, Hobart
7.   Shaw, *A History of Clan Shaw,* p. 70
8.   Shaw, *Bernard's Brethren,* p. 78; Mr Edward Shaw, Hobart
9.   Lands Department. Letter from Edward Carr Shaw's mother to Recorder of Land Entitlements
10.   Shaw family papers; Mrs Carr to Fanny Greene, 1832; Mr Charles Shaw, Red Banks, Swansea
11.   Shaw, *Bernard's Brethren,* p. 64
12.   Obituary, E.C. Shaw, 1885
13.   CS01/361/240
14.   CS01/141/2493, 65
15.   CS01/360/240
16.   *ADB*; and Reid, *The East Coast,* p. 6
17.   CS01/361/271
18.   CS01/361/240
19.   *The True Colonist,* Apr. 16, 1833
20.   C0257/280/46, 109
21.   Levy, *Governor George Arthur,* p. 171
22.   C0257/280/46
23.   CS01/361/262
24.   CS01/361/261
25.   Meredith, 'Memoir of the late George Meredith'; (TC 920 MER)
26.   ibid., p. 42
27.   Hughes, *The Fatal Shore,* p. 486
28.   ibid.,
29.   CS01/361/250
30.   Amos papers; Adam Amos to W. Pringle, 1834. (NS323/4)

CHAPTER 12

1. LSD1/6/369
2. *The True Colonist,* May 21, 1833
3. *Hobart Town Courier,* Mar. 12, 1834
4. Steel papers; Will Green to Michael Steel, 1834. (NS174)
5. Backhouse, *A Narrative of a Visit to the Australian Colonies,* p. 184
6. Travers, *Pioneers at Piermont,* p. 69
7. 'Home Life in V.D.L.', Frances Cotton; THRA, PP
8. Diary Notes of Charles Meredith, Royal Society of Tasmania
9. Parker papers, UTA; (P1/6, Introduction)
10. ibid., (P1/6, P1/1)
11. AOT, 76/899
12. Meredith, 'Memoir of the late George Meredith'; (TC 920 MER)
13. O'May, *Wrecks in Tasmanian Waters,* p. 20
14. Parker papers, UTA; (P1/6, App. B)
15. *Hobart Town Courier,* May 3, 1833
16. Meredith, 'Memoirs of the late George Meredith'; (TC 920 MER)
17. CS01/715/43
18. CS01/135/81
19. Parker papers, UTA; (P1/6, C12)
20. CS01/305/8929
21. Parker papers, UTA; (P1/6, C12)
22. CS05/122/2826
23. CS01/791/16937
24. Castle family papers; Miss Jess Castle, Hobart
25. Appendix to Report to Select Committee on Transportation, 1837; pp. 354-5
26. Ellis, *Louisa Anne Meredith,* p. 38
27. *The True Colonist,* July 9, 1833
28. Ellis, *Louisa Anne Meredith,* p. 53
29. Shaw family papers; Notes by Bernard Shaw, 1901; Mr Charles Shaw, Red Banks, Swansea
30. Shaw family papers; Anne Shaw's Day Book; Mr Charles Shaw, Red Banks, Swansea
31. Parker papers, UTA; (P1/6, P1/9)
32. Meredith, *Tasmanian Friends and Foes,* p. 236
33. CS01/79/1764
34. Levy, *Governor George Arthur,* p. 171
35. Meredith, 'Reminiscences and Experiences of an Early Colonist', p. 10 (TC)

36.   ibid.
37.   Diary Notes of Charles Meredith; Royal Society of Tasmania
38.   Robertson and Craig, *Early Houses of Northern Tasmania, Vol. 2*
39.   Robson, *A History of Tasmania,* p. 196
40.   Meredith, 'Memoir of the late George Meredith', p. 23 (TC 920 MER)
41.   ibid., p. 16
42.   CS01/884/18, 765
43.   Diary Notes of Charles Meredith; Royal Society of Tasmania
44.   CS01/884/18765, 160
45.   Allen family papers; John Allen to his sister Hannah, 1839; Mrs Ruth Amos, Swansea
46.   Amos family papers; Financial records; Mr Bruce Amos, Cranbrook

CHAPTER 13

1.   Parker papers, UTA; (P1/6, C14)
2.   LSD1/10/21
3.   Robertson and Craig, *Early Houses of Northern Tasmania, Vol. 2*
4.   Parker papers, UTA; (P1/6, App. B)
5.   CS05/122/2826
6.   Parker papers, UTA; (P1/6, App. B)
7.   Robertson and Craig, *Early Houses of Northern Tasmania, Vol. 2*
8.   Allen family papers; John Allen to his sister Hannah, 1838. Mrs Ruth Amos, Swansea
9.   Amos papers; Diary of James Amos, Dec. 1840. (NS323/2)
10.   Allen family papers; John Allen to his sister Hannah, 1838. Mrs Ruth Amos, Swansea
11.   ibid., John Allen to Sir George Arthur, Apr. 1838
12.   ibid., John Allen to Board of Assignment, Hobart Town, May 1838
13.   Reid, *The East Coast,* p. 34
14.   Allen family papers; John Allen to his sister Hannah, Jan. 1839; Mrs Ruth Amos, Swansea
15.   Parker papers, UTA; (P1/6, G6)
16.   Amos family papers; Mr Bruce Amos, Cranbrook
17.   Smith, John Lee Archer - *Tasmanian Architect and Engineer*
18.   LSD1/2/2201
19.   *Priceless Heritage,* National Trust of Tasmania, p. 129

20.   Amos papers; Diary of James Amos. (NS323/2)
21.   Allen family papers; John Allen to W. Lyne Jnr., July 1839; Mrs Ruth Amos, Swansea
22.   'East Coast Excursion, 1968', G. Crawford; Royal Society of Tasmania (Northern Branch)
23.   Amos papers; Diary of James Amos. (NS323/2)
24.   *Franklin's Map of Tasmania, 1837*
25.   Allen family papers; John Allen's Day Book; Mrs Ruth Amos, Swansea
26.   Amos papers; Adam Amos to his sons, July 1843. (NS323/4)
27.   Meredith, 'Memoir of the late George Meredith'; (TC 920 MER)
28.   Meredith, Reminiscences and Experiences of an Early Colonist, (TC)
29.   Ellis, *Louisa Anne Meredith,* p. 64
30.   ibid., p. 89
31.   Meredith, *My Home in Tasmania,* p. 25
32.   ibid., p. 32
33.   Ellis, *Louisa Anne Meredith,* p. 37
34.   ibid., p. 117
35.   Reid, *The East Coast,* p. 29
36.   Sims, *'The Life, Times and Family of Captain Peter Maclaine of Scotland and Van Diemen's Land'*
37.   Meredith, *Tasmanian Friends and Foes,* p. 42
38.   Parker papers, UTA; (P1/6, App. B)
39.   *The Mercury, Oct. 27, 1926*
40.   Allen family papers; John Allen to Police Magistrate, Swansea, Dec. 1838. Mrs Ruth Amos, Swansea

CHAPTER 14

1.   Beattie, J.W.; Lives and Times of Early Governors; (Lectures, 1903)
2.   Syme, *Nine Years in V.D.L.*
3.   Heyer, *The Presbyterian Pioneers of V.D.L.,* p. 160
4.   Amos papers; Diary of James Amos, Apr. 1843. (NS323/2)
5.   ibid., Jan. 25, 1844
6.   Shaw, *Bernard's Brethren,* p. 36. Mr Edward Shaw, Hobart
7.   Meredith, *My Friends and Foes,* p. 130
8.   von Stieglitz, *Pioneers of the East Coast,* p. 64
9.   Parker papers, UTA; (P1/6, App. B)
10.   Allen family papers; John Allen's Day Book; Mrs Ruth Amos, Swansea

11. Radcliff family papers; Mr James Radcliff, Devonport
12. Amos, *Amos and Lyne Family History,* p. 13
13. Amos papers; Adam Amos to his sons, May 1842. (NS323/4)
14. Parker papers, UTA; (p1/6, App. B)
15. Amos, *Amos and Lyne Family History,* p. 13
16. Cotton family papers; F. Cotton to J. Mather; (UTA)
17. Parker papers, UTA; (P1/6, App. B)
18. *The Mercury,* Feb. 18, 1984; 'Kelvedon Diaries uncover a Story', Andrew Fisher
19. Hurburgh, *The Royal Tasmanian Botanical Gardens,* 1818-1986, p. 20
20. *ADB*
21. Travers, *Pioneers at Piermont,* p. 73
22. ibid., p. 79
23. Robson, *A History of Tasmania,* p. 285
24. ibid., p. 348
25. Cotton, *Kettle on the Hob,* p. 21
26. ibid., p. 24
27. Robson, *A History of Tasmania,* p. 366
28. Reid, *The East Coast,* p. 16
29. Ellis, *Louisa Anne Meredith,* p. 124
30. Meredith, *My Home in Tasmania,* p. 146
31. Ellis, *Louisa Anne Meredith,* p. 127
32. Heyer, *The Presbyterian Pioneers of Tasmania,* p. 161
33. Meredith, *My Home in Tasmania,* p. 57
34. 'Excursion to Swansea, 1960'; Geoffrey Stilwell and Eric Reed; THRA PP
35. Amos family papers; 'The Amos Family, Cranbrook', M.B. Amos; Mr Bruce Amos, Cranbrook
36. Amos papers; Gala Kirk. (NS977/1-6)
37. ibid., (NS323/4)
38. Personal communication, Mrs Ruth Amos, Swansea
39. Amos papers; Letter from W. Pringle, Scotland. (NS323/5)

CHAPTER 15

1. SC195/16/1284
2. Ellis, *Louisa Anne Meredith,* p. 59
3. HRA III, IV, p. 497
4. SC285/320/987
5. *Southern Star,* Feb. 5, 1883
6. LSD/SLTX/AO/LS5
7. LSD/Pembroke Book 3a/77

8.   Calder papers, SLV; John de Courcy Harte; (O/N50215)
9.   SC285/320/987
10.   Swansea Anglican Church Records, Swansea
11.   *Colonial Times,* May 11, 1852
12.   'East Coast Excursion, 1968', G.H. Crawford; Royal Society of Tasmania (Northern Branch)
13.   Amos, *Amos and Lyne Family History,* p. 14
14.   Ellis, *Louisa Anne Meredith,* p. 154
15.   SC195/16/1284
16.   Ellis, *Louisa Anne Meredith,* p. 155
17.   ibid., p. 156
18.   Cotton, *Kettle on the Hob,* p. 72
19.   von Stieglitz, *Pioneers of the East Coast,* p. 32

CHAPTER 16

1.   Radcliff family papers; Mr James Radcliff, Devonport
2.   von Stieglitz, *Pioneers of the East Coast,* p. 52
3.   Parker papers, UTA; (P1/6, App. B)
4.   Radcliff family papers; Agreement. Mr James Radcliff, Devonport
5.   *Illustrated London News, Oct. 17, 1856;* (Parker papers)
6.   Parker papers, UTA; (P1/6, P1/9: Introduction)
7.   Radcliff family papers; Mr James Radcliff, Devonport
8.   Parker papers, UTA; (P1/6, P1/9: Introduction)
9.   ibid.
10.   ibid.
11.   Ellis, *Louisa Anne Meredith,* p. 163
12.   ibid., p. 167
13.   *The Hobart Town Advertiser,* Oct. 23, 1861
14.   Ellis, *Louisa Anne Meredith,* p. 178
15.   Diary Notes of Charles Meredith; Letter to Captain Despard, 1856; Royal Society of Tasmania
16.   Shaw family papers; Anne Shaw's Day Book; Mr Charles Shaw, Swansea
17.   HSD/52/7
18.   Told to Mr Tylney Cotton by his father; author's communication with Mrs Tylney Cotton, Swansea
19.   Amos papers; Diary of James Amos. (NS323/2)
20.   Parker papers, UTA; Mr Fred Rapp to Dr Parker, 1928; (P1/6, P1/1)
21.   ibid., (P1/6, App. B)
22.   Cotton, *Kettle on the Hob;* Foreword, Mr W.N. Oats

23.   ibid., p. 77
24.   'East Coast Excursion, 1968', G.H. Crawford; Royal Society of Tasmania, (Northern Branch)
25.   Allen, *The Homestead,* Bicheno
26.   Parker papers, UTA; (P1/6, P1/9)
27.   *The Southern Star,* Feb. 5, 1883
28.   Parker papers, UTA; (P1/6, P1/8)
29.   ibid.
30.   ibid., (P1/6, P1/2)
31.   ADB
32.   Cotton, *Kettle on the Hob,* p. 66
33.   *The Mercury,* Apr. 23, 1883; Obituary, Francis Cotton

INDEX

Aborigines: 23, 27, 31, 35, 36, 40, 42, 50, 55, 56, 58, 60, 70, 71, 77, 78, 79, 80, 81, 82, 87, 91, 92, 96, 98, 99, 101, 107, 108, 109, 113, 114, 120, 140, 149, 151, 155, 169.

Addison, John & Hugh: 51, 52, 67, 87, 152, 167, 172.

Allen, Ann (Bell): 183, 197.

Allen, Anne (Mrs Tilney Cotton): 197.

Allen, Ann Eliza (Mrs John Allen): 166, 182, 183, 194.

Allen, Edwin: 182.

Allengrove: 149, 155, 165, 166, 167, 182, 194.

Allen, John: 62-64, 78, 79, 115, 148, 149, 155, 156, 165-167, 181, 183, 184, 194, 197.

Allen, Joseph: 62, 64, 78, 82, 149, 155, 197.

Allen, Richard: 62-64, 78, 85, 107, 182.

Allport, Joseph: 33, 69.

Amos, Adam, Jnr: 55, 112, 124, 127, 151, 152, 155, 167.

Amos, Adam, Snr:
    English life: 3, 4, 5, 7, 9.
    V.D.L. 1821-1830: 12, 13, 23, 28, 29, 34-36, 40-43, 46, 49, 52, 55, 57, 58, 63, 64, 91, 97, 108.
    V.D.L. 1830-1845: 121, 122, 125, 150, 151, 156, 167, 175, 176, 179, 193.
    Land: 15, 16, 21, 22, 25, 27, 83, 85, 106, 112, 152, 174, 199.

Amos families: 6, 7, 9, 32, 34, 65, 69, 124, 150, 161, 174.

Amos, Caroline (Mrs Will Lyne): 161.

Amos, Hannah (Mrs John Amos): 4, 6, 29, 31, 70, 184, 187.

Amos, James (son of John): 112, 138, 141, 150, 151, 174, 175, 184, 194.

Amos, James (son of Adam): 12, 18, 41, 47, 49, 50, 55, 58, 134, 166, 169, 174.

Amos, John (son of Adam): 18, 32, 55, 79, 112, 122, 154, 177, 194.

Amos, John (Snr):
    English life: 4, 7, 9.
    V.D.L. 1821-1848: 10, 12, 18, 19, 23, 27, 28, 31, 32, 40, 78, 140, 148, 156, 163, 174, 175.
    Land: 15, 16, 21, 22, 27, 33, 47, 69, 70, 85, 86, 112, 140, 141, 184.

Amos, Lavinia: 31, 187.

Amos, Mary (Mrs Adam Amos): 4, 64, 152, 167, 176.

Amos, Mary Collins (Mrs James Amos): 150, 151, 184.

Amos, Matilda: 31, 191.

Amos, Robert: 107.

Apslawn: 63, 65, 127, 155, 162.

Apsley: 63-65, 77, 78, 81, 84, 107, 112, 114, 124, 127, 129, 161, 174, 186, 192.

Apsley, Lord: 61, 77.

Archer, John Lee: 152.
Archer, Joseph: 7, 9.
Arthur, Governor George: 44-46, 48, 52, 53, 57, 58, 61, 62, 68-70, 74, 77, 79, 82, 83, 85, 97, 108, 109, 110, 113, 115, 117, 122, 123, 125, 126, 132, 140, 141, 149, 157.
Aubin, Francis: 108, 117, 121, 122, 125, 126, 143.

Backhouse, James: 129.
Banwell: 74, 82, 88, 98-100, 134.
Bark Mill: 174.
Bathurst, Lord: 7, 16, 23, 45, 47, 57, 58, 59, 61, 64, 68, 83, 85.
Baynton, James: 107.
Bedford, Rev. William: 134.
Belbrook: 22, 23, 28, 33, 64, 85, 91, 100, 107, 109, 113, 179, 181, 182, 189, 190, 191, 199.
Belle, Vue: 11, 157.
Belmont: 68, 71, 72, 82, 86, 122, 125, 130, 136, 148, 186, 191, 197.
The Bend: 112, 197.
Betsey Island: 69, 115.
Bicheno: 183, 184, 197.
Black Drive (Black War): 108, 120.
Botanical Gardens: 169.
Brady, Matthew, 38, 40, 41, 50, 54.
Breakneck Hills: 181.
Break-o'Day: 46, 62, 83.
Briskfields Invalid Depot: 200.
Brisbane, Sir Thomas: 22-24, 37, 59.
Brook Lodge: 107, 109, 130, 190.
Buckland: 35, 37.
Burrows, Mary (Mrs Thomas Watson): 103, 115, 182.
Burst-my-Gall: 181.
Burt, Andrew: 5,6.
Bushby, William: 155.
Bushrangers: 39, 40, 49-53, 60, 61, 91, 123, 149, 163, 165, 173, 174, 187.
Butler, Agnes: 116, 149, 167, 197, 200.
Butler, Anna Maria: 167.
Butler, Gamaliel: 69.
Butler, Joseph: 116, 149, 167, 192, 200.
Buxton, Ellen: 29, 33, 82, 184, 194, 195.
Buxton, George: 29, 33, 195.
Buxton, Mary Ann (nee Radford): 33, 130, 157, 179, 199.
Buxton, Thomas (Jnr): 33, 108, 195, 196.
Buxton, Thomas (Snr): 17, 19, 23, 30, 33, 36, 43, 50, 55, 56, 82, 87, 92, 154, 181, 195.

Calder, James E: 179, 180.
Cambria: 139, 140, 156, 158, 159, 177, 184, 186, 191, 192, 194.
Cameron, Margaret: 190.

Campania: 120.
Campbell Town: 63, 87, 134, 149, 156, 163, 197, 199.
Cape of Good Hope: 6, 9.
Castle Bromich Hall: 1, 68.
Castle, Edith: 74, 99, 134.
Castle, John: 74, 99, 134.
Castle, Joseph (Jnr):74.
Castle, Joseph (Snr): 74, 82, 88, 98, 134.
Castle, Phoebe: 74, 99.
Castle, Robert: 74, 99.
Champ, William: 188.
Clare, Thomas: 29.
Cogil, —: 58, 86.
Coles Bay: 13.
Collins, Lt-Gov. David: 12, 91.
Compton, Richard: 9.
Conolly, Patrick: 179, 181.
Conolly, Father Philip: 22, 106, 107, 179, 181.
Convicts, female: 132, 138.
Cooke, Richard: 127, 129, 165.
Coombend: 70, 155, 167.
Cope, Emma (Mrs Edward Shaw): 193, 199.
Coswell: 52, 67, 87, 88, 152, 172.
Cotton, Anna: (Mrs Joseph Mather): 172.
Cotton, Anna Maria (Mrs Francis Cotton): 92-94, 172, 173, 187, 200; 201, 202.
Cotton, Edward: 197, 202.
Cotton family: 172, 187.
Cotton, Francis: 92-96, 108, 112, 129, 140, 143, 172, 173, 194, 197, 201, 202.
Cotton, James: 197.
Cotton, Joseph: 197.
Cotton, Henry: 169, 187, 194.
Cotton, Mary: 172.
Cotton, Tilney: 197.
Courland: 167, 200.
Craigie Knowe: 151, 152, 174.
Cranbrook: 70, 107, 112, 134, 141, 150-152, 154, 160, 161, 163, 174, 184.
Cranbrook - Syde: 22.
Creek Hut: 19, 27, 29, 33, 38, 40, 42, 43, 62, 141.
Cumming, James C: 33, 41, 87, 103, 112.
Cygnet River: 15, 21, 58, 64, 159, 161.

Darling, Governor Sir R: 59.
de Gillern, Major William: 163, 165.
Degraves, John: 189.
Denison, Governor Sir W: 181.
Desailly, Dr Francis: 9.
Devil's Royals: 181.
Dido: 187.

The Douglas: 149, 155, 161, 165, 166.
Dove, Rev. Thomas: 174.
Duffy, Patrick: 107, 109, 190.
Dunalley: 13.

Eardley-Wilmot, Lt-Gov. Sir John Eardley: 173.
Eastern Marshes: 88.
Eastern Tiers: 15, 84, 174.
Egg Farm: 79, 116, 149, 165.
Enstone Park: 90, 129, 155.
Evans, George: 16, 17, 20, 22, 52, 69.
Evans, Mary (Mrs George Meredith): 1, 3, 5, 6, 7, 156, 186.
Evans, Nurse: 5, 6, 29.

Falmouth: 155.
Fenton, Ann (Mrs Edward Shaw): 137, 138, 193.
Fenton, Mrs: 137, 143.
Ferguson, John (Jnr): 163.
Ferguson, John (Snr): 122.
Ferndene: 167.
Fingal: 179, 196.
The Fisheries: 39, 40, 131, 138.
Forster, Matthew: 125.
Franklin, Lady Jane: 143.
Franklin, Sir John: 143, 173.
Freycinet Peninsula: 13, 15, 21, 38, 67, 76, 113.

Gala: 152, 154, 174, 176.
Gala Kirk: 174, 175, 177, 197, 200.
Gala Mill: 153, 169.
Gatehouse, Charles: 147.
Gatehouse, George: 30, 35, 36, 60.
Gatehouse, Silas: 13, 30, 60, 97, 108, 147.
Gatehouse, William: 60.
Gay, Robert: 32, 40.
Gellibrand, Joseph: 115, 169.
Glamorgan (Great Swan Port): 138, 192, 199.
Glencoe: 155, 197.
Glen Gala: 25, 27, 28, 31, 36, 38, 41, 50, 52, 62, 64, 65, 70, 83, 85, 107, 108, 134,
    151, 152, 154, 156, 160, 163, 167, 174.
Glen Gala Mill: 31, 154.
Glen Heriot: 122, 194.
Gould: 36.
Government House: 12, 87, 110, 157.
Graham, John Alexander: 191, 194.
The Grange: 33, 107, 115, 163, 169, 187, 197.

Great Swan Port (Glamorgan): 15-18, 22, 23, 29, 31-33, 36, 45, 47, 49, 52, 58, 62, 63, 67, 69, 73, 77, 91, 93, 95, 106, 108, 115, 121, 125, 126, 132, 136-138, 143, 156, 157, 166, 169, 170, 172, 173, 177, 179, 182, 184, 199.
Greene , Arthur: 119, 120.
Greene, Fanny: 119, 120.
Gregson, Thomas G: 7, 9, 193.
Grindstone Bay: 30, 35, 36, 41, 87, 99, 101.
Grueber, Helen (Mrs Edward Cotton): 202.
Grueber, Stephen: 188.
Gunn, Lt. William: 40-42, 50, 52, 117.
Gunning, George W: 11, 12.

Hammond, Maria (Mrs John Meredith): 186, 193.
Harte, John de Courcy (Paddy): 16, 22, 23, 28, 33, 36, 37, 82, 85, 87, 91, 106-108, 129, 130, 179, 180, 181, 190, 200.
Haverfordwest: 4.
Hawkins, John: 82, 87, 108.
Hawthorn, Miss: 127, 128.
The Hazards: 13.
Hazard, Richard: 38.
Hell's Gates: 181.
Hepburn, Jacobina: 76.
Hepburn, Robert (Jnr): 190, 191.
Hepburn, Robert (Snr): 74, 76, 77, 84, 106, 122-124, 131, 132, 166, 196.
Hepburn, William (Jnr): 177.
Hepburn, William (Snr): 75, 196.
Heriot: 4.
Heriot Mill Farm: 3.
Hibberd, George: 58, 91.
Hobart Town: 7, 10, 15, 19, 22, 25, 29-34, 37-39, 41, 53, 60-63, 72, 74, 79, 88, 92, 97, 99, 101, 103, 106, 108-110, 120-123, 127, 129-132, 137, 152, 155, 157, 160, 166, 172, 180, 182, 188, 197, 199.
Hobart Town Courier: 118, 160, 188.
Hobart Town Gazette: 101.
Hobart Town Intelligencer: 10.
Hobbs, James: 143.
Hollyoak, William: 32, 35.
The Homestead (The Guest House):133.
Honner, Richard: 23, 24, 28, 32, 47.
Hooley, Thomas, 30, 40.
Hume, James: 149, 161.
Hume, Lillias: 161.
Humphrey, Adolarius W. H: 33, 37, 41.
Huntingfield: 182.
Hurst, James: 194.

Inns: *The Morning Star*, 149; *Rose & Brown*, 177; *Swan Inn*, 130, 157, 180; *Swan Inn*, Swansea, 177, 191.
Isabella: 75, 196.

Jackson, Isabella: 197.
Jamaica: 75.
Jericho: 25, 29, 58.
Jorgensen, Jorgen: 91, 92.
Jutland: 175, 176.

Kangaroos: 23, 27, 31, 40, 48.
Kangaroo Island: 177, 178.
Kelly, Captain J: 131.
Kelvedon: 95, 96, 108, 112, 129, 140, 169, 172, 187, 194, 197, 200, 202.
Kermode, William: 76.
Kew Gardens: 169.
King, Elizabeth (nee Webber): 147, 170, 171.
King, James (Jnr): 69, 108, 115, 169.
King, James (Snr): 68, 69, 70, 85, 107, 112, 115.
King, John Perkins: 170-172, 177, 194.
Kirby, George: 107, 177, 179, 189.
Kullaroo Estate: 87.

Lane, Richard: 91, 95, 96.
Lapham Samuel: 145.
Launceston: 28, 88, 133.
Lavender, William: 163.
Leard, William: 98, 108, 131.
Lewis, Fred: 177.
Lilla Villa: 162.
Lillie, Rev. J: 174.
Lippscombe: 120.
Lisdillon: 87, 103, 133, 143, 167, 188, 189, 195, 199.
Little Swanport: 28, 30, 36, 37, 41, 74, 79, 82, 87, 108, 109, 157, 174, 180.
Little Swanport River: 13, 87, 94, 103, 106, 130, 132, 158, 200.
Llandaff: 184.
Llanstinnan: 177.
London: 5, 6, 7, 24, 93.
Lord, Edward: 7, 11, 30.
Lord, Thomas Daunt: 48, 97, 108, 122-126, 132, 133.
Luttrell, Dr. Edward: 42.
Luttrell, Maria Antonet: 134.
Lyne, Betsy: 66, 78.
Lyne, Henry: 70, 90, 155.
Lyne, John: 71, 78, 81, 109, 112, 124, 125, 127, 151, 161, 194.
Lyne, Sarah: 59, 63, 64, 81, 161, 174.
Lyne, Susan: 66, 70, 78, 151, 152, 155.
Lyne, William (Jnr): 62, 161, 174, 194.
Lyne, William (Snr): 58-64, 70, 77-79, 81, 84, 90, 103, 108, 113, 114, 124, 152,
    161, 174, 184, 192, 199.

231

McArthur, John: 7.
McCabe, James: 54.
McGregor, Rob Roy: 75, 196.
McIntyre, Archibald: 155, 156.
McKenzie, Alexander: 192.
McLeod, Margaret (Mrs Francis Cotton, Jnr): 197.
Maclaine, Frances: 97, 145, 160.
Maclaine, Hugh: 160.
Maclaine, John: 160.
Maclaine, Peter: 97, 98, 108, 109, 113, 133, 160.
Macquarie, Governor Lachlan: 7, 15, 16, 25, 37.
Malahide: 16, 24, 25, 30, 35, 41, 43, 46, 48, 68, 179.
Maria Island: 15, 42, 48, 52, 82, 94, 97, 98, 122, 132.
Mather, Joseph: 172, 173.
Mather, Robert: 95, 172.
Mayfield: 33, 36, 55, 56, 82, 87, 92, 107, 163, 191, 195, 196.
Mayfield Beach: 165.
Mayfield Mill: 153, 154.
Mayson, Rev. Joseph: 160.
Melrose: 13, 83.
Meredith, Charles: 27, 29, 31-34, 48, 50, 71, 94, 136, 157-161, 173, 174, 184, 186, 191, 192.
Meredith, Edwin: 184, 186.
Meredith, George (Jnr): 12, 23, 27, 31-35, 42, 49, 56, 68, 71, 86, 117, 118, 136, 137, 177, 178, 184.
Meredith, George Campbell: 157.
Meredith, George (Snr):
    English life: 1, 4-7.
    Emigration: 9-11.
    V.D.L. 1821-1830: 15-18, 24-28, 30, 32-34, 40, 43, 47-50, 52, 56, 57, 61, 62, 71-73, 78, 83, 86, 94, 97, 101, 107, 108.
    V.D.L. 1830-1856: 113, 117, 118, 121-126, 130, 131, 135, 138-140, 148, 155, 156, 160, 172, 178, 184-186, 191.
    Politics: 38, 52, 140.
    Land: 15, 16, 21, 23, 29, 45, 57, 68, 69, 112, 141, 142.
    Family fued: 191-193.
    Death: 193.
Meredith, Henry: 5, 6, 9, 34, 156, 184.
Meredith, John: 29, 34, 71, 157, 184, 186, 191-195.
Meredith, John (cousin): 7, 10, 12, 15, 16, 21, 22, 25, 28, 29, 47, 136.
Meredith, Louisa (Mrs John Bell): 72, 136, 157.
Meredith, Louisa Anne (Mrs Charles Meredith): 72, 135, 136, 157, 158, 160, 173, 186, 191, 192.
Meredith, Maria (Mrs John Meredith): 186, 193.
Meredith, Mary (Mrs George Meredith): 1, 3, 5-7, 27, 29, 31, 34, 38-42, 50, 56, 72, 73, 115, 136, 148, 156, 159, 184, 186, 193.
Meredith River: 13, 15, 18, 21, 23, 43, 58, 86, 139.
Meredith, Rosina: 192.

Meredith, Sabina (Mrs John Boyes): 72, 136, 184.
Meredith, Sarah (Jnr) (Mrs James Poynter): 72, 136.
Meredith, Sarah (nee Hicks): 1,6, 7, 29, 72, 186.
merinos: 7, 27.
Milligan, Dr. J: 161.
Milton: 64, 78-81, 85, 115, 148, 149, 155, 175.
Mitchell, John: 188, 191, 194, 195.
Mitchelmore, Mrs: 199.
Moreton Bay (Brisbane): 140.
Morey's Store: 199.
Morris, James: 191.
Moulting Lagoon: 13, 21, 40, 49, 53, 62-64, 77, 79, 80, 103, 104, 116, 124.
Muirlands: 106, 107, 130, 179.
Murdock, Peter: 48, 83, 88.
Murray, David: 161.
Murray, Hugh: 161.
Murray, Robert Lathrop: 136.
Muskitoo: 35, 36, 40, 42.
Musters: 28, 32, 78, 165.

New Norfolk Asylum: 194.
New Town: 11, 15, 16, 152, 167, 175, 188.
New South Wales: 7, 18, 31, 38, 52, 59-61, 97, 107, 133, 140, 157.
New Zealand: 177, 186, 191, 195.
Nicholson, John: 122, 123.
Nine Mile Beach: 13.
Nixon, Bishop R: 193.
Noyes, W. T: 156.

O'Connor, Roderic: 83, 84, 86, 88, 103.
O'Connor, William: 190.
Okehampton: 97, 98, 132.
Old Bull: 139, 140, 148, 159.
Omoroe (Rheban): 133, 134, 146, 147, 167.
Orr, William M: 118, 121.
Oyster Bay: 13, 17, 18, 21, 37, 42, 48, 52, 62, 63, 67, 69, 70, 79, 86-88, 91.
Oyster Bay Guest House (Resthaven): 177, 191.

Paradise: 181.
Parsons, Charles C: 115.
Picnic Point: 183, 197.
Pur Hotel: 194, 195.
Purmont: 96, 97, 146-148, 171, 172.
Pirates Bay: 25.
Pittwater: 35, 36, 52.
The Plains: 85, 197.
Plas Newydd: 192.
Point Puer: 188.

Police Magistrates: 12, 34, 36, 79, 87, 95, 108, 121-126, 132-134, 149, 150, 165, 173, 186, 192.
Port Arthur: 122, 123, 134, 188.
Port Dalrymple: 28, 50.
Port Phillip: 179.
Port Sorell: 173, 174, 184.
Presbyterian: 4, 174-176.
Pringle, William: 55, 176.
Pritehard: 28.
Prossers Plains: 35, 37, 129.
Prosser River: 13, 20, 41, 134, 146, 181.
Pyke, —: 94.

Quaker (Society of Friends): 93, 95, 129, 130, 197.
Quin, Kevin: 119.

Rapp, Fredrick: 195.
Radcliff, Anna Maria (Mrs James Radcliff): 167, 188, 189.
Radcliff, James: 101, 102, 112, 133, 134, 143, 145-147, 167, 188, 189.
Radcliff, Richard: 103, 133, 138, 145-147.
Radford, John: 29, 30, 35, 109, 110, 130, 178-180, 199.
Radford, Mary Ann (Mrs John Radford): 130, 157, 179, 199.
Ravensdale: 82, 130, 143.
Raynor, David: 40, 50.
Raynor, George: 40, 49, 86, 149, 155.
Raynor, John: 40, 101.
Red Banks: 22, 33, 35, 42, 47, 50, 52, 53, 58, 62, 68, 117, 121 137-139, 141, 165, 187, 190, 192, 199.
Redcliffe: 191.
Reid, Alexander: 18, 30, 79, 107, 109, 113, 121, 161, 163, 174, 177.
Reid, Eliza (Mrs Alexander Reid): 161.
Resthaven (Oyster Bay Guest House): 177, 191.
Rheban (Omoroe): 133, 167, 188.
Rhyndaston: 1, 4, 7.
Rice, Henry: 12, 13, 15.
Riversdale: 22, 32, 69, 86, 148, 159, 184, 186, 191.
Riversdale Mill: 147, 148.
Robinson, George Augustus: 108, 109.
Rocky Hills: 87, 95, 163, 165, 170, 180.
Rostrevor: 98, 131.
Rowlands, T. W: 118, 123.
Roy, Mary Ann: 75, 196.
Roys Hill: 77, 84, 196, 197.

St Andrews Presbyterian Church: 152.
St Davids Church, Hobart Town: 130, 137, 197.
Salmon, Samuel: 160, 187.
Salt Works: 87, 133, 145.

Schouten House: 191.
Seaford: 87, 145.
Sealing: 87, 138.
schools: 171, 172, 191.
Scott, Thomas: 20, 22.
Shaw, Ann (Mrs Edward Shaw, nee Fenton): 137, 138, 193.
Shaw, Bernard: 138, 199.
Shaw, Edward Carr: 118-121, 137, 138, 143, 156, 163, 165, 188-190, 193, 194, 198, 199.
Shaw, Frederick: 199.
Shaw, George Bernard: 161.
Shaw, Joseph: 31, 32, 37, 38.
Sherbourne Lodge: 104-106, 167, 182.
Ships: *Albion*, 38; *Amelia*, 131; *Ann*, 116; *Breeze*, 172; *Black Swan*, 43; *Britomart*, 147; *Caroline*, 34; *Cygnet*, 172; *Dancing Wave*, 195; *Defiance*, 118; *Eagle*, 120; *Emerald*, 7, 10, 27, 141; *Greenoah*, 70; *Henry & Mary Jellico*, 92, 94; *Hugh Crawford*, 59, 60, 62, 66; *Independent*, 48, 172; *Jean*, 128; *Lady Castlereagh*, 110; *Mayflower*, 125; *Mercia*, 188; *Orelia*, 74, 97; *Prince Leopold*, 16, 48, 94; *Rockingham*, 119; *Sir George Arthur*, 157; *Science*, 115; *Swan*, 171, 172; *Wave*, 103; *Westmorland*, 34.
Simpson, James: 87.
Society of Friends (Quakers): 93, 95, 129, 130, 197.
Sorell: 115.
Sorell, Governor William: 11, 15-17, 22-24, 34, 40, 69.
South Australia: 184, 186, 191, 197.
Spiky Bridge: 165.
Spring Bay: 13, 30, 97, 108, 109, 112, 132, 149, 197, 202.
The Springs: 64, 78, 85, 107, 163, 174, 182.
Spring Vale: 15, 22, 25, 40, 64, 85, 122, 158, 160, 173.
Steel, Jane (Mrs Richard Cooke): 59, 60, 127, 129, 155.
Steel, Michael: 59, 60, 90, 127-129.
Steel, William: 90, 128, 129, 155.
Story, Dr. George Fordyce: 92-94, 96, 108, 112, 130, 143, 160, 169, 173, 182, 183, 187, 194, 195, 197, 200, 202.
Swan Motor Inn: 196.
Swan Port: 13, 17, 29, 33, 56, 58, 60, 62, 121, 199.
Swan River: 15, 21, 22, 25, 33, 47, 58, 63, 69, 70, 77, 105, 107-109, 112, 131, 152, 154, 159, 160.
Swansea: 118, 172, 174, 177, 191, 192, 194, 199, 200.
Swanwick: 76, 77, 85, 106, 132, 149, 166, 197.
Sydney: 15, 16, 22, 24, 27, 30, 31, 35, 103, 106, 107, 118, 130, 140, 157, 177, 179.

Talbot, William: 16-19, 23, 24, 28, 30, 33-37, 43, 45-47, 57, 68, 86, 179.
Tasmania: 196, 197, 199.
Tasmanian Austral-Asiatic Review: 136.
Templestone: 149, 161.
Teuch, Frederick Dr: 170.
Theatre Royal, Hobart Town: 157.

Thompson Villa (Enstone Park): 90, 129, 155.
Thunderbolt: 181.
Ticket-of-Leave: 91.
Tingley, Henry: 134, 135.
Tirzah: 165.
Tracoon (Traquhoun): 167.
Travers, Thomas: 171.
True Colonist: 121, 126.
Two-Mile Creek: 87, 103, 143.
Twamley, Louisa Anne (Mrs Charles Meredith): 136, 157.

Van Diemen's Land: 6, 7, 9, 10, 23, 25, 30, 33, 45, 48, 52, 55, 59, 61, 69, 74, 76, 83, 90, 91, 94, 97, 98, 101, 103, 110, 116, 120, 136, 140, 143, 156, 157, 172, 179, 184, 188.
Villeneuve (Twamley): 188.

Wales: 4, 7, 29, 156, 186.
Walker, George Washington: 129.
Wardlaw, Robert: 134.
Waterloo, Battle of: 58.
Waterloo Bridge: 189.
Waterloo Point (Swansea): 58, 67, 77, 79, 82, 86, 90-94, 96, 108, 118, 121-123, 125, 126, 138, 149, 156, 158, 160, 163, 165, 172, 193, 195, 199.
Watersmeeting: 109, 113, 161, 163.
Watson, Brereton: 106, 107, 182, 189.
Watson, Dorothy (Mrs Thomas Watson, Jnr): 115, 148.
Watson, Mary (Mrs Thomas Watson, Snr) (Mrs Richard Allen) nee Burrows: 103, 115, 182.
Watson, Robert: 103, 105, 106.
Watson, Thomas (Jnr): 103, 105, 106, 115, 148.
Watson, Thomas (Snr): 103, 182.
Waubs Harbour: 149, 161, 162, 167.
Webber, Elizabeth (Mrs John King): 147, 170, 171.
Webber, Jane: 171.
Webber, John: 67, 171.
Webber, Mary (Mrs Robert Webber): 66, 67, 147.
Webber, Robert: 66, 67, 87, 147-149, 170.
Webber, Walter: 171, 172.
Webber, William: 67, 148, 171.
Western Australia: 119.
Whaling: 38-42, 72, 86, 131, 138.
Wollis Charles: 189, 190.
Wolfe, —: 189.
Woodstock: 97, 98, 109, 160.
Woollet, Miss: 195.
Wye River: 15, 21-23, 27, 47, 58, 64, 106, 112.

Milton Keynes UK
Ingram Content Group UK Ltd.
UKHW021945101123
432363UK00004B/69

9 781915 115263